# New Horizons
## in Special Education

## Evidence-Based Practice in Action

*Edited by*

Barry Carpenter *and* Jo Egerton

Sunfield Publications
*living, learning, growing*

First published in Great Britain
by Sunfield Publications 2007.

*Cover image by*
*Reggie Price,* copyright © 2007

Published by
Sunfield Publications
Sunfield, Woodman Lane, Clent, Stourbridge DY9 9PB.
www.sunfield.org.uk

ISBN: 0-9550568-2-9

Printed and bound in Great Britain by
PCL WOLLASTON PRINT LIMITED
Richmond House, Richmond Road, Smethwick, West Midlands B66 4ED

*This book is dedicated to the many staff at Sunfield
who daily display amazing skills of education and care.
We celebrate you, with thanks.*

# Contents

**Page no.**

Acknowledgements     vi

Contributing Authors     viii

Foreword     xiii
*Roy McConkey*

## Part 1: Introduction to Evidence-Based Practice

Chapter 1     Introduction     3
*Barry Carpenter and Jo Egerton*

Chapter 2     Developing the Role of Schools as Research Organisations:     9
The Sunfield Experience
*Barry Carpenter*

## Part 2: Building Communication

Chapter 3     Play: An Interactive Approach Supporting Behavioural     23
and Developmental Growth
*Kellyanne Thornton and Emma Taylor*

Chapter 4     'Sherborne @ Sunfield': An Adapted Approach Used to     37
Support the Social Engagement of Young People with
ASD through Sherborne Developmental Movement
*Jotham Konaka*

Chapter 5     Why Do You Do That?: Stories to Support Social     59
Understanding for People with ASD
*Iain Chatwin*

## Part 3: Enhancing Health and Well-Being

Chapter 6     Identifying and Responding to the Needs of Young People     77
on the Autistic Spectrum with Mental Health Problems:
Implications for Organisation, Practice and Research
*Barry Carpenter, Barry Coughlan, Nick Logan and
Teresa Whitehurst*

Chapter 7    Mental Health Difficulties in People with Intellectual          89
             Disability: Integrating Theory and Evidence-Based Practice
             *Barry Coughlan*

Chapter 8    Zippy's Friends: Developing Curriculum Resources to             110
             Support the Mental Health Needs of Young People with
             Special Educational Needs
             *Gill Rowley and Jan Cook*

Chapter 9    Reconnecting Thinking, Feeling and Willing: Children            127
             with Autism in a Colour-Light Environment
             *Diana Pauli*

**Part 4: Inclusion in the Community**

Chapter 10   Journeys of Enquiry: Working with Families in a                 145
             Research Context
             *Barry Carpenter, Sally Conway, Teresa Whitehurst
             and Elizabeth Attfield*

Chapter 11   Changing Perspectives on Inclusion and Disability:             155
             'The Monkey King' Arts Project
             *Teresa Whitehurst*

**Part 5: The SIECCA Curriculum**

Chapter 12   Implementing TEACCH in Support of a 24-Hour                    171
             Curriculum
             *Iain Chatwin and Val Harley*

Chapter 13   Transference of Training into Practice: The                     181
             TEACCH Training Programme at Sunfield
             *Iain Chatwin and Deb Rattley*

**Part 6: Preparing for the Future**

Chapter 14   Preparation for Adulthood: Pathways in Recognised               195
             Attainment
             *Maureen Porter*

Chapter 15   Transition Solutions: Looking to the Future                     212
             *Jo Egerton*

Chapter 16   Research Tools for Evidence-Based Practice                     222
             *Teresa Whitehurst*

# Acknowledgements

There are many, many people, both within and outside Sunfield, whom we would like to thank for contributing to the development of a growing evidence-based practice and research culture at Sunfield. Those who have directly supported the projects described within this book, we are able to thank by name in the following paragraphs. However, there are many more professionals who, through their specialist advice and contributions to staff professional development, or through personal conversations, have generated the vision for reflection and change in practice, and inspired valuable developments for the young people at Sunfield over the last 10 years. We do not have the space to thank you as individuals, but please accept our deep gratitude. We also extend heartfelt thanks to funding organisations who have financially supported past or on-going research projects not described in this volume.

We would like to recognise particularly the commitment of Sunfield's Trustees to supporting the development of research at Sunfield over many years, which led incrementally to their founding the Sunfield Research Institute in 2005. Our thanks go, not only to them, but also to the professionals who give their time to offer informed guidance and act as critical friends through the following groups: Sunfield's Autism Advisory Group, chaired by Penny Lacey of the University of Birmingham; the Advisory Council; the Research Institute's International Advisory Board, Management Group and Research Associates; the Directors of the Professional Development Centre and the associated PDC Advisory Group.

Our grateful thanks go to all the Sunfield research participants – families, students and staff – for their involvement, enthusiasm and commitment, and also to the following external professionals and organisations for their support for the projects described in this book:

- To Penny Lacey, University of Birmingham, and Roy McConkey, University of Ulster, for their encouragement in the publication of this volume

- To Melanie Peter of Anglia Ruskin University and Dave Sherratt of Mowbray School, Andrew Cooksey (autism consultant) and Clare Tatterson (developmental psychologist), for their advice and support (Chapter 3)

- To Cyndi and George Hill of the Sherborne Association UK for their consultancy and work on the Sherborne @ Sunfield project; to Jackie Buscombe, Senior Occupational Therapist at Sunfield and to Cate Detheridge of Widgit Software for the development of the Sherborne @ Sunfield Symbols; and to the Three Guineas Trust, for their generous financial support (Chapter 4)

- To Stuart Cumella of the University of Birmingham for his advice in structuring the investigation of the impact of Social Stories (Chapter 5)

- To Caroline Egar and Chris Bale of Partnership for Children for their involvement in the adaptation of Zippy's Friends for young people with severe and complex intellectual disabilities; to the Specialist Schools and Academies Trust in London for funding the pilot project (Chapter 8)

- To the Michael Wilson Foundation, who funded the specialist lighting and its installation for the colour light environment; to Harkness Hall Ltd and ROMPA for donating items for this environment; to John Watson of Creative Lighting Design; and especial thanks to Diana Pauli herself for giving of her own time so generously to the students at Sunfield (Chapter 9)

- To the Parents Advisory Group for their insight and commitment; to Fran Russell for her consultancy support of the research into families' experiences of induction to Sunfield (Chapter 10)

- To the Shyster's Theatre Company and the Open Theatre Company from Coventry, under the directorship of Richard Hayhow, to David Gaukroger, ex-musical director at Sunfield, and the musicians from the Birmingham Conservatoire, to The Patrick Centre at the Hippodrome Theatre in Birmingham, and to the pupils and staff of Haybridge High School, Hagley (formerly Hagley Middle School) for their involvement, enthusiasm and commitment (Chapter 12)

- To Dr Mary E. Van Bourgondien and all the Division TEACCH consultants, past and present, from the University of North Carolina for their training, inspiration and advice on implementing TEACCH at Sunfield; and likewise to Sandra Patillo and Jackie Wadlow (Chapters 12 and 13)

- To Nick le Mesurier, Helen Bradley and Qulsom Fazil from the University of Birmingham for their advice and support in structuring and reporting on 'The Far Side' transition project, and to Melanie Smart and Jan Millward for their contributions; to Annette English and Bridget Jones of the West Midlands Regional Partnership and to Phil Madden of the Home Farm Trust for their support of the Transition Solutions project (Chapter 15)

- To Clare Tatterson, developmental psychologist, and to Patrick Holford, Lorraine Perretta and Deborah Colson from the Bio Brain Centre, London, for their involvement in the Sunfield Nutrition Project; to Christopher Beaver of GA Architects, London, for his work on the ASD-specific living environment (Chapter 16).

And last, but by no means least, to Ian Jones and the appeals team for ensuring financial support for the large-scale research initiatives undertaken at Sunfield.

If we have inadvertently overlooked anyone who ought to have been mentioned, please accept our apologies and our thanks.

# Contributing Authors

**Elizabeth Attfield** began her career as a language teacher in secondary schools. After retraining to work with primary-age children, she held a variety of posts in mainstream and special educational settings, before moving to the voluntary sector as parent partnership officer. She joined autism.west midlands over seven years ago and, in her current role as training officer – family and education, her specific remit is to provide more support for families through training workshops and to develop accredited courses for professionals working with individuals with autistic spectrum disorder (ASD) across the age and ability range. She is the mother of a 20-year-old son with ASD and severe intellectual disabilities, who now lives in an autism-specific adult residential setting in Lincolnshire, having previously been a pupil at Sunfield School. She has recently co-authored a book on living with ASD.

**Barry Carpenter** joined Sunfield as chief executive/principal in 1997. He has over 30 years' experience in special education, having held the leadership roles of head teacher, inspector of schools, and principal lecturer. In 1992, he established the Centre for the Study of Special Education at Westminster College, Oxford, which became a national teaching and research centre. As part of his role at Sunfield, he now directs the recently established Sunfield Research Institute. He has been awarded honorary professorships by the Universities of Northumbria and Worcester. Barry has written extensively in the field of special educational needs. His book, *Enabling Access,* won the National Association of Special Educational Needs' Academic Book Award. He has recently edited, with Jo Egerton, *Early Childhood Intervention: International perspectives, national initiatives and regional practice.* He lectures nationally and internationally, and most recently in Greece, Austria, Holland, Finland, Australia and Japan. He represents the UK on the European Union Working Group on Early Intervention, and Europe at the International Society for Early Intervention. He has been appointed by the Disability Rights Commission as their representative on the General Teaching Council for England. Barry is the father of three children, one of whom, Katie, has Down syndrome. He was awarded the OBE by the Queen in 2001 for services to children with special educational needs.

**Sally Conway** has a background in intellectual disability nursing, and has worked in a variety of settings supporting adults with intellectual disabilities. She is now head of family services at Sunfield School, and was instrumental in developing the service from its infancy in 1999 to its current profile. She has undertaken extensive research regarding family issues.

**Jan Cook** is the information and communications technology (ICT) training officer at Sunfield, and is responsible for the delivery of all aspects of ICT to the large staff team. She has 15 years' experience of working with students with intellectual disabilities and challenging behaviour. She is a TEACCH-trained practitioner, and she is also a Widgit Software trainer, educating staff in the use of Widgit Software's 'Writing With Symbols' (WWS) and 'Communicate in Print2' (CIP2) programs. Jan has an Adult Education Teaching Certificate, and is currently studying for a Professional Certificate of Education at Newman College in Birmingham.

**Barry Coughlan**, BA, Ph.D., D.Psych.Sc. (Clin. Psych.) is currently employed as a senior clinical psychologist with the Brothers of Charity Services, Bawnmore, Limerick, Ireland. Prior to this, he was employed as a clinical psychologist with the Health Service Executive, Mid-West Region, in Ireland, and worked in the area of adult mental health. Barry also works as a research associate at Sunfield School with children and adolescents with complex intellectual disability and ASD. As part of his current post, he works with adults with intellectual disability from the ages of 18 years to over 65 years of age, in both residential and community settings. He is involved in on-going research with the Brothers of Charity, the Health Service Executive in Ireland, the University of Limerick and with Sunfield School. Recent publications include papers on the areas of obsessive compulsive disorder, alcohol and drug abuse in adolescents, decision-making, and psychotropic drug prescribing. He presents lectures and workshops nationally and internationally, and teaches on postgraduate clinical psychology, psychotherapy and other educational programmes in University Colleges Cork, Galway and Dublin, and in the University of Limerick, Ireland. He presently sits on the Clinical Division Committee of the Psychological Society of Ireland and is a member of the Board of Examiners for the Society's Clinical Diploma.

**Iain Chatwin** is a qualified social worker with 25 years' experience of working with children and young people with intellectual disabilities and ASD. Following posts as team leader and care manager with responsibilities for developing ASD-specific services, he has more recently taken on a training role. As staff development co-ordinator at Sunfield, Iain is responsible for the development and delivery of innovative and specialised training programmes, specifically in approaches to working with people with ASD. This has also included the development of university-accredited courses for teaching assistants and social care staff. His role involves being a National Vocational Qualification assessor, a practice teacher for master's and bachelor's degree courses in social work, and a TEACCH trainer. Iain is also an associate tutor with the Institute of Education and the Institute of Health and Social Care at the University of Worcester. Iain conducts training courses throughout the UK and has presented at conferences nationally and internationally. Iain conducts training courses throughout the UK and has presented at conferences nationally and internationally.

**Jo Egerton** is research fellow/publications manager at Sunfield School for young people with severe and complex intellectual disabilities in Clent, Worcestershire. She has worked in the field of special education for 10 years, and during that time has held posts in teaching, research, residential care, leisure and development. She holds a Postgraduate Certificate in Education and has a master's degree in learning disability studies. She has trained as a TEACCH practitioner, and holds a master's level module in the TEACCH approach. She has co-edited two books with Barry Carpenter, and has authored and co-authored several journal articles. While working in Oxfordshire, she developed *On Track,* a Mencap-funded accessible newspaper for young people with intellectual disabilities in the county. She has presented at a number of conferences.

**Val Harley** is a senior care manager with responsibility for recruitment and training specifically in the field of National Vocational Qualifications in Health and Social Care. She also holds the post of TEACCH trainer within the Sunfield organisation. Her career in the caring profession, working specifically with students who have severe and complex intellectual disabilities, spans 23 years. She has predominantly focused her work on the residential care of these students, although she has trained a variety of professionals including psychologists, speech and language therapists and teachers in her TEACCH trainer capacity. She has also spent time supporting families to implement the approach at home and supporting staff to implement a social curriculum within a residential setting. Her role has developed over time as she has been given educational opportunities to broaden her knowledge and gain professional qualifications. She has a Certificate in Social Services qualification in Social Work and a bachelor's (BA Ed.) honours degree in special education.

**Jotham Konaka** is a teacher/researcher with over 25 years' teaching experience in the area of special educational needs. He is currently working at Sunfield School for young people with severe and complex intellectual disabilities, including Autistic spectrum Disorders (ASD). As a founder member of the Specials Schools Sports Association of Kenya, he contributed immensely towards the development of a physical education curriculum for children with physical and neurological disabilities in the country. Jotham is a holder of an MA degree in special education as well as being a level 3 Sherborne Developmental Movement (SDM) practitioner. He has recently completed a two-year research project exploring the use of SDM programme to support social engagement with young people with severe ASD. Jotham is currently exploring ways of extending this work as part of his doctorate studies. He has presented at conferences nationally and internationally, and run training courses based upon the 'Sherborne @ Sunfield' programme. He has contributed chapters about the programme to several publications.

**Nick Logan** presently heads the psychology and therapies department at Sunfield, and for the last year has been responsible for leading on the Sunfield Assessment and Outreach Service. Having a professional background as a chartered psychologist, throughout his time at Sunfield, Nick has co-ordinated the policy and practice on challenging behaviour. Due to the changing nature of the needs of the students coming to Sunfield, his research on behaviour has inevitably led him to the field of mental health needs. Nick is currently an honorary national adviser for the Down Syndrome Association which partially requires him to present papers to conferences. He is also honorary lecturer for the University of Worcester. He has contributed a number of articles to professional journals.

**Roy McConkey** is professor of learning disability at the University of Ulster, Northern Ireland: a post jointly funded by the Eastern Health and Social Services Boards. A psychologist by training and a native of Belfast, he has previously held posts at the University of Manchester, in Dublin and in Scotland. He has worked in the field of intellectual disability for over 30 years, and has authored, co-authored and edited over 15 books, and published over 100 book chapters and research papers in learned journals. He has acted as a consultant to various United Nations agencies and international non-governmental organisations. This work has taken him to some 20 countries in Africa, Asia and South America.

**Diana Pauli**, MA Cantab., Ph.D. is a research associate of the Research Institute at Sunfield School. Originally a science teacher in a mainstream school, she has been involved in autism research for the past eight years.

**Maureen Porter** is an assistant head teacher at Sunfield, with responsibility for 14–19 education. She is also responsible for the delivery of accreditation, both internal and external, and is a national workshop deliverer for the Award Scheme Development and Accreditation Network (ASDAN). Maureen holds a bachelor's (BA) honours degree in education and a master's degree (MA) in special and inclusive education, a Postgraduate Certificate in Education, a Certificate of Education (Further and Higher Education) and a Certificate in Special Education. Maureen began her career in special education in 1967 and, for the last 19 years, has worked at Sunfield, rising from teaching assistant to her present position. During these 19 years, she has obtained all her qualifications through the personal development programme facilitated by Sunfield, and the programme of in-service training. Most of her work is school-based. She has been head of department for both 14–16 years and further education (16–19) years. She has designed the school's further education curriculum, and has introduced the external accreditation programme throughout the school and residential houses. She regularly delivers ASDAN workshops, both internally and externally, and hosts moderation meetings.

**Deb Rattley** is an assistant head teacher at Sunfield, with responsibility for curriculum, professional development and training. She is a TEACCH trainer and an associate tutor with the Institute of Education at the University of Worcester. Over the last 20 years, Deb has gained experience teaching in mainstream schools, special schools and specialised unit provision for children with moderate intellectual difficulties and children with specific speech and language difficulties. She has also worked as an outreach teacher. Prior to working at Sunfield, Deb was teacher in charge of two speech and language units within a mainstream school. Deb holds a Bachelor of Education degree (B.Ed.), her main subject being special educational needs, a Master of Education degree (M.Ed.) in the management of special needs, and the National Professional Qualification for Headship (NPQH). The majority of Deb's work is school-based; however, she works closely with families to implement TEACCH beyond Sunfield. She is responsible for assessment, and teaching and learning within her curriculum role.

**Gill Rowley** is an assistant head teacher at Sunfield, currently responsible for Key Stages 1, 2, and 3; she is also the subject leader for personal, social and health education (PSHE) and citizenship. She qualified as a teacher with a Bachelor of Education (B.Ed.) degree in special education in 1980, and since then has taught in a range of day and residential special schools for children and young people with severe intellectual disabilities and autistic spectrum disorders. She has worked in schools within the maintained sector, a National Autistic Society school, where she began working on curriculum development, and also a local autistic society school, where she first became responsible for PSHE and citizenship. Sunfield has recently been inspected by Ofsted (October 2006) which reported that, *'the wider provision for pupils' personal, social and health education and citizenship is outstanding.'*

**Emma Taylor** and **Kellyanne Thornton** have worked closely with children and young people with intellectual disabilities for six years in the psychology and therapies department at Sunfield. Both graduated from university with a degree in psychology. Emma continued to complete a master's degree in community care (learning disabilities) at Keele University. While both were employed as psychology assistants at Sunfield, they became particularly interested in the role of play in the developing child with intellectual disabilities and ASD. They began a research project, the results of which have been published in the UK journal, *Good Autism Practice,* and have presented their research at various conferences. They are now training to become play therapists at Canterbury Christchurch University, whereby they hope to apply their knowledge of play therapy philosophy to their current approach.

**Teresa Whitehurst** has been research and development officer at Sunfield for three years. She has a B.Sc. honours degree in psychology, and postgraduate research qualifications, and undertook a range of research projects prior to joining Sunfield, primarily evaluating services for vulnerable populations. She is currently studying for a master's degree in neuroscience. Teresa's role focuses on developing and sustaining a dynamic and productive research culture within the school in addition to conducting focused research projects. Research projects are determined by a person-centred, family-focused approach, and include topics such as nutrition and ASD, mental health issues, inclusion, the voice of the child and sleep problems. Teresa has published a number of articles in academic journals, and presented research at various conferences.

# Foreword

*Roy McConkey*

Isn't it odd how often we use words without stopping to reflect fully on their meaning? Take the word 'complex', for example. It is freely used in education – as in children with complex needs; or undertaking complex assessments; or managing complex family problems. As an adjective, it transforms the simple to the difficult, the mundane into the exceptional, the insignificant to the profound. Conquering complexity seems a noble challenge, undertaken more in hope than in certainty.

What do we really mean when we use the word 'complex'? Is it a euphemism invoked by politicians for 'I don't understand what's going on' or by plumbers to mean 'This is going to cost you a fortune'? My dictionary says 'complex' means intricate or complicated, but that merely replaces one abstraction with others. I read that it can mean a neurotic or obsessive feeling, as in having a complex about something. Now, that strikes a chord with me – thinking of some of the people I know in special needs education – but perhaps these are the outcomes of dealing with complexity rather than the phenomena itself?

Another meaning, derived from psychology, shows promise: 'a group of repressed ideas or emotions in conflict with others already accepted'. Certainly in that sense, much of special needs education deserves to be called complex. It is only a generation past since children with severe learning difficulties were accepted *into* the educational system, but it would be a step too far to claim they have become *part of it*. It is easy to label mainstream educators as unaccepting, but I wonder if the complexity of creating an inclusive system lies more with the special needs sector and their repression of the ideas and emotions inherent in their educational endeavours, some of which do conflict with those of the mainstream. As a result their efforts are undervalued by educationalists, but more crucially their influence on mainstream education has been muted.

If you accept this argument, then this book is especially welcome. It details in wonderful practicality what it means to deliver a complex curriculum to children with complex needs and produce ordinary, mundane and, dare I say, simple outcomes; the sort that parents want for their children – that they would be happy, have friends, and engage in activities to help them to grow and develop while keeping them out of trouble.

There is yet another meaning of complex: 'consisting of several closely related parts'. In this sense, this is certainly a complex book, and that is meant as a compliment!

The many different disciplines involved with children who have special needs still try to dissect the developing child into discrete parts for assessment and therapy, and then expect that somehow these parts will magically re-assemble into a new improved child. Even more surprisingly, many teachers have colluded with this notion, and allowed themselves to become just one more professional, when it is they who could and should be the integrator, the co-ordinator, the educator.

But to take on that role is complex. It means bringing together closely related parts of every child's life within and beyond school. Sunfield may be a unique school; one of its kind in these islands. Yet what is really special about it, as you will discover through these pages, are the interrelated processes that they use to help children to develop a fuller and richer life. These are not bound by places and personalities, but rather can be implemented by any educator. That includes you and me! We are indebted to Sunfield for sharing with us the complexity they strive to manage – in all its meanings.

Roy McConkey
*Professor of Learning Disability*

# PART 1

# Introduction to
# Evidence-Based Practice

# CHAPTER 1

# Introduction

*Barry Carpenter and Jo Egerton*

There is a changing pattern of disability emerging in childhood (Carpenter, 2005). Foetal Alcohol Spectrum Disorder, Fragile X Syndrome, prematurity and an array of chromosomal abnormalities are now major causes of disability in our child population. For a voluntary sector disability organisation such as Sunfield, two fundamental questions underpin provision and development – 'Who are our students now?' and 'Who will our future population of students be?' Sunfield provides education and residential care, alongside psychology, health and therapy support, for young people with severe and complex intellectual disabilities aged between 6 and 19 years. In recent years, for a majority of our students, these severe learning needs have arisen from profound autistic spectrum disorder (ASD).

The UK government's 1997 Green Paper, *Excellence in All Schools: Meeting special educational needs,* heralded the move to include children with a full range of special educational needs within the mainstream education system. However, the government recognised that those with the most severe and complex difficulties would continue to need specialist support (Department for Education and Employment, 1997). Indeed, subsequent national studies have reported a co-morbidity in this child population, with mental health needs being particularly prevalent (Foundation for People with Learning Disabilities (FPLD), 2002)

Children with profound ASD were then ill-served by the UK education system. The lack of provision, appropriate curriculum and clear rationale for teaching and learning disenfranchised these children from education, put huge amounts of pressure on their families, and led to a worrying trend of social exclusion. In a climate of inclusion, these children were the victims of an inequality of educational opportunity.

In response to the educational and social disadvantage that children with profound ASD were suffering, Sunfield launched the Sunfield Integrated Education and Care Curriculum Approach (SIECCA) in 1998 (Carpenter, Ashdown and Bovair, 2001; Carpenter, Chatwin and Egerton, 2001; see also Chapter 12). The SIECCA programme was developed with reference to contemporary research and is regularly reviewed and updated to ensure it continues to meet the changing needs of Sunfield's students (Bondy and Frost, 1996; Jordan, 2001; Mesibov, 1997; Mesibov and Howley, 2003; Powell, 2000). Through its focus on profound autism, Sunfield also became involved with the regional autism initiative investigating best practice (West Midlands SEN Regional Partnership, 2002).

As professionals, we are all entering a new phase in learning about childhood disabilities. We have found out much of what we need to know about their causes and aetiology (Guralnick, 2004). Evidence from practitioners will help us to connect to new challenges – to address the needs of students who will be in our classrooms in the future (Carpenter, 2005; General Teaching Council for England (GTCE), 2004, 2006). Our professional knowledge will depend upon our observations of young people in the context of our work with them and our academically informed analyses of those observations. If we, in our varying professions, do not continue to change to meet the needs of the children and young people we serve, then our schools, and the pedagogy they employ, will become obsolete.

The Sunfield Research Institute was founded by Sunfield's Trustees in 2005. It aims to develop understanding within the organisation of the nature and impact of severe and complex intellectual disabilities and to find new and improved ways of supporting our young people and their families through research which is:

■ *Child- and family-centred* – our inspiration for change must be the students we are working with

■ *Practice-informing* – the only justifiable outcome is improvement for those students

■ *Inclusive* – students and families should be welcomed as research partners in their own right

■ *Collaborative* – everyone involved can contribute a valuable perspective, no matter what their role.

At the Institute's launch in 2005, Professor Lesley Saunders, Policy Adviser for Research at the General Teaching Council for England, encouraged all practitioners to reclaim the language of professional discussion through research. This is what the contributors to this book have sought to do both at Sunfield, and now, with this publication, further afield. As Teresa Whitehurst emphasises in Chapter 16, there is still much to be learned and assimilated about the research process but, as early practitioner researchers, we have made a commitment to establishing the ethos of evidence-based development to improve the life chances of the young people we support and meet their changing needs.

### The teacher as researcher

For many years, research has been the preserve of academics, and many teachers feel overawed by the prospect of carrying out research alongside their classroom commitments. Below, Maureen Porter, assistant headteacher (14–19 education) at Sunfield, describes her experience of becoming a practitioner researcher.

> The first principle of teaching must surely be that we as teachers have a responsibility to provide the best quality of education that is possible for each individual student. All our attitudes to the students we teach and the educational methods we employ are cultivated over the years by the acquisition of our own principles and values. Not every teacher is aware that they hold personal educational philosophies, but most would be able to describe their approaches to practice in detail. What we believe to be simply practical approaches to getting through our daily routines in the classroom or care environment can, upon investigation, often be traced to theories which have precedent, proof and justification. However well

can justify our approaches, we need to be reflective practitioners – striving for professional self-development through critical consideration of our practices. Only by constant evaluation of our practice, embracing innovative approaches and through continuing professional development that broadens our knowledge, can we hope to impact upon future practice. As Blandford (2000) tells us:

*...the art of self-evaluation is acquired against a background of continual learning.* (p. 183)

My attitudes to my students and the educational methods I employ to teach them have been assembled, expanded and reconsidered over the years as my understanding of students with intellectual disabilities has improved, but I reached a point in my career when I began to question my method of teaching. Why was I using a particular approach, what information was I presenting to my students, and how was I managing their challenging behaviour? However long we have been teaching, 'There is a time when people's experience runs out...' (Horton and Freire, 1990).

Research enables us to move forward from a personally held view towards a proven approach which can be shared with others. Many of us may identify with Rousseau, who wrote:

*What can I do? I have not written about other people's ideas of education but about my own. My thoughts are not those of others.* (Rousseau, 1969)

However, as researchers, we must be ready to move on, to look objectively at why and how, and to evaluate, improve and justify. Upon my promotion to head of Sunfield's further education department, I felt empowered to ask if the teaching methods we were using in the department were the best possible. Did our further education curriculum really 'serve the pupil in promoting personal development and preparing the pupil for adult life' (Her Majesty's Inspectorate (HMI), 1991). These questions led to the start of my research (see Chapter 14).

The staff in any school are its major resource, and as such should be willing to examine and research their own practices, critically reflecting and discussing in as many forums as possible. In order to develop we must hold up our values and beliefs to scrutiny, and this takes strength of mind, particularly in some climates of low professional morale and confidence. Ultimately, the objective is to enrich our profession and make us more efficient practitioners.

Although the enquiry cycle of research can seem never ending, remember to celebrate your achievements. As David Miliband, School Standards Minister in the UK, said:

*One should never be satisfied, one should always want to do better, but one should be proud of progress that has been made.* (2004)

## This book

The chapters in this volume are a series of evidence-based reports which reflect the journeys of key practitioners at Sunfield in taking up the challenge of research; their goal – to meet students at their points of learning need. Over time, Sunfield has built on the initial evidence-based work and evolved into a research-focused organisation (see Chapters 2 and 16. Research approaches, ethically underpinned, now provide the framework for seeking access to the learning pathways of students with very complex ASD. This approach has been validated in the 2006 inspection report (Office for Standards in Education (Ofsted), 2006) which identified the school as being 'a significant contributor…to the debate about autism'. Inspectors identified that this reflective practice had had a direct impact within Sunfield and was evident in the meticulous provision made for students.

The UK government's current focus for children's learning is articulated in *Every Child Matters: Change for children* (Department for Education and Skills, 2004). Their aim is that they should be healthy, stay safe, enjoy and achieve, make a positive contribution and achieve economic well-being. At Sunfield, our research programme reflects these concerns and seeks to identify ways in which these aims can become reality for our students.

Many of the children and young people at Sunfield have profound ASD; others have a range of developmental disabilities. In the field of education, they would usually be described as having severe learning disabilities. However, the generic term we have chosen to cover these different diagnoses is 'intellectual disability', which is more widely in use across different disciplines and internationally.

The chapters in the book are organised into sections which reflect different areas of research at Sunfield – from laying the foundations of learning and social relationships, 'Building communication', through to the point when young people begin their adult life, 'Preparing for the future'.

### Section 1: Introduction to evidence-based practice
This chapter and Chapter 2 (Barry Carpenter) introduce Sunfield and place the school's approach within the context of the wider, evolving practitioner research climate.

### Section 2: Building communication
Communication has always been a central focus in the education and care practice of Sunfield. Chapter 3 (Kellyanne Thornton and Emma Taylor) and Chapter 4 (Jotham Konaka) explore the foundations of pre-verbal communication through play and movement approaches. In Chapter 5, Iain Chatwin has adapted the concept of Social Stories (Gray, 2004) to enable access to social self-management for young people with a higher conceptual understanding.

### Section 3: Enhancing health and well-being
Young people with intellectual disabilities, and especially those with ASD, are at greater risk of developing mental health problems than their typically developing contemporaries. Until recently, the co-morbidity of mental health issues and intellectual disabilities had been largely ignored. Chapters 6 (Barry Carpenter, Barry Coughlan, Nick Logan and Teresa Whitehurst) and 7 (Barry Coughlan) discuss the mental health issues arising among children and young people with intellectual disabilities and the development of a mental health training package for staff at Sunfield to equip them to recognise and support the mental health needs of students at Sunfield.

Chapter 8 (Gill Rowley and Jan Cook) describes the adaptation of 'Zippy's friends', a mainstream Personal, Social and Health Education (PSHE) programme, for students with severe and complex intellectual disabilities with the goal of supporting and strengthening their emotional well-being. In Chapter 9, Diana Pauli investigates the development of thinking, feeling and willing among students with profound ASD within a responsive coloured light environment.

## Section 4: Inclusion in the community
Chapters 10 (Barry Carpenter, Sally Conway, Teresa Whitehurst and Elizabeth At-tfield) and 11 (Teresa Whitehurst) describe two different inclusive approaches. In Chapter 10, the authors describe how Sunfield families and staff have collaborated in investigating how families feel about their welcome into the school community. Chapter 11 describes how young people with severe and complex intellectual disabilities have, within the structure of an Arts project, contributed to and commented on the wider community outside Sunfield.

## Section 5: The SIECCA Curriculum
The SIECCA approach has received recognition in literature (Jones, 2002; FPLD, 2002; Lacey, 2001), and was described by Ofsted (2006) as 'outstanding...a genuine 24-hour curriculum in which pupils flourish because it is meticulously planned and implemented by dedicated teams of staff, both in residences and the school'. Chapters 12 and 13 describe the development of the curriculum and the implementation of a transdisciplinary staff training programme to support students' achievement within that approach.

## Section 6: Preparing for the future
In this section, the focus is upon the future for both the young people at Sunfield and the staff as practitioner researchers. In Chapter 14, Maureen Porter describes the development of the Further Education curriculum with a particular emphasis on vocational achievement and accreditation for young people about to move to adult residential placements. Chapter 15 (Jo Egerton) describes Sunfield's ongoing research into the transition needs of young people and their parents. Finally, Chapter 16 (Teresa Whitehurst) describes current and evolving research practice among practitioners at Sunfield and explores future possibilities.

## References
Blandford, S. (2000) *Managing Professional Development in Schools*. London: Routledge.

Bondy, A. and Frost, L. (1996) 'Educational approaches in preschool: behavior techniques in a public school setting'. In: E. Schopler and G.B. Mesibov (eds) *Learning and Cognition in Autism*. New York : Plenum Press.

Carpenter, B. (2005) 'Real prospects for early childhood intervention: family aspirations and professional implications'. In: B. Carpenter and J. Egerton (eds) *Early Childhood Intervention: International perspectives, national initiatives and regional practice.* Coventry: West Midlands SEN Regional Partnership.

Carpenter, B., Ashdown, R. and Bovair, K. (eds) (2001) *Enabling Access: Effective Teaching and Learning for Pupils with Learning Difficulties (2nd Edition).* London: D Fulton

Carpenter, B., Chatwin, I. and Egerton, J. (2001) 'An evaluation of SIECCA: an intensive programme of education and care for students with profound autistic spectrum disorders', *Good Autism Practice*, 2 (1), 52–66.

Department for Education and Employment (1997) *Excellence for All Children: Meeting special educational needs.* London: DfEE.

Department for Education and Skills (2004) *Every Child Matters: Change for children.* Nottingham: DfES.

Foundation for People with Learning Disabilities (2002) *Count Us In: Report of the Committee of Inquiry into the Mental Health of Young People with Learning Disabilities.* London: Mental Health Foundation.

General Teaching Council for England (2004) *GTC Research Digest 2000–2004.* London: GTCE.

General Teaching Council for England (2006) 'Using research in your school and in your teaching: research engaged professional practice'. [Online at: http://www.gtce.org.uk/tplf]

Gray, C. (2004) 'Social Stories 10: the new defining criteria and guidelines', *Jenison Autism Journal*, 15 (4), 2–21.

Guralnick, M. (2004) 'Early Intervention for children with intellectual disabilities: current knowledge and future prospects.' Keynote address to the 12th IASSID World Congress, Montpellier, France (15 June 2004).

Her Majesty's Inspectorate (HMI) (1991) *Education Observed: The implementation of the curricular requirements of ERA.* London: HMSO.

Horton, M. and Freire, P. (1990) *We Make the Road by Walking: Conversations on education and social change.* Philadelphia: Temple University Press.

Jones, G. (2002) *Educational provision for children with autism and Asperger syndrome – meeting their needs.* London: David Fulton.

Jordan, R. (2001) *Autism with Severe Learning Difficulties.* London: Souvenir Press.

Lacey, P. (2001) *Support Partnerships: Collaboration in action.* London: David Fulton.

Mesibov, G.B. (1997) 'Formal and informal measure on the effectiveness of the TEACCH programme', *Autism* 1 (1), 25–35.

Mesibov, G. and Howley, M. (2003) *Accessing the Curriculum for Pupils with Autistic Spectrum Disorders.* London: David Fulton.

Office for Standards in Education (Ofsted) (2006) 'Inspection report: Sunfield School (2–5 October 2006)'. [Online at: www.ofsted.gov.uk]

Porter, J. and Ashdown, R. (2001) *Children with Complex Learning Difficulties.* Tamworth: NASEN.

Powell, S. (ed.) (2000) *Helping Children with Autism to Learn.* London: David Fulton.

Rousseau, J.J. (1969) *Emile (Reprint).* London: Dent and Sons.

West Midlands SEN Regional Partnership (2002) *Report on Autistic Spectrum Disorders: A comprehensive report into identification, training and provision focusing on the needs of children and young people with an autistic spectrum disorder and their families within the West Midlands region.* Coventry: West Midlands SEN Regional Partnership.

# CHAPTER 2

# Developing the Role of Schools as Research Organisations

## The Sunfield Experience

*Barry Carpenter*

### Changing children; changing practice?

As professionals, we are entering a new phase in learning about childhood disabilities. We have found out much of what we need to know about their causes and aetiology. Michael Guralnick (2004) observes that:

> *We now know so much about childhood disability that we must move to second generation research. This must be practitioner led and evidence based.*

With such a shift in research focus, the answers to many of the challenges posed by the changing pattern of childhood disability (Carpenter, 2005) will come from the evidence base held by practitioners. For as the recent report from the Parliamentary Hearings on Services for Disabled Children (October 2006) stated:

> *In 2006, the population of disabled children looks dramatically different to thirty years ago. It is now acknowledged that 7% and not 3% of all children have a disability or long-term condition, a total of 770,000 children and young people in the UK.* (HM Treasury/Department for Education and Skills (DfES), 2006)

### The changing locus of research

In the light of such a dramatic reconfiguration of the face of special educational needs, the locus of research, which is practitioner-led, needs to change. The General Teaching Council for England (GTCE, 2004) encourages practitioners to:

> *Create, interpret, share and rigorously evaluate practical evidence about teaching and learning in and for different contexts.*

They argue further (GTCE, 2006) that research inquiry aims to solve problems by achieving deeper understanding. Our professional knowledge will depend upon our observations of young people in the context of our work with them and our academically informed analyses of those observations. This approach will require us to understand the new challenges and change in order to go forward'. For, as Furlong (2000) argues:

> *The issue is not whether teachers naturally engage in theorising their practice – they do. Rather the issue is whether they have been justified and developed by being exposed to the critical scrutiny of other practitioners; whether they are based on a consideration of evidence from research and from elsewhere; whether they have been interrogated in terms of the values and assumptions on which they are based.*

If we, as teachers, do not continue to change to meet the needs of the children and young people we serve, then our schools, and the pedagogy they employ, will become obsolete. I would endorse completely Olson's (2003) statement:

> *There is no way to ignore the goals, beliefs and intentions of the teachers and learners…pedagogy is the professional competence involved in making timely, informed decisions about drawing individual minds and cultural resources together.*

Do we have the pedagogy to hand that will enable us to meet the many and varied teaching challenges posed by these children with different patterns of learning who engage, or rather do not engage, with the classroom-based experiences presented? Do we have the capacity as a profession to touch these children at their point of learning need?

Bluntly, my assessment at the moment is that we do not; we are not able to present rich learning environments capable of addressing the full spectrum of need. However, I am in no doubt that with the wealth of experience of children with traditional special educational needs held in the teaching profession, and the talent and ingenuity of many teachers for devising creative solutions, new pathways will be found. But all of this must be informed by a rigorous process of practitioner-led, evidence-based research. Only by working with and through the children, will we discover their learning profiles and evolve the teaching strategies that will deliver an education of quality. The power truly is in our hands; but then so are the answers to some very great needs in an exceptionally challenging and vulnerable group of children – those with complex special educational needs arising from the 'new' causes of disabilities – foetal alcohol syndrome, drug abuse, etc.

## The relationship between academic and practitioner research

Frequently, academics perceive practitioner research as lacking rigour, and practitioners view much academic research as impracticable. However, the relationship between academic and practitioner research is symbiotic in two ways. The first is that practitioner research offers a context in which existing academic theory can be tested (translational research; Shirley, 2005), so that its 'real life' impact, day-to-day, for a young person with a special need or disability can be assessed. Rose (2002) notes that:

> *Teachers are more likely to participate in classroom-based inquiry when they perceive that this will have benefits to their own practice and to the needs of the pupils in their classrooms.*

The second is that new ideas and concepts can emerge from a foundation of existing good practice and theory (GTCE, 2004), and these can then be investigated by academics for a wider population of young people. Both Rose and Grosvenor (2001) and Kershner and Chaplin (2001) have cited examples of teacher research projects that have increased understanding of methods, approaches, teaching and learning in a variety of different special needs settings. Additionally Watkins (2006), in a statement that can apply equally well to practitioners from other disciplines, postulates that:

> *Only through developing opportunities for teachers to research their own personal conceptions of what special needs education is – and isn't – will the wider educational community really move forward in its thinking.*

The recent workforce remodelling in many schools has raised the profile of teaching assistants. They find themselves engaged in classroom-based enquiry, and for some this leads to foundation degree studies or higher level teaching assistant (HLTA) qualifications. Taylor, Wilkie and Baser (2006) specifically write about supporting learning professionally and the developing role of teaching assistants. They quote the reflections of Leanne (a teaching assistant) upon the importance of research:

> *In the past, I have successfully contributed and played an active role in research-based developments within our school, working alongside colleagues, children and parents… as a result, I am aware of the positive impact that research can have in future developments, and how it informs the raising of standards.*

All practitioners have a role to play in improving both standards and the quality of teaching and learning in schools. Therefore a whole-team approach, which we have chosen to call 'transdisciplinary', to evidence-based research practice has the potential to have a positive and lasting impact upon teaching and learning in a wide variety of educational settings. It also offers the opportunity to seek solutions to the complex profile of learning needs presented by this ever-changing population of children with special educational needs. If we are professionally honest with ourselves, we do not have the pedagogy to touch some of these children at their point of learning need.

With the comparatively recent emphasis on researchers' accountability to the subjects of their study, the effective application of research to professional practice has become an increasingly important, ethical consideration, and resonates with the seminal message first articulated by Stenhouse (1981).

**Practitioners as researchers**
It is easy for practitioners to become over-awed by the concept of research, and to perceive it as a lofty, academic concern removed from their own activity. Education practitioners are engaged in 'research' as part of the routine of day-to-day work in school. Whether it be using the internet to gather up-to-date information on a previously unknown genetic condition, observing a student to find out why certain behaviours are occurring, or analysing the latest assessments for a cohort of students; all of these activities constitute 'research'. However, as Whitehead (Shepherd, 2004; see also Whitehead and Hartley, 2005) states:

> *Research…is not distant from practice, but its lifeblood. It feeds the cycle of reflection/evidence/evaluation/teaching and learning. It's what excellent teachers do.*

The practitioner working with a child or young person with special educational needs is the means by which research – carried out by both academics and other practitioners – can make a difference to their daily lives. This has been ably demonstrated through a whole series of articles promoted by journals serving the field of special educational needs (cf. *British Journal of Learning Support*, volume 21). These articles expound creative, insightful approaches, which ultimately enhance the quality of learning for children and the effectiveness of teaching for teachers (Doveston and Keenaghan, 2006; Johnson, 2006).

Practitioners, while ideally placed to carry out 'real world' research (Robson, 2002), often need support in carrying out setting-based inquiry (Roberts-Holmes, 2005). This may be in structuring the research so that it meets important academic criteria – e.g. justification, rigour, dissemination, recognition of participant rights (Porter and Lacey, 2004). It may also require organisational solutions to the practical issues of time and staffing. Action research models have contributed greatly to bringing clarity to this process (Zuber-Skerritt, 1989)

### Developments at Sunfield School
#### An evolving service
At Sunfield, as a residential special school for young people with profound autistic spectrum disorders (ASD) and complex needs, there is a need to plan ahead and to explore new ways of intervening in order to improve life for the continually changing generations of young people with severe/complex intellectual disabilities and their families. The school's capacity to be a responsive organisation, offering high quality services, underpinned by a sound evidence base and a dynamic research process, is crucial to both its future children, and its current children's futures. The school enables staff to be responsive in developing approaches that will be innovative, dynamic and, at times, ground-breaking to meet the children and young people at their point of learning.

Practitioner research is a dynamic process owned by all staff working with young people and families. From their different perspectives comes a greater appreciation of specific contextual detail and its implications for the young people. All have a contribution to make to transdisciplinary research along a continuum of involvement. Projects may include practitioners who have traditionally been excluded from research – for example, school dinner ladies (Smith, 2002) and catering staff (Sunfield Nutrition Research Project; see Chapter 16). These staff bring insights from alternative perspectives, which can address problematic elements of research design and add value to the cumulative evidence base.

The perspectives of families and young people in the research context are also vital and address the aim of seamless support for the young person. In a recent piece of research undertaken by Carpenter, Conway, Whitehurst and Attfield (Chapter 10), a Parent Advisory Group were involved in the analysis of interview transcripts which explored other parents' experiences of induction to Sunfield. In another piece of work, Sunfield's Student Council carried out their own inquiry into the school's Mission Statement and what everyone thought of it (Ross, Kelly, Lee and Pearson, 2003). They found out that some of the students could not read the symbols used, and therefore they decided that the best way of embodying what Sunfield stood for was a photograph of a cross-section of familiar people who made up the Sunfield community.

### Supporting the research process

The trustees and senior management team at Sunfield deemed that its future provision development would be reliant upon the answers and insights staff generated from their research endeavour and practice-based evidence through inquiry. Thus the assimilation of research as a dimension of work-related practice, generating evidence for evaluation and future development, became essential.

At Sunfield, there are many professionals who come from evidence-based disciplines (e.g. from Care, Therapies, Education, Psychology), who in the course of their work, look for outcomes which will benefit young people, families and staff. Sunfield evolved an effective model of transdisciplinary practice, in which collaborative teamwork was an embedded feature (see Chapters 12 and 13). Upon this platform, a fundamentally transdisciplinary research approach was developed, and this has been successfully trialled in reported research projects (Logan, Cowley, Winstanley and Gallivan, 2005; Whitehurst and Howells, 2006). A recent project around nutrition for young people with ASD involved a chef from the catering department as a key player in the research process, alongside teachers, care workers, therapists and support staff.

Acknowledging that practitioner-led research should not be equated with an approach that is tardy, ad hoc and unsubstantiated, Sunfield encourages a robust research process, identified by Porter and Lacey (2004) as one which:

- Has integrity
- Is rigorous
- Is well-planned
- Is carefully executed
- Is meticulously reported
- Is transparent
- Is ethical.

Recognising the importance of the efficacy of research carried out in the school, senior managers and trustees ring-fenced money in the school's budget to support the appointment of a research officer, who would be able to develop and guide research within the school. This development was underpinned by the formulation of a Research Policy. Its aims and objectives (see Figure 2.1) constitute the framework within which the research officer operates, and its stated aims and objectives provide criteria against which research proposals can be evaluated.

Currently, the governance, policy and research development instituted by Sunfield with the aim of supporting its staff in becoming flexible practitioners include:

- *A research policy:* Sunfield's research policy is not lofty; it was drawn up in consultation with staff engaged in research, including those studying for NVQ III
- *Training:* Sunfield's 'Professional Development Centre' offers a wide range of professional courses which give an opportunity for participants to reflect on present practice and gain new knowledge

- *Literature*: Sunfield's lending library is continually updated with new publications, and also has a selection of journals; these provide a resource to inform practice and support research

- *The publications brochure*: a useful reference for all staff, particularly new staff who want background information on projects. It also serves as an ongoing means of dissemination to interested practitioners in other organisations

- *A specialist research post*: Sunfield has developed the post of research officer to provide specialist research support for the institution and the staff

- *Opportunities for dissemination (external):* staff are encouraged to write up their work for external professional journals, to submit papers to conferences and, where appropriate, to deliver external training

- *Opportunities for dissemination (internal):* in addition to contributing to external professional journals, Sunfield has an 'Innovations Forum' where staff who have been carrying out research present it to the rest of the staff; research is also disseminated through Research Briefing Sheets

- *The Research Institute*: this was founded by Sunfield's trustees in January 2005 in acknowledgement that working with a population of young people who have severe and complex intellectual disabilities and a changing pattern of need requires creative exploration and adaptation of existing approaches

- *Sunfield's Research and Ethics Group*: chaired by a trustee, the group evaluates staff research applications to make sure that they comply with its criteria for ethical research

- *Sunfield Research Institute Strategic Management Group:* chaired by a trustee, the group ensures the aims and objectives of current and future research remain responsive to the changing population need.

### Raising research consciousness

Many staff at Sunfield engage with some form of small-scale research in their study towards National Vocational Qualifications (NVQs) or a Foundation Degree in Learning Support. During a research awareness-raising exercise conducted with several staff groups at Sunfield prior to undertaking their research module, they were simply asked, 'What do you think we mean by research?' The words generated by staff often varied according to work-related perspective (see Figure 2.1), but all were descriptors of facets of the research process. For example:

- Enquire
- Probe
- Observe
- Collect evidence

- Investigate
- Evaluate
- Disseminate
- Report.

- Examine
- Hypothesise
- Search

With many staff from different levels and disciplines engaged in research, both they and their colleagues have come to value inquiry into practice and recognise the importance of implementing of evidence-based change for the young people with whom they work.

### How can staff engage?

There is a potentially rich source of evidence already in the practitioner research domain from the wide range of staff who work with the young people – daily logs and evidence collected against personalised learning targets (care and education staff),

## Figure 2.1. Excerpt from Sunfield's Research Policy: Aims and objectives

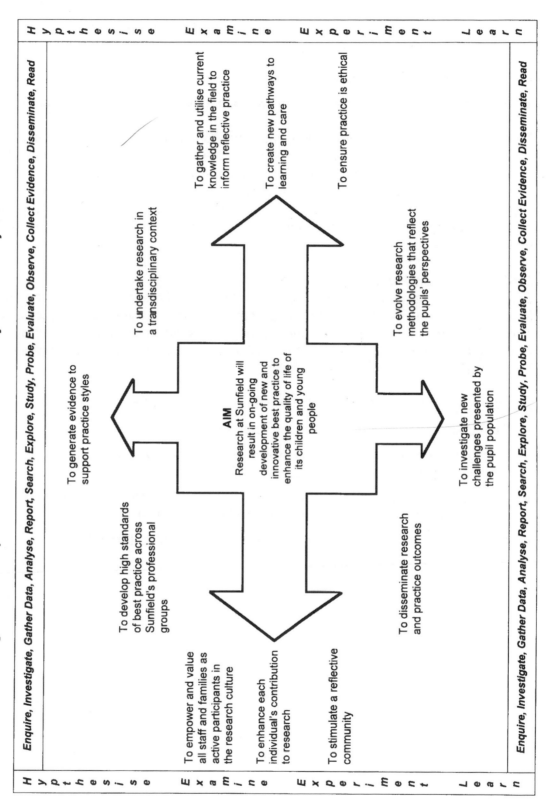

Enquire, Investigate, Gather Data, Analyse, Report, Search, Explore, Study, Probe, Evaluate, Observe, Collect Evidence, Disseminate, Read

**Hypothesise**

**Examine**

**Experiment**

**Learn**

To gather and utilise current knowledge in the field to inform reflective practice

To create new pathways to learning and care

To ensure practice is ethical

To undertake research in a transdisciplinary context

To evolve research methodologies that reflect the pupils' perspectives

To generate evidence to support practice styles

**AIM**

Research at Sunfield will result in on-going development of new and innovative best practice to enhance the quality of life of its children and young people

To investigate new challenges presented by the pupil population

To develop high standards of best practice across Sunfield's professional groups

To empower and value all staff and families as active participants in the research culture

To enhance each individual's contribution to research

To stimulate a reflective community

To disseminate research and practice outcomes

Enquire, Investigate, Gather Data, Analyse, Report, Search, Explore, Study, Probe, Evaluate, Observe, Collect Evidence, Disseminate, Read

**Hypothesise**

**Examine**

**Experiment**

**Learn**

behaviour and functional analysis reports (psychology and occupational therapy staff), etc. If this data is to be used for research purposes, however, it is important that the data recorded is of a high enough quality to support the research.

The purpose and motivation for staff to engage in research lie in two questions posed by Porter and Lacey (2004):

■ What influence will my research have?

■ What contribution will it make to the lives of people with intellectual difficulties?

The issue of concern, once identified, has to be worked in a clear, researchable question. Topics can be stimulated by many different influences, such as a new development or initiative, a recurring difficulty, a long-standing personal interest or another piece of research. Moving from a research topic to a research question is an important step, and is the point at which many staff fail to proceed with their investigations (Rickman, 2005). Consultation with the research officer often enables staff to make that transition.

### Staff research projects

Sunfield staff have, to date, taken part in a wide range of research projects that inform the care of our young people with severe and complex intellectual disabilities. These have focused on inclusion, the experience of siblings, counselling and Social Stories (cf. Howley and Arnold, 2005), health resources and play therapy, among other areas. Some current projects include:

■ Interactive play (see Chapter 3; Thornton and Taylor, 2005)

■ Staff training and mental health (see Chapters 6 and 7)

■ Engaging the thinking, feeling and will of young people with autism through the medium of colour (see Chapter 9; Pauli, 2006)

■ Families' experience of induction (see Chapter 10; Carpenter, Conway and Whitehurst, 2005; Conway, Powell and Whitehurst, 2005)

■ Evaluation of an autism-specific living environment (Whitehurst, 2006)

■ Body percussion in music therapy

■ A curriculum response to *Every Child Matters* (DfES, 2003).

### Enabling school research
### External project funding

Some projects receive external funding through grant applications. For example, the Sherborne Developmental Movement Project was externally sponsored enabling a recontextualisation of this long-established programme (Sherborne, 2001) specifically for young people with profound ASD. In partnership with a Sunfield research associate from the Sherborne Movement Foundation, who brought insight and rigour to this project (Hill, 2006), this research moved from internal trials to multi-site trials involving 10 other schools, and has resulted in the 'Sherborne @ Sunfield' Movement Programme, launched in Autumn 2006 (see Chapter 4). It has revealed much about engagement as a key feature of the learning pattern of the young person with ASD.

Other projects are co-commissioned and co-sponsored by and with organisations sharing similar concerns. Transition from school to adult provision is a major factor in the lives of young people with ASD and their families. Sunfield's initial baseline research (Smart, 2004) revealed a high level of placement breakdown. In conjunction with Home Farm Trust and the West Midlands SEN Regional Partnership, the Transition Solutions Project has been established. This is a three-year project focusing on supporting families of young people with complex learning needs moving from a residential school to adult services (see Chapter 15).

The need for knowledge acquisition, practice-sharing and debate as a means for solution formulation should not be underrated in the research process. Alongside this project, the West Midlands SEN Regional Partnership has sponsored, through Sunfield's Professional Development Centre, three seminars for practitioners in the region to come together to share curriculum concerns around ransition for young people with ASD and to gather information about materials and practice models currently available. These debates and their outcomes will be fed into the Transition Solutions project.

### Collaboration with higher education

Collaboration with higher education institutions is another way of stimulating and supporting research within a school culture. However, as opposed to the traditional pattern of locating the research at a university, the model adapted at Sunfield allows for the researcher's main base to be the school. An international teacher fellowship was established for a teacher-researcher from the University of Andolou in Turkey, who accepted half-time, class-based teaching alongside an experienced Sunfield teacher. They collaborated on a project which focused on the comparison of two main pedagogical approaches in the field of ASD. The teacher-fellow led on the research style and approaches, but gained much from the dialogue with a colleague from another culture. What evolved here was ipsative research as it examined child-centred learning in a very specific, skill area. At the time of writing, Sunfield, together with the University of Worcester, have collaborated in offering a Ph.D. studentship, to be located at Sunfield, and focused on the development of ASD-specific learning environments which can be built in some new classrooms.

### Inter-school collaboration

Close collaboration with other schools has been a key feature of Sunfield's work, and this resulted in a particular Arts-based inclusion project. 'The Monkey King' project (see Chapter 11) took place over a two-year period, and took the form of a musical performance. The project involved Sunfield young people and staff, and the young people from a mainstream middle school, with professionals from the Open Theatre Company and the Shysters Theatre Company in Coventry (both for actors with intellectual disabilities) (Whitehurst, 2007, in press; Whitehurst and Howells, 2006). The project culminated in a major theatre production presented at the Birmingham Hippodrome over five performances.

The research strand of this project looked specifically at how perceptions of mainstream students changed as a result of working closely alongside peers with autism and severe and complex intellectual disabilities (Whitehurst and Howells, 2006). A process of Positive Social Construction was formed from this research, building on current theories relating to inclusion (Carpenter and Shevlin, 2004; Mittler, 2007, in press). The project has been disseminated through performance, presentation to staff at an Innovations Forum, through seminars at Universities and through a presentation at the National Teacher Research Panel Conference (http://www.livegroup.co.uk/ntrp).

## Conclusion

As practitioners, working with our young people day by day, it is impossible not to appreciate Rose's (2002) comment that:

> *Researching <u>with</u>, rather than <u>on</u>, people with disabilities is an important distinction and must guide the motivations and actions of all who engage in the process.*

The following four tenets of practice form the foundations of our commitment to continuing research alongside our young people and their families. We value practice that is:

- Evidence-based: through robust recording of young people's developmental progress and attainment, reflecting on our practice

- Research-focused: through asking ethical questions that improve our knowledge and understanding of the young people and the quality of our service to them

- Family-orientated: through resources and support that enable families to grow in their love and commitment

- Child-centred: through individually tailored, high-quality education, care, psychology and therapeutic services.

Sunfield has a long and proud tradition established in 1930 based on the premise that our support for young people with intellectual disabilities must meet them at their point of greatest need. Sunfield offered education to young people with intellectual disabilities long before the 1971 watershed. During 1959–1960, Nordoff and Robbins developed their music therapy programme there (Nordoff and Robbins, 1992). As Wilson (2002) stated:

> *If educational research is to change practice for the better, it can…only do this by operating through the minds and the understanding of practitioners.*

We need to respond to the new challenges presented by our young people. They will provide the key to developing effective specialist schools. We must accept the challenge for the sake of our young people, change and go forward.

## Acknowledgements

I would like to thank those staff at Sunfield who shared their thoughts and experiences with me in formulating this chapter, especially Jo Egerton (research fellow/publications manager) and Teresa Whitehurst (research officer).

## References

Carpenter, B. (2005) 'Early childhood intervention: possibilities and prospects for professionals, families and children', *British Journal of Special Education,* 32 (4), 176–183.

Carpenter, B. and Shevlin, M. (2004) 'Creating an inclusive curriculum'. In: P.N. Noonan Walsh and H. Gash (eds) *Lives and Times: Practice, policy and people with disabilities.* Dublin: Wordwell.

Carpenter, B., Conway, S. and Whitehurst, T. (2005) 'First impressions', *Special Children,* August, 28–32.

Conway, S., Powell, S. and Whitehurst, T. (2005) 'Parents as research partners:

working together to explore family experiences of their induction to a residential special school', *PMLD–Link* (Summer), 26–29.

Department for Education and Skills (DfES) (2003) *Every Child Matters.* Nottingham: DfES Publications.

Doveston, M. and Keenaghan, M. (2006) 'Improving classroom dynamics to support students' learning and social inclusion: a collaborative approach', *Support for Learning,* 21 (1), 5–11.

Furlong, J. (2000) *Higher Education and the New Professionalism for Teachers: Realising the potential of partnership.* London: Committee of Vice-Chancellors and Principals.

General Teaching Council for England (2004) *GTC Research Digest 2000–2004.* London: GTCE.

General Teaching Council for England (2006) 'Using research in your school and in your teaching: research engaged professional practice'. [Online at: http://www.gtce.org.uk/tplf]

Guralnick, M. (2004) 'Early intervention for children with intellectual disabilities: current knowledge and future prospects.' Keynote address to the 12th IASSID World Congress, Montpellier, France (June).

Hill, C. (2006) *Communicating through Movement: Sherborne Developmental Movement – towards a broadening perspective.* Clent: Sunfield Publications.

Her Majesty's Treasury/Department for Education and Skills (DfES) (2006) *Parliamentary Hearings on Services for Disabled Children.* London: Council for Disabled Children. [Online at: http://www.edcm.org.uk, http://www.cafamily.org.uk and http://www.mencap.org.uk]

Howley, M. and Arnold, E. (2005) *Revealing the Hidden Social Code: Social stories for people with autistic spectrum disorders.* London: Jessica Kingsley.

Johnson, D. (2006) 'Listening to the views of those involved in the inclusion of pupils with Down's syndrome into mainstream schools', *Support for Learning,* 21 (1), 24–29.

Kershner, R. and Chaplin, R. (2001) *Understanding Special Educational Needs: A teacher's guide to effective school-based research.* London: David Fulton.

Logan, N., Cowley, B., Winstanley, C. and Galivan, A. (2005) 'Developing a counselling service for students with severe intellectual disabilities and profound autism', *Good Autism Practice,* 6 (2), 61–64.

Mittler, P. (2007, in press) 'Education: the missing link at transition', *Tizard Review of Learning Disabilities.*

Nordoff, P. and Robbins, C. (1992) *Therapy in Music for Handicapped Children.* London: Gollancz.

Olson, D. (2003) *Psychological Theory and Educational Reform: How school remakes mind and society.* Cambridge: Cambridge University Press.

Pauli, D. (2006) 'Contact through Colour', *Special Children,* 173, 30–33.

Porter, J. and Lacey, P. (2004) *Researching Learning Difficulties: A guide for practitioners.* London: Sage.

Rickman, M. (2005) *Tool-Kit for Planning your Research Project Topic.* Slough: NFER.

Roberts-Holmes, G. (2005) *Doing your Early Years Research Project.* London: Paul Chapman/Sage.

Robson, C. (2002) *Real World Research: A resource for social scientists and practitioner researchers (2nd edn).* Oxford: Blackwell.

Rose, R. (2002) 'Teaching as a "research-based profession": encouraging practitioner research in special education', *British Journal of Special Education,* 29 (1), 44–48.

Rose, R. and Grosvenor, I. (2001) *Doing Research in Special Education: Ideas into practice.* London: David Fulton.

Ross, L., Kelly, L., Lee, S. and Pearson, M. (2003) 'The student council at Sunfield', *The SLD Experience,* 36 (Summer), 27–30.

Shepherd, A. (2004) 'Only active learners need apply', *Times Educational Supplement,* 11 June. [Online at: http://www.tes.co.uk]

Sherborne, V. (2001) *Developmental Movement for Children: Mainstream, special needs and pre-school (2nd edn).* London: Worth Publishing.

Shirley, S. (2005) 'Challenges to autism research'. Paper presented to 'Autism and Asperger Syndrome' Conference, Royal Society of Medicine/National Autistic Society, Manchester (June).

Smart, M. (2004) 'Transition planning and the needs of young people and their carers: The Alumni Project', *British Journal of Special Education,* 31 (3), 128–137.

Smith, N. (2002) 'Transition to the school playground: an intervention programme for nursery children', *Early Years: An International journal of research and development,* 22 (2), 129–146.

Stenhouse, L. ( 1981) 'What counts as research?', *British Journal of Educational Studies*, 29 (2), 103–114.

Taylor, C., Wilkie, M. and Baser, J. (2006) *Doing Action Research: A guide for school support staff.* London: Paul Chapman.

Thornton, K. and Taylor, E. (2005) 'Play and the reduction of challenging behaviour in children with ASD and learning disabilities', *Good Autism Practice,* 6 (2), 75–80.

Watkins, A. (2006) 'So what exactly do teacher-researchers think about doing research?', *Support for Learning*, 21 (1), 12–18.

Whitehead, M. and Hartley, D. (eds) (2005) *Major Themes in Education: Teacher education.* London: Routledge/Taylor Francis.

Whitehurst, T. (2006) 'The impact of building design on children with autistic spectrum disorders', *Good Autism Practice,* 7 (1), 31–38.

Whitehurst, T. (2007, in press) 'Liberating silent voices: perspectives of children with profound and complex learning needs on inclusion', *British Journal of Learning Disabilities.*

Whitehurst, T. and Howells, A. (2006) '"When something is different, people fear it": children's perceptions of an arts-based inclusion project', *Support for Learning,* 21 (1), 40–44.

Wilson, J. (2002) 'Researching special needs', *British Journal of Special Education,* 29 (3), 141–143.

Zuber-Skerritt, O. (ed.) (1989) *New Directions in Action Research.* London: Falmer Press.

# PART 2
# Building Communication

CHAPTER 3

# Play

## An Interactive Approach Supporting Behavioural and Developmental Growth

*Kellyanne Thornton and Emma Taylor*

### Introduction

This project began four years ago with the main aim being to investigate the role of play in the developing student with autistic spectrum disorder (ASD). As the study has developed, the objectives of the study have evolved, becoming more specific and defined. They include:

- To explore the influence of play on challenging behaviour

- To investigate how play can reduce challenging behaviour through the exploration of behaviour management strategies

- To investigate how play can reduce challenging behaviour through promoting the enhancement of under-developed skills

- To encourage and facilitate the development of cognitive, emotional, social and personal skills through play

- To promote the importance of play with the student with ASD and severe intellectual disabilities.

### The role of play

Play is at the heart of being a child. As McMahon (1992) states, 'It is a spontaneous and active process in which thinking, feeling and doing can flourish. It provides a powerful energy that overcomes all obstacles of childhood existence:

> *Among the many painful scenes there were unique instances when the prisoners, and sometimes their executioners stood with tears in their eyes, watching the playing child entering the gas chambers. The children spent their precious last moments in play.* (Eisen, 1988)

Above, Eisen portrays a scene during the Holocaust whereby spontaneous play occurred without consideration to environmental conditions. This clearly illustrates that children's impulse and desire to play survives even in the most devastating circumstances.

As human beings, we have an undeniable need to play. Play is a vehicle for acquiring knowledge and learning skills that are essential for development. It also assists in enhancing well-being. As Oaklander (1988) explains:

*Playing is how children try out and learn about their world. Play is therefore essential for healthy development. For children, play is serious purposeful business through which they develop mentally, physically, and socially.*

There is a vast amount of literature outlining the benefits of play. For typically developing children, research affirms that play assists in the growth of cognition, in that children develop an awareness of the functions and meanings of objects (Fenson and Schell,1986), learn to problem-solve, and enhance their language and verbal communication (Garvy, 1990; Levy, 1984). Furthermore, cognition is facilitated through encouraging flexibility and creativity in behaviour and thought (Sutton-Smith, 1967; Sylva, Bruner and Genova, 1976).

Play also facilitates social development, as it encourages a drive for social interaction. Consequently, the child becomes aware of others and begins to learn from others, thereby moving away from egocentricity, acknowledging the significance of friendships, relationships, shared meanings, co-operation, trust, intimacy, negotiation and compromise (Dunn, 1988; Haight and Miller, 1993; Hartup and Sansilio, 1986; Howes, Unger and Matheson, 1992; Jordan, 2003; Parker and Gottman, 1989; Rubin, 1980). Emotional growth is encouraged through play as it allows the child to recognise, express and explore their own and others' emotions and feelings. Play also enables the child to discover coping strategies for anxieties and inner tensions in a safe environment (Hetherington and Park, 1993).

Erikson (1950) assumed that children learn how to cope with the demands of reality through creating similar situations in their play. In particular, they learn to master emotions and frustrations through re-enacting and rebuilding traumatic or upsetting situations. Play can act as an emotional release, cleansing the child from negative feelings relating to difficult events (Wolfberg, 1999). As Jeffree, McConkey and Hewson (1977) argue, play acts as a 'safety valve which prevents the build up of frustration' leaving the child emotionally refreshed and motivated.

Finally, play contributes to personal maturation in that it provides a safe space in which to explore autonomy (McMahon, 1992; West, 1996). It also encourages sense of achievement and self-worth through mastery, and increases self-esteem, self-identity and self-confidence (Moyles, 1989; Piaget, 1951). As McConkey (1986a) writes; 'I doubt if teaching and therapy can ever inculcate a sense of autonomy, self-sufficiency and cooperativeness to anything like the same extent as play can do.'

If play is an innate and compelling drive that is prominent in childhood, where does this leave the child with ASD? For those that theoretically struggle with play, as it is typically understood, will the spirit and magic of play be lost or can they too gain from its power?

## Play and children with ASD

For children with ASD, some would argue that a distinguishing feature is an absence of developmentally typical play (Wolfberg, 1999). The rationale for this argument is associated with the triad of impairments, namely difficulties in social interaction, communication and imagination (Hill and McCune-Nicolich, 1981; Kanner, 1943; Lahey, 1988; Lifter, 2000). Furthermore, numerous studies suggest that spontaneous symbolic play and spontaneous functional play are affected due to the complexities of autism (Jarrold, Boucher and Smith, 1996; Wulff, 1985). Generally, children with ASD engage in fewer varied functional play acts (Mundy, Sigman, Ungerer and Sherman, 1986; Sigman and Ungerer, 1984) and seldom initiate more sophisticated forms of pretend play, such as object substitution, role play or creating fictitious beings (Baron-Cohen, 1987; Lewis and Boucher, 1988; Ungerer and Sigman, 1981). Rather, they are drawn to repetitive play activities (Wolfberg, 1999). As play requires elements of language, imagination and social interaction, the child with autism is likely to feel 'lost and confused and resort to activities that are meaningful and comforting only to him' (Moor, 2002).

Other professionals argue that children with ASD have a suppressed, latent potential for play which can be unleashed with adult support. Research suggests that when prompted by an adult without the presence of peers, children with autism may be able to understand and produce more complicated and diverse forms of play (Boucher and Lewis, 1990; Charman and Baron-Cohen, 1997; Jarrold, Boucher and Smith, 1996; Lewis and Boucher, 1988; Mundy, Sigman, Ungerer and Sherman, 1986; Riguet, Taylor, Benaroya and Klein, 1981; Sigman and Ungerer, 1984). Duffy (1998) says that the adult role in releasing play potential is to generate situations whereby creativity and imagination are stimulated and encouraged through interactions with an adult. Furthermore, Sherratt and Peter (2002) suggest that adult support involves addressing internal and external factors and resources. External prompts may include play equipment, organising the environment and instructions. An internal prompt may involve encouraging motivation and confidence through emotional affect. These children require diverse and innovative learning and play opportunities due to the unique nature of their play and learning styles. Adults need to take responsibility for encouraging engagement, expanding their play experiences and interests, and assessing, reviewing and adjusting their play approach (Thornton and Cox, 2005). Jeffree, McConkey and Hewson (1977) also argue that it is important for adults to encourage play opportunities, as through play the foundations for future learning are established:

> *[Play] will also mean that the child will become more active and less passive, he can start deciding for himself what he wants to do. It will widen his interests and in so doing will literally broaden his mind.*

Therefore, if play can be encouraged with children with ASD, surely it is then detrimental to underestimate its impact on the child's development. As McConkey (1986b) writes, 'If children normally use play to help them make sense of their world, then a child with disabilities may be doubly handicapped if this need is not met'. These professionals suggest that the benefits of play are universal, and *all* children's emotional, cognitive, social, and personal development can be enhanced.

Another significant influential element of play is its potential to motivate behavioural change. Many children with ASD display challenging behaviours due to an inability to communicate their needs effectively. For Oaklander (1988), behaviours perceived by others as inappropriate and disruptive are attempts to restore a 'social connection'. Due to an inability to communicate their feelings in any other way, the child may resort to inappropriate behaviour as they are unaware of how else to manage or express themselves. Play can be a valuable tool for addressing these behaviours as the child can learn more appropriate ways of meeting their needs, in turn developing strategies for self-regulatory behaviour (Thornton and Cox, 2005). In this way, play can indirectly promote positive behaviours through enhancing social, emotional, personal and cognitive development. Furthermore, through play behaviour management strategies can be explored, thereby reducing the need to engage in challenging behaviours.

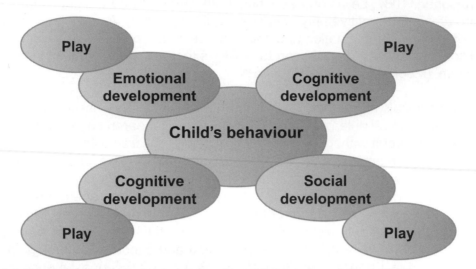

**Figure 3.1. The influence of play on behaviour (Thornton and Cox, 2005)**

## Methodology

This study was a piece of action research undertaken with a small sample size within a single school. It was decided to pursue a case study approach due to the individuality of the participants, the uniqueness of the approach and as no two cases are the same. As Coolican (1999) writes:

> *Whether or not case studies of special circumstances lead to later, more formal, structured and quantitative studies, the richness they provide is their unique strength. Very often we could not possibly imagine the special experiences of the person studied, and we could not possibly draw up the appropriate questions to find out.*

Comparisons between participants were not undertaken as the children did not comprise a homogenous group.

### Participants

Participants included boys and girls aged chronologically between 7 and 18 years. Many had a diagnosis of ASD, although all displayed autistic tendencies. All had a diagnosis of severe intellectual disabilities, some with dual diagnosis including Down syndrome and attention deficit/hyperactivity disorder (ADHD). In terms of expressive language, most of the participants communicated through Makaton, symbols, pictures, and photographs. Some participants were able to communicate verbally; however, this was often limited to one- or two-word phrases, and was sometimes echolalic.

### Procedure

Play was tailored to the individual as it was essential to acknowledge the developmental level of the student concerned for it to be successfully utilised as a vehicle for supporting development. Although developmental ages were taken into consideration, each participant encountered the same play process (see Figure 3.2).

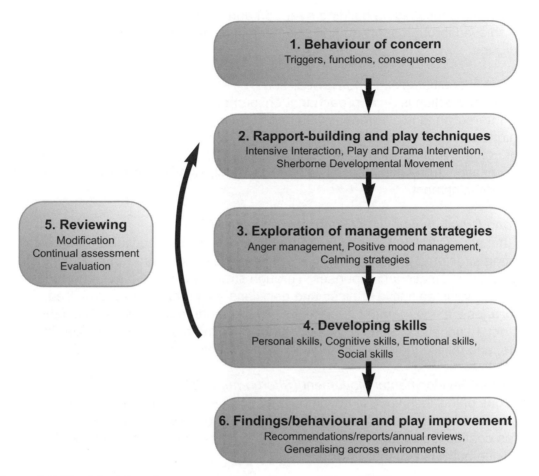

**Figure 3.2. Model of the play process (Thornton and Cox, 2005)**

All students participating in the study were referred by care, education or therapy staff for play intervention resulting from concerns about their behaviour and play. There were various reasons for referral, including poor self-confidence, failure to exercise control appropriately, difficulties in developing rapport with peers, low self-esteem, lack of play skills, lack of understanding of feelings, or problems with initiating social interaction appropriately.

Before play sessions began, the students were assessed to find out whether play sessions would be helpful in addressing the concerns of staff. Triggers, functions and consequences of challenging behaviours were analysed and explored. If it was deemed that play sessions were likely to be beneficial, parental consent was obtained for the students to take part in the study, and then weekly 45-minute sessions were scheduled. The majority of students received two-to-one staff support.

Sessions took place in a large room that was exclusively utilised as the 'play room'. Part of the play room was screened off, enabling sessions to occur either in the smaller area behind the screen for those who found it difficult to channel their attention, or in the larger area when the focus was gross motor movement. Potential distractions were minimised with only relevant materials and equipment being accessible to the student. Photographs and symbols were, however, accessible to the student so they were able to choose items that were not readily available or out of view.

Initial sessions focused on building a rapport and relationship with the student. This was achieved through applying principles and ideas from three well-established techniques.

*Intensive Interaction (Nind and Hewett, 2001)*
Intensive interaction is an approach that encourages learning, communication and social interaction, and awareness with people with severe intellectual disabilities. The technique attempts to assist individuals in gaining knowledge about the fundamentals of communicating such as eye-contact, listening, and waiting. They also learn about imitation, turn-taking, social cause-and-effect, all of which are crucial for successful development.

*Play and Drama Intervention (Sherratt and Peter, 2002)*
With this approach, the key elements are: incorporating the individual's interests; providing structured play opportunities; and engaging them through provoking stimulating affective emotional responses. Through structured social play opportunities, perimeters for imaginative choices and decisions are progressively extended. This encourages the engagement in pretence. Furthermore, drama allows the individual to reflect, to understand and regulate their own feeling responses to similar life events, and realise their own influential capability on others.

*Sherborne Developmental Movement (Sherborne, 2001)*
The focus of this technique is how movement can assist in the formation of relationships and increase awareness of self and others. Consequently, movement enhances confidence, independence, trust, initiative and positive self-image. The underlying belief is that individuals:

> *...need to feel at home with their bodies and so gain body mastery, and they need to be able to form relationships.* (Sherborne, 2001, xiii)

A very recent study (see Chapter 4) has developed an adapted approach to Sherborne Developmental Movement specifically for young people with ASD.

**Building relationships**
Once a connection with the student was formed using these approaches, and they appeared comfortable and familiar with the play environment and expectations, sessions then focused on exploring behaviour management strategies to address the behaviour of concern. During these sessions, skills that aided the enrichment of social, cognitive, personal and emotional development were practised and rehearsed with the student until they were embedded in the student's behavioural repertoire. Subsequently, positive play experiences and positive behaviours were promoted, thus the urge to display challenging behaviours was diminished.

Throughout the play process, the play approaches and behavioural strategies were continually being assessed and evaluated, and, when necessary, modified specifically for the individual student. Findings from the sessions were then distributed to staff through various media, such as written reports, video evidence, photographs, guidelines and the student's creations. Successful behavioural strategies were incorporated into Priority Behaviour Development Plans (PBDP), which addressed a specific behaviour through a series of defined step-by-step goals. Each PBDP clearly stated proactive and reactive strategies, the effectiveness of which was continually monitored by education and residential care staff using behaviour charts, through which it was possible to ascertain their appropriateness or the need for their further modification.

## Results

Data was collected from observational analysis undertaken after each session to monitor for change and progression. To illustrate progression and the beneficial impact of the play process for students with ASD and challenging behaviour, a case study is summarised below.

### *Stuart*[1]

*Background:* Stuart is an adolescent boy with a diagnosis of ASD and severe intellectual disabilities. At the time of referral, Stuart was 12 years old and living in a residential house with five other students with intellectual disabilities, two of whom were female and three, male.

*Referral:* Stuart was initially referred by residential care staff due to increasing concerns relating to self-injurious behaviours. Through liaising with the leading psychologist and through our own observations, it became evident that these behaviours correlated with anxiety provoked by the following antecedents: requests being denied; verbal input, including demands; waiting; changes within the environment, particularly an increase in noise or number of people; and, finally, pain and physical discomfort due to a chronic physical condition. His anxieties were expressed through biting his fingers and applying direct force to his forehead with his fist. This pressure could also be achieved through pushing his head against the bodies of staff or peers. His behaviour suggested that he was actively seeking to gain a particular sensory input required to self-regulate and calm himself at times of distress.

*Initial sessions:* Weekly individual play sessions commenced, as it was deemed that they would be beneficial in attempting to reduce his negative behaviours through teaching and enhancing skills to communicate *appropriately* and self-regulate his behaviour. Sessions focused on developing a rapport between staff and Stuart. It was vitally important for Stuart to feel comfortable and relaxed in the play environment, and that he was fully aware of boundaries and expectations before teaching could begin. To create a positive and inviting atmosphere, Stuart's interests were incorporated into sessions. At that time, he had a particular interest in Batman and Superman, and appeared to enjoy the sensation of spinning. Therefore, an activity from the Sherborne Developmental Movement programme (Sherborne, 2001) was introduced whereby Stuart was moved around on a duvet to the theme tunes from Batman and Superman films. To encourage interaction between staff and student, the principles of intensive interaction and play and drama were applied, whereby staff would withhold a response until eye-contact was given.

*Subsequent sessions:* Subsequent sessions involved exploring behaviour management strategies that sought to teach Stuart alternative and appropriate ways of communicating his feelings and needs. Sensory equipment and games were introduced when Stuart was calm and relaxed, providing him with the opportunity to experience and explore the different sensations. At this point, no teaching took place, sessions were purely exploratory and child-led. Examples of sensory equipment were vibrating snakes, vibrating pillows, vibrating teether, a hand massager and a facial massager with alternative heads available.

When it was possible to identify Stuart's preferred equipment, teaching commenced.

Stuart was first encouraged to request the equipment through photographs. Concurrently, when Stuart displayed self-injurious behaviours during sessions, his behaviour was interrupted with the consistent phrase 'Hands down,' and he was offered a piece of sensory equipment to provide alternative stimulation. Thus, Stuart learnt to associate the decrease in anxiety with the sensory equipment, weakening the previous relationship between anxiety reduction through self-injurious behaviour. Furthermore, Stuart was then prompted to communicate his need for the desired equipment spontaneously through photographs when anxious, thereby increasing his autonomy, control, freedom, communication skills and self-awareness.

*Developing skills*: Through sessions, Stuart gained competence in the following areas.

Cognitive skills: Stuart's cognitive ability was strengthened as, through the sessions, he gained an awareness of the function and meaning of certain objects. As Stuart was able to modify his responses, this signified an increased capacity for flexibility and creativity in behaviour. In addition, decision-making was practised and improved, which was reflected in his being able to choose the desired piece of sensory equipment. Finally, communication skills and memory were also reinforced as he was able to successfully communicate through photographs.

Emotional skills: Play sessions revealed development in emotional skills as Stuart became able to recognise, express and explore his feelings of anxiety and frustration appropriately. As he learnt alternative ways of coping, his self-injurious behaviours decreased. Sessions also increased his motivation to want to learn, interact and control his own behaviour. Emotional enhancement was also observed through his responses to play equipment through recognising and communicating his preferences and dislikes.

Personal skills: As sessions progressed, personal development was enhanced. Stuart's confidence increased as he became more able to self-regulate his behaviour appropriately. This ability provided a sense of achievement, thereby increasing his self-esteem, reflected in his body language. As Stuart was able to control his behaviour effectively, his sense of autonomy and independence matured. This resulted in an increase in spontaneous communication.

Social skills: Play sessions facilitated social development as Stuart demonstrated an increased desire to interact socially with staff for tangible gains. Through this, he mastered the skills of listening, waiting and turn-taking, and experienced the value of social cause and effect. Enhanced social skills were conveyed through increased eye-contact, increased attempts in initiating interactions, closer proximity to others, imitative behaviours, and longer periods of joint attention.

Findings from the sessions were distributed to care and education staff and Stuart's parents through various media including video footage, reports, PBDPs and discussions with all involved. All sensory equipment, techniques and communication aids were recommended and implemented on house, in school and at his parental home.

Following the implementation of recommendations, observations were carried out to monitor progress and assess whether the frequency and intensity of self-injurious behaviours had decreased. These revealed a significant decrease of challenging behaviours compared to baseline observations. Furthermore, Stuart seemed calmer and more relaxed in his surrounding environment. Generalisation of skills was successfully accomplished, as he was able to request appropriately the desired input to calm at times of distress rather than engaging in self-injurious behaviours. His social tolerance and interest also seemed to improve outside sessions, as it was reported that Stuart's focus and participation in group activities had increased.

The above case study clearly demonstrates how play can assist in the modification of challenging behaviours through enhancing and teaching skills. Collation of findings from sessions of all students involved in play sessions resulted in the following general observations:

- Students receiving play sessions revealed that although they had a diagnosis of ASD, they can and do play, but often in distinctive ways

- Data collected from play sessions indicated that play did influence development and assist with the acquisition of skills. This in turn seemed to lead to a reduction in the frequency and intensity of inappropriate behaviours.

- Generally, it was observed that, during sessions, eye-contact, imitation, turn-taking, sharing, waiting and communication skills were improved

- All students involved in the study required adult input to aid development of play skills. This input involved the adult being responsible for engaging the student, stimulating their thoughts and motivation, providing internal and external motivators, offering encouragement, adjusting the type and amount of adult support, broadening their play experiences, modelling play behaviours, extending skills, and assessing and evaluating their progress.

## Discussion

This study reveals that children with ASD involved in the study *did* have the potential to play, and, when this potential was unleashed, they actively engaged in the process of playing. This process enhanced the child's well-being, stimulated development and assisted in addressing challenging behaviours through teaching skills and promoting pro-social behaviours. Furthermore, the study illustrated that the essential ingredient needed to unleash this potential is adult involvement and encouragement. Figure 3.3 illustrates the qualities needed for adult intervention.

Adult involvement and encouragement, however, needs to be balanced and tailored to the individual. For adult participation to be successful, the adult must be prepared to lose their inhibitions, physically get down to the child's level, and become an active playmate. Every child senses when an adult is enjoying interacting and being with them. When this shared experience is fun, emotionally rewarding and stimulating, the child will want to engage in the process again. Play must provide a balance between adult-led/directed and child-led/non-directive approaches. In this way, adults must be sensitive to sharing the lead role. It is vital that the adult also considers the child's developmental age, and introduces activities and techniques that are suitable. Overwhelming expectations can result in feelings of failure and dissatisfaction. It is vital that adult intervention assists in empowering the child through play.

With this involvement, the drive to want to play is stimulated for the child with ASD. This was indicated by the fact that, generally, all students were eager to attend play sessions, and wanted to participate actively and contribute to their sessions. This therefore supports the finding of Jeffree, McConkey and Hewson (1977) that play has the potential of moving the child away from passivity to more active involvement.

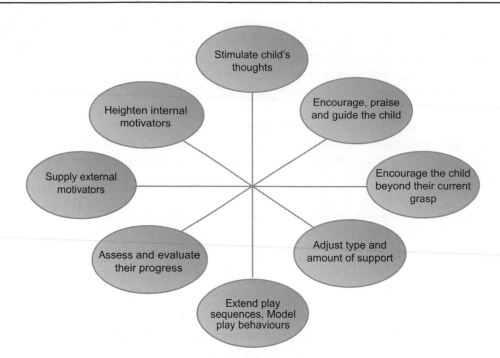

**Figure 3.3. Roles of an adult involved in intervention**

The study also encourages a movement away from a deficit perspective – that the impairments experienced by children with ASD in the areas of communication, social interaction and imagination (the 'triad of impairments') inhibit and restrict play – to a positive one: that, through the process of play, communication, social interaction and imagination can be enhanced. It is time to think more optimistically and realise the powerful impact that play contributes to the life and development of a child with ASD instead of focusing and seeking to explain the impact of autism on children's play. This shift in thinking is reflected in Figure 3.4.

Brooks (2001) and Sherratt and Peter (2002) hold similar view points. Brooks describes all youngsters as having 'islands of competence'; these islands represent areas of strength which can be built upon. He also emphasises the adult's role in identifying and reinforcing these islands, thereby creating hope and optimism. Sherratt and Peter suggest a triad of competence focusing on abilities and achievements, and argue that through play the child will develop more creative, flexible thinking, leading to improvements in communication and social interaction.

**Concluding comment**
This study has enabled us to enter and observe the playful world of students with ASD and witness the benefits on their development and behaviour. Addressing challenging behaviours requires an element of teaching and learning. Successful learning requires an essence of fun for it to become more meaningful. The very nature of play breeds enjoyment, and is therefore a logical medium for teaching new and alternative skills to combat inappropriate behaviours. The approach is a simple but effective and powerful way of working and connecting with children with ASD.

These shared experiences have challenged traditional beliefs and begs the question 'if play is a means of helping children to make sense of the world, why are we not *all* making vast efforts to promote its importance with children with ASD? Surely the time has arrived to passionately campaign and support play for *all* children.

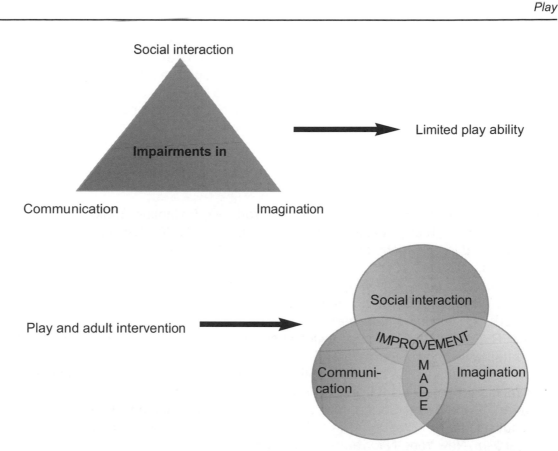

**Figure 3.4. The relationship between the triad of impairments, play and play intervention**

## The next step

When beginning this piece of work, the focus was to explore how students with ASD played and the impact play could have on social skills development and challenging behaviour. Through exploration, various models and theories were incorporated, transforming it into a piece of action research.

On this journey, many lessons have been learnt, and limitations of the current study have been acknowledged. The main limitation was the difficulty in obtaining quantitative results due to the small sample size and case study approach. Furthermore, it is difficult to generalise effective behavioural strategies discovered in sessions due to the individuality of each student. Play must be personalised and modified to the individual, and the method by which play can assist in reducing challenging behaviour is subject to knowledge, understanding and practice acquired through various encounters with each student with ASD. What works for one may not work for another.

The study initially examined the broad areas of development, challenging behaviour and their relationship with play. Analysis of data led to the formation of foundations and generation of openings for the study, which led to a need to investigate the areas of development in greater detail. Due to the growing number of children with autism experiencing mental health problems (Carpenter, 2004), the next logical step would appear to be to explore further the link between play, emotional support and emotional development. Play can be utilised as a tool for facilitating emotional growth, individuation *and* for providing emotional support as it encourages expression, exploration and acceptance of feelings, the self and the child's inner and outer worlds. A flourishing approach that attempts to connect all three is Play Therapy (Axline, 1967; McMahon, 1992; Oaklander, 1987; West, 1996).

The next phase of the research will explore the benefits and impact of play, whether as a developmental or therapeutic aid, with students with ASD who are experiencing emotional difficulties in their lives (e.g. exploring the cognitive and affective processes experienced during play that can enhance a student's emotional state and well-being). Through this process, it is anticipated that knowledge of play therapy principles and practice will influence the play approach by offering a conceptual and theoretical framework, thereby further developing, refining and extending current thoughts already presented in this chapter.

## References

Axline, V. (1967) *Dibs in Search of Self.* New York, NY: Ballantine Books.

Baron-Cohen, S. (1987) 'Autism and symbolic play'. In: P.J. Wolfberg (ed.) (1999) *Play and Imagination in Children with Autism.* New York, NY: Teachers College Press.

Boucher, J. and Lewis, V. (1990) 'Guessing or creating? A reply to Baron-Cohen'. In: P.J. Wolfberg (ed.) (1999) *Play and Imagination in Children with Autism.* New York, NY: Teachers College Press.

Brooks, R. (2001) 'How can parents foster self esteem in their children?'. [Online at: http://www.schwablearning.org]

Carpenter, B. (2004) 'The mental health needs of young people with profound and multiple learning disabilities' *PMLD–Link,* 16 (1), 9–12.

Charman, T. and Baron-Cohen, S. (1997) 'Brief report: prompted pretend play in autism'. In: P.J. Wolfberg (ed.) (1999) *Play and Imagination in Children with Autism.* New York, NY: Teachers College Press.

Coolican, H. (1999) *Research Methods and Statistics in Psychology.* London: Hodder and Stoughton.

Duffy, B. (1998) *Supporting Creativity and Imagination in the Early Years.* Buckingham: Open University Press.

Dunn, J. (1988) 'Understanding others: evidence from naturalistic studies of children'. In: A. Witten (ed.) *Natural Theories of Mind.* Oxford: Blackwell.

Eisen, G. (1988) *Children and Play in the Holocaust: Games among the shadows.* Amherst: University of Massachusetts Press.

Erikson, E.H. (1950) 'Childhood and society'. In: P.J. Wolfberg (ed.) (1999) *Play and Imagination in Children with Autism.* New York, NY: Teachers College Press.

Fenson, L. and Schell, R.E. (1986) 'The origins of exploratory play'. In: P.J. Wolfberg (ed.) (1999) *Play and Imagination in Children with Autism.* New York, NY: Teachers College Press.

Garvy, C. (1990) *Play.* Cambridge, MA: Harvard University Press.

Haight, W. and Miller, P. (1993) *The Ecology and Development of Pretend Play.* Albany: State University of New York Press.

Hartup, W.W. and Sansilio, M.F. (1986) 'Children's Friendships'. In: P.J. Wolfberg (ed.) (1999) *Play and Imagination in Children with Autism.* New York, NY: Teachers College Press.

Hetherington, E.M. and Park, R.D. (1993) *Child Psychology: A contemporary viewpoint (4th edn).* New York, NY: McGraw Hill.

Hill, P.M, and McCune-Nicolich, L. (1981) 'Pretend play and patterns of cognition in Down's Syndrome Children', *Child Development,* 52, 611–617.

Howes, C., Unger, O. and Matheson, C.C. (1992) *The Collaborative Construction of Pretend.* Albany: State University of North York Press.

Jarrold, C., Boucher, J. and Smith, P. (1996) 'Generativity deficits in pretend play in autism'. In: P.J. Wolfberg (ed.) (1999) *Play and Imagination in Children with Autism.* New York, NY: Teachers College Press.

Jeferee, D.M. McConkey, R. and Hewson, S. (1977) *Let Me Play*. London: Souvenir Press.

Jordan, R. (2003) 'Social play and autistic spectrum disorders: a perspective on theory, implications and educational approaches', *Autism,* 7 (4), 347–360.

Kanner, L. (1943) 'Autistic disturbances of affective contact', *Nervous Child*, 2, 217–250.

Lahey, M. (1988) *Language Disorders and Language Development*. New York, NY: Macmillan.

Levy, A.K. (1984) 'The language of play: the role of play in language development', *Early Child Development and Care,* 17 (1) 49–61.

Lewis, V. and Boucher, J. (1988) 'Spontaneous, instructed and elicited play in relatively able autistic children'. In: P.J. Wolfberg (ed.) (1999) *Play and Imagination in Children with Autism.* New York, NY: Teachers College Press.

Lifter, K. (2000) 'Linking assessment to intervention for children in developmental disabilities or at-risk for developmental delay: Developmental Play Assessment (DPA) Instrument'. In: K. Gitlin-Weiner, A. Sandgrund and C. Schaefer (eds) *Play Diagnosis and Assessment (2nd edn).* Hoboken, NJ: John Wiley.

McConkey, R. (1986a) 'Play it again, chum'. In: L. McMahon (ed.) (1992) *The Handbook of Play Therapy.* London: Brunner-Routledge.

McConkey, R. (1986b) 'Changing beliefs about play and handicapped children'. In: L. McMahon (ed.) (1992) *The Handbook of Play Therapy.* London: Brunner-Routledge.

McMahon, L. (1992) *The Handbook of Play Therapy.* London: Brunner-Routledge.

Moor, J.M. (2002) *Playing, Laughing and Learning with Children on the Autism Spectrum: A practical resource of play ideas for parents and carers.* London: Jessica Kingsley.

Moyles, J. (1989) *Just Playing: The role and status of play in early childhood education.* Milton Keynes: Open University Press.

Mundy, P., Sigman, M.D., Ungerer, J., and Sherman, T. (1986) 'Defining the social deficits in autism: the contribution of non verbal communication measures'. In: P.J. Wolfberg (ed.) (1999) *Play and Imagination in Children with Autism.* New York, NY: Teachers College Press.

Nind, M. and Hewitt, D. (2001) *A Practical Guide to Intensive Interaction.* Kidderminster, Worcs.: BILD.

Oaklander, V. (1988) *Windows to Our Children: A Gestalt Therapy approach to children and adolescents.* Highland, NY: Gestalt Journal Press.

Parker, J.G. and Gottman, J.M. (1989) 'Social and emotional development in a relational context: friendship interaction from early childhood to adolescence'. In: P.J. Wolfberg (ed.) (1999) *Play and Imagination in Children with Autism.* New York, NY: Teachers College Press.

Piaget, J. (1951) 'Play, dreams and imitation in children'. In: R. Gross (ed.) (1996) *Psychology: The science of mind and behaviour (3rd edn).* London: Hodder and Stoughton.

Riguet, C., Taylor, N., Benaroya, S. and Klein, L. (1981) 'Symbolic play in autistic, Downs and normal children of equivalent mental age'. In: P.J. Wolfberg (ed.) (1999) *Play and Imagination in Children with Autism.* New York, NY: Teachers College Press.

Rubin, K.H. (1980) 'Fantasy play: its role in the development of social skills and social cognition'. In: K.H. Rubin (ed.) *Children's Play.* San Francisco, CA: Jossey-Bass.

Sherborne, V. (2001) *Developmental Movement for Children: Mainstream, special needs and pre-school (2nd edn).* London: Worth Publishing.

Sherratt, D. and Peter, M. (2002) *Developing Play and Drama in Children with Autistic Spectrum Disorders*. London: David Fulton.

Sigman, M. and Ungerer, J.A. (1984) 'Cognitive and language skills in autistic, mentally retarded, and normal children'. In: P.J. Wolfberg (ed.) (1999) *Play and Imagination in Children with Autism.* New York, NY: Teachers College Press.

Sutton-Smith, B. (1967) 'The role of play in cognitive development'. In: P.J. Wolfberg (ed.) (1999) *Play and Imagination in Children with Autism.* New York, NY: Teachers College Press.

Sylva, K., Bruner, J.S. and Genova, P. (1976) 'The role of play in the problem solving of children three to five years old'. In: P.J. Wolfberg (ed.) (1999) *Play and Imagination in Children with Autism.* New York, NY: Teachers College Press.

Thornton, K. and Cox, E. (2005) 'Play and the reduction of challenging behaviour in children with ASD and learning disabilities', *Good Autism Practice*, 6 (2), 75–80.

Ungerer, J.A. and Sigman, M. (1981) 'Symbolic play and language comprehension in autistic children'. In: P.J. Wolfberg (ed.) (1999) *Play and Imagination in Children with Autism.* New York, NY: Teachers College Press.

West, J. (1996) *Child Centered Play Therapy (2nd edn)*. London: Arnold.

Wolfberg, P.J. (1999) *Play and Imagination in Children with Autism.* New York, NY: Teachers College Press.

Wulff, S.B. (1985) 'The symbolic and object play of children with autism: a review'. In: P.J. Wolfberg (ed.) (1999) *Play and Imagination in Children with Autism.* New York, NY: Teachers College Press.

**Endnote**

[1] The student's name has been changed to protect their identity.

# CHAPTER 4

# 'Sherborne @ Sunfield'

## An Adapted Approach to Support Social Engagement of Young People with ASD through Sherborne Developmental Movement

*Jotham Konaka*

### Introduction

As one of the key training bases for Sherborne Developmental Movement (SDM) in the UK, Sunfield was interested in investigating the resonance of SDM with the concept of engagement for students with autistic spectrum disorder (ASD). This formed the focus of a two-year study (September 2004 – August 2006) – a collaborative piece of work between Sunfield and Cyndi and George Hill, two experienced Sherborne consultants/trainers from the Sherborne Association UK. The project was supported financially by the Three Guineas Trust.

### Sherborne Developmental Movement

'Developmental Movement' was pioneered and developed by Veronica Sherborne (Sherborne, 2001), based upon Rudolf Laban's principles and theory of human movement. Laban advocated 'self-exploration and self-expression of responses to inner feelings and impulses, within an environment which is not bound by specifics and restrictive techniques' (Hill, 2006). Sherborne drew on his ideas of developing confidence in the body, spatial awareness and exploring human relationships through movement to provide a framework for her work with children with special educational needs (Sherborne, 2001; Hill, 2006). Her technique was based upon the belief that relating to oneself and relating to other people is essential for the satisfactory development of every human being. It placed equal importance on the development of physical abilities, a good self-esteem and the ability to form positive relationships with others through shared 'movement experiences'. The movement experiences used took many forms, but all were designed to encourage specific developments in the child.

SDM has been recognised as highly effective in promoting communication and sociability in individuals with severe and complex intellectual disabilities (Department of Education and Science, 1991; Dibbo and Gerry, 1994; Sheppard, 1996; Peter, 1997; Sherborne, 2001; Sugden and Wright, 2001; Thornton and Taylor, 2005; Hill, 2006). Those who use SDM suggest that it encourages development of body awareness, a positive self-concept and relationship-building, all of which form the basis of social engagement (Dibbo and Gerry, 1994; Peter, 1997; Hill, 2006). Any meaningful engagement also requires an awareness of others, and it has been argued that SDM has the potential to contribute towards the development of this awareness by enabling individuals to work together in a caring and safe partnership (Dibbo and Gerry,

1994; Sheppard, 1996). It has been used successfully by Sunfield with this group of students, and is a feature of Sunfield's curriculum; however, the areas addressed are all areas of challenge for a student with ASD.

At the time when Sherborne was working, little was known about ASD, and it was not widely acknowledged as an intellectual disability. Therefore her original 'Developmental Movement' did not take account of the very different engagement and learning needs of students with ASD. Our work has led to questions being raised about how best to engage students with ASD in the development opportunities offered by SDM.

## Young people with ASD

An increasing number of the young people who are referred to Sunfield have ASD. The Committee of Enquiry into Meeting the Mental Health Needs of Young People with Learning Disabilities (Foundation for People with Learning Disabilities, 2002) found that young people with ASD are 40% more likely to develop a mental health problem than other young people with disabilities. This report suggested that one positive strategy to support emotional well-being and reduce stress and anxiety levels in these young people was through focused physical activity.

Many individuals with ASD have atypical body and environmental awareness, they can experience hyper- or hyposensitivity in all the senses – touch, sound, smell or sight (Grandin, 1995; Worth, 2005), and they also experience communication difficulties (American Psychiatric Association, 2000; Wing, 2002). Social interaction and access to the curriculum is consequently very problematic. In SDM, the potential benefits to the person with ASD are substantial as physical activity is combined with social interaction and relationship development. However, many of our students with ASD were experiencing difficulties with access to SDM sessions.

## Social engagement and movement

In the 21st century, much of what there is to know about the aetiology of disabilities is already known (Guralnick, 2004), and the focus of educators and researchers is upon 'engagement' of individuals with intellectual disabilities as the foundation for effective learning (Guralnick, 2004; Mesibov and Howley, 2003). The term, 'engagement', has received many interpretations. The National Research Council (2001) defines it as 'sustained attention to an activity or person'. SDM, focusing on the interactive relationship between participant and facilitator,[1] has engagement as its central tenet, although at the time when Sherborne developed it, the term was not in use. Engagement with another person is the platform on which interactive and communicative relationships can be built (Kellett and Nind, 2003).

Movement is considered to be the most fundamental aspect of a young child's life contributing to early social-communicative development (Davis, 1997; Greenspan, 1995; Maurer, 2003). Due to their sensory sensitivities and social difficulties, many children with ASD have been unable to engage fully in the experiences necessary to enable them to develop even the very basics of social interaction and communication as a foundation for exploring relationships, and developing confidence, intentionality and social protocol (Aitken and Trevarthen, 1997; Werner, Dawson, Osterling and Dinno, 2000). Under normal circumstances, children assimilate these during infant play (Stern, 1989; Thornton and Taylor, 2005; Seach, 2006) and movement experiences (Davis, 1997). Maurer (2003) and Teitelbaum (1998) argue that deficiencies in early motor development in individuals with autism are predictive of subsequent developmental difficulties in communication and social interaction. Peter (1997) and Filer (2006) suggest that SDM offers an important compensatory opportunity to capture early sensori-motor experiences (Piaget, 1969) for individuals for whom such experiences may have been impossible at an earlier life stage.

Greenspan (1995) and Maurer (2003) suggest that shared spatial and temporal scaffolds can encourage incipient social relationships in children with ASD. SDM can provide such a scaffold. Hill (2006) describes it as:

> *...a form of therapeutic intervention, which seeks to engage participants in interactive learning, through shared movement experiences which have their origins in the normal patterns of human development.*

## Aims and objectives of the research

The aim of this research was to develop an adapted teaching approach to the SDM to support the development of social engagement for students with ASD and to explore staff perceptions of the effectiveness of the adapted approach.

## Project design

The project took place within a supportive research management structure which provided the researcher with opportunities for professional development and consultancy from two experienced Sherborne Association UK consultant/trainers to ensure consistency of high quality SDM delivery, and with access to constructive discussion with other experienced professionals in the areas of special educational needs and research through a project management group.

The study adopted a qualitative action research method (Robson, 2002), using a cyclical approach to research – beginning with an idea of how practice could be improved (hypothesis), followed by cycles of trial, evaluation and modification within the context of the focus environment. This led to a refining of the original hypothesis and finally implementation. As with many action research projects, this one adopted a collaborative approach, involving other professionals in data collection and analysis.

The research was organised in four phases:

Phase 1    (September 2004 – January 2005) Introduction of SDM using a traditional approach and identification of gaps in methods of delivery. Adaptations to be made in response to data collected using facilitator/leader observation and corroborative video footage.

Phase 2    (February – October 2005) Trial of SDM incorporating Phase 1 adaptations. Further adaptations to be made in response to data collected from facilitator/leader observation and corroborative video footage in the Phase 1 participant group, and participant groups from two other schools.

Phase 3    (November 2005 – February 2006) Verification trial of the final adapted SDM programme among 11 schools, including those taking part in the earlier phases. Data collected to be analysed with reference to variables.

Phase 4    (February – August 2006) Data analysis, research write-up and implementation of adapted SDM approach.

In order to implement the phases, it was important that:

■ Staff involved in SDM delivery received training in both SDM, the adapted approach and data collection techniques

■ An adapted programme was developed during Phase 1

■ Data collection instruments were identified or devised.

## Research participants

The research participants were a purposive sample, which comprised student and facilitator/leader groups from Sunfield and 10 other schools who were involved variously during the three phases of active research. The student group included 100 individuals all of whom had diagnosis of severe/profound ASD. They ranged between the ages of 7 and 19 years and comprised male and female students:

Phase 1    Sunfield students (n=29) shared among six groups, each group including four to six students

Phase 2    Phase 1 students (n=29), and students from two other schools (n=14)

Phase 3    Phase 2 students (n=14 from the two Phase 2 schools), and students from seven other schools (n=45) and a new group of students from Sunfield (n=11).

There were 23 staff involved in leading, and 120 in facilitating, various SDM sessions, in addition to the researcher and one Sherborne consultant. Students were supported on a one-to-one basis by facilitators, with the session leaders and non-participant observers being supernumerary.

Participating schools, in addition to Sunfield, were selected by the researcher and project management group according to the schools' ability to support the proposed research and their provision to students with complex intellectual disabilities including ASD. The individual schools were then asked to identify a student group with a session leader and facilitators from among their staff to fit these criteria:

■ Students were diagnosed as having severe or profound ASD

■ The leader(s) were able to commit to leading every session

■ Maximum possible consistency of facilitator support for students.

## Staff training

Prior to the start of the project the researcher was trained to SDM Level 3 standard, and was supported throughout the project in terms of session support and consultation by the two Sherborne Association UK consultants/trainers. Facilitators also received training:

Phase 1    All facilitators were given preliminary training by the two consultants and the researcher.

Phase 2    Training for session facilitators for Sunfield and the additional two schools involved was delivered by the researcher supported by a Sherborne Association UK consultant/trainer. In addition to teaching basic SDM delivery, training also covered use of lesson plans, visual cues, and observation/evaluation forms developed in Phase 2.

Phase 3    A training day at Sunfield was delivered jointly by the Sherborne Association UK consultant/trainer and the researcher, for the staff from 10 additional schools who had been identified as session leaders (n=23). This included the staff from the two Phase 2 schools and two teachers from Sunfield who would work with two new groups of students. Training was cascaded down to facilitators in the schools.

## Structure of SDM sessions

The researcher prepared four lesson plans to support the delivery of the SDM sessions in advance of Phase 1. This is atypical of traditional SDM session delivery, in which the progression of movement experiences offered by the leader is dependent upon a responsive relationship between leader and participants. In traditional delivery, the leader responds to cues from the participants, both verbal and non-verbal. No two sessions are the same, but are thus driven by the participants, enabling the free-flow of ideas. However, the lesson plans were important in maintaining consistency of sessions across different venues for data collection purposes and later comparison.

The Sherborne movement experiences chosen for the lesson plans were taken from those described in *Developmental Movement for Children* (Sherborne, 2001) with reference to four stages of developmental progression documented by Hill (2006).The lesson plans incorporated movement experiences based on three distinct inter-personal relationship experiences – 'with', 'against' and 'shared'. In the facilitator–participant dyad, the adult's body becomes the conduit for the student's experience of movement. Each of the plans focused on specific movement dynamics, social and communication skills, class organisation and assessment opportunities. Each was intended to be delivered three times consecutively to facilitate a more representative assessment of students' responses.

The SDM sessions were delivered during all three phases, with adaptations to the model being incorporated at the end of each phase:

Phase 1    Each of the six groups of students had twice-weekly Sherborne sessions delivered by the researcher. Each group was given the same movement experiences for a period of six weeks, using the SDM teaching methods.

Phase 2    The SDM teaching model was adapted based upon Phase 1 outcomes. Twelve directly comparable sessions were delivered to each group by the researcher and one Sherborne Association UK consultant/trainer.

Phase 3    Further adaptations were incorporated into the model trialled in Phase 2 to create the 'Sherborne @ Sunfield' model. The 'Sherborne @ Sunfield' SDM sessions were delivered by session leaders identified by each of the 11 schools with consultancy support from the researcher and one Sherborne consultant. Sessions were held at least twice weekly for eight weeks.

**Data collection**
Baseline data on students' social and communicative needs and abilities was obtained from teacher profiles, and school assessments and reports. This information was used in deciding what SDM movement experiences to include in the initial lesson plans.

Baseline data on the students' levels of engagement in their initial SDM sessions was collected through researcher and facilitator evaluation using a standard form immediately following the session and triangulated through documentary video evidence.

Throughout the three project phases, data was collected using a variety of methods, including:

■ *Informal observation by session leader and facilitators (Phases 1, 2 and 3)*
During Phase 1, instead of using a prescriptive observation schedule, a post-session discussion group was convened in order to allow key elements relating to students' sociability to emerge. It was decided that a prescriptive, fixed observation schedule would be limiting since the capacity of SDM in supporting social communicative development with people with ASD was still unclear.

■ *Formal observation/evaluation by session leader, facilitators and non-participants (Phases 2 and 3)*
Participant and non-participant observers were given a pre-determined observation/evaluation grid which focused on key research themes including sociability indicators, prompting strategies, types and/or levels of engagement, as well as teaching techniques. Non-participant observers recorded data during sessions, while facilitators completed the evaluation sheet immediately after each SDM session.

■ *A research diary (Phases 1, 2 and 3)*
This was an on-going record of field notes from SDM sessions, key points from informal discussions (e.g. those leading to programme modification) and informal observations.

■ *Facilitator survey through questionnaires (Phase 3)*
A questionnaire was distributed to all the leaders and facilitators at the end of the practical work with the students. The format and content was similar to the interview schedule.

■ *Semi-structured interviews with facilitators and session leaders (Phases 2 and 3)*
Pre- and post-intervention interviews were carried out. The questions within the semi-structured interview schedule related to the focus of the research and invited participant opinion upon adaptations made to the SDM session delivery. Although interviews were tape-recorded, key interviewee responses were noted as the interviews proceeded.

■ *Documentary video evidence (Phases 1, 2 and 3)*
Video evidence was used to corroborate other data collection.

**Data analysis**
Data collected during semi-structured interviews with facilitators were transcribed and subjected to categorical content analysis (Lord et al., 2000; Robson, 2002). Coded data was then organised into themes and subcategories. The categories drawn were embedded in implicit, as well as explicit, data (Radnor, 1994).

The explicit data covered different views of the staff on the effectiveness of the programme, while the implicit data was derived from the researcher's personal judgement of the students' responses and facilitator/leader perceptions (Cohen, Manion and Morrison, 2000). Hycner (1985) refers to this as 'delineating units of general meaning, entailing a thorough scrutiny of both verbal and non-verbal gestures to elicit a participant's meaning' (cited in Cohen, Manion and Morrison, 2000).

## Ethical issues

An outline for this research project was submitted to and approved by the Sunfield Research and Ethics Committee. There were a number of ethical issues associated with the project. Fully informed written consent for students' to take part in the project was obtained from parents/carers. While students with severe/profound ASD were unable to understand the implications of their taking part in the project, they were able to give their assent to taking part in sessions. Fully informed consent was also obtained from facilitators/leaders. All participants were told of their rights in respect of the research – to withdraw without prejudice at any time for any reason and to have the opportunity to see reports on the research outcomes.

As SDM involves extensive body contact, there were important ethical issues around touch and safeguarding students to be explored in the context of the schools' child protection policies and national guidelines. As Hill (2006) explains, where the school's policy prohibits touch, SDM cannot take place. However, in most schools it is possible to implement SDM within the policy guidelines in consultation with the head teacher.

There is also a human rights issue around individual choice and touch for students with ASD. Many are touch aversive, and therefore it may appear that SDM, with its dependence on physical contact, would infringe their human rights. However, most students appeared to accept touch during the movement sessions – perhaps because in this context it was not irrational; rather, it was focused and part of a cohesive, predictable experience incorporated into their kinaesthetic sense (Jones, 2002). Although facilitators actively encouraged students to take part in movement experiences, they were asked not to coerce students into taking part.

There may also be issues of student sexual appropriateness associated with close physical contact. This situation had to be addressed sensitively for one student in consultation with staff who knew him well. It was decided during Phase 1 that the student should withdraw from the project.

Health and safety issues are another consideration, especially for facilitators, due to the physicality of SDM. Staff supporting participants need to be physically fit, and there was discussion about this with facilitators taking part in the project.

On completion of the research, there were two main considerations – the sustainability of the adapted programme, and dissemination of information. It is important that Sunfield continues to support and encourage the schools involved in the research project to retain the momentum they have gained through the adapted approach to SDM. The researcher and Sunfield, in association with the Sherborne Association UK, have made the adapted training programme, 'Sherborne @ Sunfield', available alongside Level 1 SDM training through Sunfield's Professional Development Centre.

This is to be supported by a training DVD (funded by the Three Guineas Trust). The adapted programme will be disseminated by Sunfield PDC, and will be included in its future publication lists.

Details of the research, its development and outcomes will be made available on the Sunfield website (http://www.sunfield.org.uk). These continue to be disseminated to potential participants and interested professionals through journals, conferences and workshops.

### Research outcomes

The initial assumption in this study was that students with ASD would find the form in which the SDM movement experiences were presented challenging, and therefore that other ways of providing the same movement experiences would have to be devised. However, during Phase 1, it emerged that most of the students were able to take part in individual movement experiences, and did not appear to find the form of the movement experiences confrontational, as originally anticipated. After observation and informal discussion between the researcher, the consultants and facilitators, it emerged that the fundamental issue to be addressed was pedagogical style.

### Phase 1 outcomes

The outcomes during Phase 1 were derived from leader and facilitator observation, video documentary evidence and diary notes of informal discussions and included:

■ Recommendations for the adaptation of SDM session delivery

■ Indicators on which observation/evaluation schedules could be based, relating to levels of student engagement in movement experiences and levels of student interaction with facilitators.

### Adaptation of SDM session delivery
#### *Environmental adaptations*

Timing of sessions: The structured SDM sessions were reduced in length to between 20 and 25 minutes as students gradually became familiar with movement experiences and the time needed reduced.

Environmental organisation: Higher levels of student engagement were noted when the environment was contained, and visual distraction (e.g. non-essential notices, tempting apparatus) was minimised.

### Communication of facilitators with students
#### *Verbal communication*

There was a majority consensus among facilitators that the use of simple, clear and consistent language by both the session leader and the facilitators was vital for supporting students' engagement. Facilitators suggested that students had become confused by complex verbal directives which appeared to increase students' levels of disengagement. This observation is commensurate with the difficulty which many students with ASD are known to have with receptive language processing (Wing, 2002). As one teacher stated:

> *...because of the information processing difficulties these children experience, it is vitally important that simple and short instructions be used at all times.*

Facilitators were therefore encouraged, when communicating verbally with their partners, to use appropriate one- or two-word statements supported by a visual prompt (see section below). They were also asked to give their partners enough time to process the information given as many students with ASD require increased processing time (Wing, 2002).

To facilitate consistent delivery and communication, an A3 sheet with written instructions, breaking down each movement experience into small achievable parts was designed and posted at a strategic position on the wall along with other visual cues (A4 symbols[2] and photographs) to guide facilitators and students.

### Visual prompts

Facilitators suggested the introduction of visual cues such as symbols and photographs as a means of communicating session developments to students. Visual communication systems build upon the strength of students with ASD as visual learners (Mesibov and Howley, 2003; Mesibov, Shea and Schopler, 2005). Most students with ASD at Sunfield routinely use visual communication and scheduling systems, both through the Picture Exchange Communication System (PECS; Bondy and Frost, 2002) and within the TEACCH model of structured teaching (Mesibov and Howley, 2003; Mesibov, Shea and Schopler, 2005). These two approaches take account of their learning patterns and needs.

To increase manageability of symbols/photographs for communication, students and facilitators were given an extendable belt attachment which held a number of visual cues relating to movement experiences. Facilitators were then easily able to cue students into the next movement experience, without having to retrieve symbols from elsewhere to do so.

### Enhancing communication using other modalities

While the significance of visual cues in facilitating communication was recognised, classroom observations and video evidence revealed that there was an increase in positive outcomes and more sustained engagement in movement experiences whenever clear demonstration preceded a movement experience. It was equally noted that when facilitators used other prompting strategies with their partners (e.g. physical prompts, gesture, signing, modelling), there was also a higher level of active engagement from the student.

## Structuring SDM sessions
### Beginnings, endings and transitions

Facilitators reported, and video evidence corroborated, that students appeared confused by transitions from one movement experience to another during sessions. Discussion suggested that this was due to lack of session structure. While the four lesson plans provided the researcher and the facilitators with a framework to follow, and formed the basis of inter-session comparability, the experiences were arranged in no particular order. There was no consistent activity which indicated the beginning or ending of the session.

Two movement experiences – 'Rocking' and 'Sliding on a blanket' – were favoured by most students, even if they had been unable to engage in the rest of the session. Following a facilitator's suggestion, it was decided that 'Rocking' would be used as an initial and transitional activity between movement experiences, and 'Sliding on a blanket' would be used as the last movement experience before the final gathering together of the group. Thus, these experiences became 'kinaesthetic cues', signifying the end of one experience and preparation for another.

### Providing familiarity and challenge

Students with ASD are often made anxious and stressed by unfamiliar situations due to their difficulties around sequencing and predicting events without reference to concrete cues (Mesibov and Howley, 2003; Mesibov, Shea and Schopler, 2005). It was therefore decided that new movement experiences, aimed at promoting specific interactional skills, would be introduced very gradually, while retaining a session framework of familiar movement experiences. Each new movement experience was repeated at least three times to consolidate the experience for the students. The retention of familiar movement experiences helped these students with severe intellectual disabilities and ASD to achieve success in the learning process, in the same SDM session as being challenged to learn new skills.

### Facilitator engagement and expertise

Analysis of video evidence showed that student engagement increased when their facilitator was engaged and animated. Partnerships were most successful when the adult was able to channel students' natural preferences for free-flow activities, intense personal contact or rough-and-tumble into positive social communicative experiences in a playful way. Students' continuing engagement also relied upon their facilitator's ability to judge how long to sustain an on-going movement experience, moving on before their partners became bored.

Most of the facilitators felt that they lacked expertise in using SDM as an interactive strategy as it was new to them. This appeared to have compromised their confidence in supporting their partners, as a learning support assistant confirmed:

> *I would have been more confident to support Lee[3] if I knew in advance what was expected of me and the child. I did not know whether I was doing the right thing or not as I had no previous experience using Sherborne Developmental Movement.*

On-project training was given; however, it was decided that, following the project, Level 1 SDM training would need to be offered to facilitators in association with the adapted SDM approach.

### Observation/evaluation instruments
### Indicators of engagement

In the course of Phase 1, five levels of student engagement with their facilitator were identified for the observation/evaluation forms to record participant and non-participant observation. These are listed in Table 4.1.

### Indicators of interaction

Following analysis of videos and notes of informal participant observation, the researcher identified the following indicators of students' level of interaction with their facilitators:

**Table 4.1. Degree of engagement associated with student interaction category**

| Categories of student interaction with facilitator | Degree of student engagement |
|---|---|
| 1. Refusal<br>• *Student moves away from group*<br>• *Does not take part in movement experience*<br>• *No interaction with facilitator* | Least engaged |
| 2. Retreatism<br>• *Student remains in proximity to the group and facilitator*<br>• *Intermittently takes part in movement experience*<br>• *Intermittent interaction with facilitator* | |
| 3. Ritualistic engagement<br>• *Student remains with facilitator*<br>• *Is a passive participant in movement experience while focusing on ritualistic activity*<br>• *No/intermittent interaction with facilitator* | |
| 4. Passive engagement<br>• *Student remains with facilitator*<br>• *Is an apparently passive participant in movement experience*<br>• *No/intermittent interaction with facilitator* | |
| 5. Authentic engagement<br>• *Student remains with facilitator*<br>• *Contributes to/initiates movement experience*<br>• *Frequent/sustained interaction with facilitator* | Most engaged |

- Eye-contact
- Turn-taking
- Joint attention
- Imitation
- Initiating interaction.

These elements were recorded into a standard form alongside information about the associated movement experience and the level of prompt for students used by facilitators. Due to its initial complexity, the form used during Phase 2 was simplified for use in Phase 3 (see Figure 4.1).

**Phase 2 outcomes**

Prior to the start of Phase 2, the first model of the adapted SDM approach was devised based upon Phase 1 outcomes. This comprised:

- Specific verbal communication strategies: minimal and focused use of simplified language in association with visual communication
- Specific visual communication strategies, which included:
  - Individual-size Sherborne symbols or photographs on an extendable belt ring for both students and facilitators
  - A4-size Sherborne symbols and photographs for students with visual difficulties

**Figure 4.1. Session evaluation sheet**

Sunfield Research

**Sunfield Research Institute**

**SDM SESSION EVALUATION SHEET**

**Date.......................... Programme no................ School/class.................. Name/ID..................**

| Movement experience | Type of prompt | | | | | | Type of engagement | | | | | | Level of engagement | | | | | Comments |
|---|---|---|---|---|---|---|---|---|---|---|---|---|---|---|---|---|---|---|
| | P | VS | V | G | S | M | TT | EC | IM | II | JA | SE | R | RT | PC | RE | AE | |
| Rocking | | | | | | | | | | | | | | | | | | |
| Sliding on hips | | | | | | | | | | | | | | | | | | |
| Exploring space with arms | | | | | | | | | | | | | | | | | | |
| Back to back push | | | | | | | | | | | | | | | | | | |
| Swaying by arms/legs | | | | | | | | | | | | | | | | | | |
| Wriggling through a tunnel | | | | | | | | | | | | | | | | | | |
| Sliding on blanket | | | | | | | | | | | | | | | | | | |

| Type of prompt: | | Type of engagement: | | Level of engagement: | |
|---|---|---|---|---|---|
| G = Gesture | M = Modelling | EC = Eye-contact | II = Initiate interaction | AE = Authentic engagement | PC = Passive compliance |
| P = Physical | S = Sign | IM = Imitation | JA = Joint attention | | R = Refusal |
| V = Verbal | VS = Visual cues | TT = Turn -taking | SE = Shared experience | RE = Ritual engagement | RT = Retreatism |

- Structural strategies, including:
    - Scheduling of movement experiences using a left-to-right sequence of A4 symbols/photographs to form a 'wall schedule' alongside A3 instruction cards
    - Kinaesthetic cues, including specific beginning, transitional and end movement experiences
- Strategies to improve consistency, including:
    - Specific guidance for facilitators in use of language (A3 cues)
    - A protocol for the introduction of new movement experience elements.

Standard recording and reporting strategies were also put into place including an observation/evaluation schedule devised to monitor levels of interaction and engagement to be filled in by facilitators at the end of each session.

Findings from the trials in the three Phase 2 schools were used to make further improvements to the adapted teaching approaches to SDM for use with individuals with severe ASD. Again, video documentation informed the process, and facilitator evaluation and discussion determined further modifications to the programme delivery. While only minimal changes were made to all the four lesson plans (see Figure 4.2) – one movement experience being replaced – the evaluation sheets were redesigned following requests by facilitators for less complex recording.

During Phase 2, there was a notable improvement in both facilitator and student engagement. The majority of students were able to respond positively to most movement experiences. The improvements were attributed to:

- *Facilitator endeavour and their ability to make the students feel safe and nurtured* This increased following additional briefing on the shared goals and objectives of the project, where concerns were resolved
- *An increase in student understanding and confidence.*

Students' communication skills also improved. Some students became able readily to recognise the visual cues and vocalise the movement experience. Many students demonstrated an improved ability to maintain eye-contact.

Students' sensory sensitivities, which had characterised Phase 1, reduced, and individual students who had shown high sensitivity to touch began to accept being held and touched.

The data collected demonstrated that, by the end of Phase 2, the majority of students showed improvement in their social communicative skills, and had remained fully engaged with their facilitators throughout the programme sessions. This showed improvement when compared with Phase 1 figures (see Figure 4.3), although some students had found elements of the SDM sessions confrontational and had persistently retreated or completely failed to join in.

**Figure 4.2. Example of a lesson plan for an adapted SDM session**

Sunfield Research

**LESSON PLAN 2.1**

| CLASS: | NO. OF PUPILS: | NO. OF ADULTS: | DATE: | DURATION: |
|---|---|---|---|---|

AIMS: 1. To develop basic skills which improve relationship play, communication, creativity and an awareness of self, others and space
2. To ensure that the quality of interaction between the caregiver and the child has positive effect on the child

### LESSON DEVELOPMENT

| Learning experience/Target | Learning activities | Class organisation | Class Development | Assessment opportunities | Dynamics |
|---|---|---|---|---|---|
| 1. Developing body and spatial awareness and an ability to move safely avoiding others | Rocking | Pairs | 1. Partners sitting one behind the other<br>2. Place hands on partner's shoulders<br>3. Rock gently forwards/backwards or sideways | 1, 3, 5, 6 | Bound/free<br>Slow/fast |
| 2. Developing creative and communication skills | Sliding on hips | Pairs | 1. Sit on the floor with straight legs and palms on the floor between the legs of a partner<br>2. Shuffle on hips saying hello to others<br>3. Use arms and feet to propel the body | 1, 2, 3 and 5 | Slow/fast<br>Straight/flexible |
| 3. Developing trust and confidence in self and others | Appearing/disappearing knees | Single/pairs | 1. Sitting on the floor with bent knees<br>2. Press and flatten knees<br>3. Bend and stretch knees | 3, 4 and 5, 6 | Strong/fine<br>Fast/slow |
| 4. Developing an ability to form positive relationships | Sliding on stomach/back | Pairs | 1. Lie on stomach next to partner<br>2. Feel parts of own body in contact with the floor<br>3. Wriggle/slide on the stomach/back towards/from a target | 1, 2, 3, 4 and 5 | Free/bound<br>Direct/flexible |
| 5. Acquiring and improving performance in basic movement skills | Wriggling through a tunnel | Pairs | 1. Adults on all fours<br>2. Partners wriggle through the 'tunnel' | 1, 3, 5 and 6 | Low/medium<br>High<br>Fast/slow |
| 6. Providing access to the curriculum | Sliding on blanket | Pairs | 1. One partner lies on blanket<br>2. Other partner pulls blanket by head or leg end | 1, 3 and 4 | Fast/slow<br>Flexible/direct |

RESOURCES: Blankets, cues (pictures and symbols)

COMMENTS:

**Case Study 1**

Paul was an 11-year-old pupil with a diagnosis of severe ASD. He was non-verbal, but attempted to vocalise some words. He was also touch sensitive but, worked very well in group situations and was often very enthusiastic about taking part. He understood turn-taking and would sit and listen when other pupils were taking their turn.

Evidence revealed that although Paul was one of the pupils capable of performing all the movement experiences during the initial stages of the project implementation, he would not allow his facilitator to touch him. Instead, he preferred to work independently beside his facilitator, but would run away whenever the adult tried to come within close proximity. However, like many other pupils who resisted close personal contact at the beginning of the project, Paul eventually overcame this barrier and started to enjoy being held and rocked. It may be that he was prepared to accept touch during SDM sessions because it was in this instance purposeful, contextual and incorporated into the his kinaesthetic experiences.

Facilitators from all three Phase 2 schools reported that the symbols/pictures helped them gain confidence in supporting their partners.

**Phase 3 outcomes**

At the beginning of Phase 3, the additional 10 schools involved were given packs containing the lesson plans, evaluation schedules, symbols and extendable belt rings for individual use, wall symbols and photographs, protocols for verbal prompting and introduction of movement experiences, and A4 ring-bound booklets of the symbols, as some of the students involved had poor vision, and hence had difficulty accessing the small cues.

During Phase 3, facilitators and leaders took part in semi-structured interviews with the researcher prior to and following the intervention to elicit their perceptions of the adapted SDM approach. The following were derived from categorical content analysis of the interview data.

**Communication**
***Visual cues***

Traditionally with SDM, the cues have been auditory, vocal and kinaesthetic, but using visual prompts is a new approach. Although it cannot be claimed that the improvement observed was due only to the use of visual cues, during sessions it was noted that, following introduction of symbol prompts, student engagement with movement experiences increased. Most of the facilitators (35 of 120) had observed that the visual communication strategies led to students feeling more in control and more confident, and a simultaneous increase in attention span, noted by eight facilitators, may suggest an association between the two. Commenting upon the use of visual cues, one facilitator remarked:

> *...the visual cues have made a big difference in the delivery of the sessions. Both the staff and pupils have found them clear and self-explanatory – immensely reducing verbal input in terms of instruction.*

Three facilitators/leaders perceived that the introduction of visual cues to augment verbal prompts had improved students' levels of engagement. The following case study illustrates this.

---

**Case Study 2**

Ron was 14 years old and had many traits of classical autism. He did make eye-contact, particularly with people he felt comfortable with. Although Ron liked to interact with familiar people, he found it uncomfortable to mix with strangers unless they were introduced to him gradually. Likewise, for him to engage in turn-taking in any new activity, it had to be explained to him in advance. Ron had good expressive language, and was happy carry on conversations, even if they were sometimes repetitive. However, occasionally he used his repetitive speech to block out the world around him. He also had poor organisational and sequencing skills and asked repetitive questions about daily or weekly events, such as 'Is it Sherborne today?', 'Are we going to the hall for Sherborne?', 'Is it Sherborne with Vicky today?'

Ron was dependent on routines and became agitated when changes were made to his daily routines without warning. Ron used a pictorial schedule booklet, which he was encouraged to carry around the school to help him follow the sequence of lessons throughout the day. His daily schedule provided room for negotiations and problem-solving. As long as changes were made clear on his schedule, he felt comfortable and coped with change.

The following extract from a teacher's diary highlighted how the structured teaching approach facilitated a dramatic change in Ron's response:

*The lad was horrendous on the first session...he was all over the place, going over the climbing frames. The second session, the change was so dramatic. I think it was the introduction of the [A4] Sherborne booklet with visual cues [instead of key rings], sequencing activities for each lesson, which immensely reduced his anxiety levels, allowing him to focus on the lesson, knowing what will happen next. The schedule provided him with opportunity to make reference to the next activity whenever he felt anxious. Ron interacted well, he counted the amount of times I did certain movements and kept rigidly to that, he was not prepared to do any more or any less! He was always looking ahead to the next movement, and clearly needed the tight structure of the lesson plan.*

Ron's repetitive questioning about activities reduced, as he was now able to see for himself what was expected. His teacher noticed his improved confidence in identifying the next activity, and intermittently encouraged him to show other pupils the visual cue for what was coming next. He enjoyed being in charge, and sometimes volunteered to support his less able peers during the session. His confidence also grew to the extent that he started to play supportive roles, as well as take on other roles in the school (e.g. taking the register to the school reception).

---

The visual cues provided the students with opportunities to communicate their preferences regarding movement experiences in a much clearer way. For example, the facilitators reported that some students would intermittently refer to the set of visual cues on key rings to ensure that their favourite movement experience was scheduled. Access to symbols associated with specific movement experiences ultimately enabled some individuals to start initiating interactions and taking the lead on certain movement experiences as a facilitator confirms:

> *Atieno's progress was amazing. She relied heavily on cue cards and would return to them between each activity. By the final session, she would keep on task for the whole activity and became more proactive in making choices of her favourite movement experiences, initiating the activity with the help of the visual cues.*

While there were many positive remarks (15) regarding the effectiveness of the visual cues, some facilitators/leaders (3) expressed the opinion that particular symbols and photographs were not clear enough, and hence required further development. However, a disadvantage of photographs is that they carry specific visual and environmental cues, all of which may deflect the student from assimilating the core message of the cue which can be isolated within a symbol (Porter and Ashdown, 2002).

## Structure of the SDM session

Seven facilitators/leaders were positive about the increased structure within SDM sessions. One teacher observed that, through her student's responses to structure, she had learnt a lot 'how an ASD child needs an ordered regime to put him at ease'.

The benefits of using 'Rocking' between movement experiences was particularly remarked upon (45 of 120 facilitators/leaders) as being useful in reassuring anxious participants. A teacher described this transitional strategy as 'very useful and reassuring [for the student]'.

The A3 and A4 cues posted on the wall were a great help to both the facilitators and students who were not very familiar with the programme. For example, there were instances when people with no previous experience in using SDM were deployed to support individual students, but because the visual cues were clear and self-explanatory, they were able to provide effective support to their student partners.

### *Familiarity and challenge*

The significance of repeating known movement experiences and gradually introducing new ones into the sessions was highlighted by 18 facilitators/leaders. One facilitator/leader pointed out that:

> *The gradual build-up by increasing the movements whilst still retaining some of the known movements gave stability to the programme with measured challenge to the participants.*

## Responses to the adapted programme

Nineteen facilitators/leaders (n=120) remarked upon the effectiveness of the adapted teaching approaches to the SDM programme in supporting students with ASD to assimilate skills in the areas of engagement (11 facilitators/leaders) and communication (8 facilitators/leaders). A head teacher asserted that:

> *In relating to those children who find interpersonal relationship very difficult and who are locked in their own worlds, our perception is that the practical*

*and interactive nature of the programme meant that those children were inter-acting without necessarily knowing that they were interacting. So relation-ships were being developed, some of the proprioceptive needs of the children were being met, and obviously the programme was fulfilling some of their needs as well as empowering their communication.*

A facilitator observed:

*During the pupils' involvement in the project, their communication skills im-proved. Some began initiating interactions. I have seen a different side to several of the pupils, actively engaged in an activity, which for some of the pupils is unusual. I feel enthused about the re-introduction of SDM to our school, and would like to explore how best to do this.*

Two facilitators/leaders reported that some students made progress from being de-pendent on visual cues to being listeners and verbal communicators. Figure 4.3 highlights the overall improvement in students' social communicative skills.

**Figure 4.3. Pupils' levels of engagement over Phases 1 to 3**

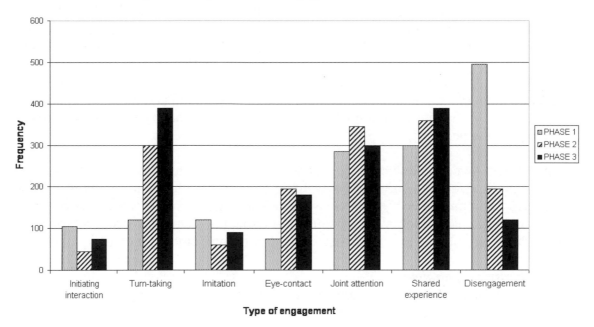

## Issues raised by the research and implications for practice

The adult facilitators remained central to the development of relationships and en-gagement in movement with individuals with profound ASD. A need for the expertise, high motivation and understanding of these adults emerged as being crucial as they have to provide effective and confident support and ensure the quality of delivery of the adapted teaching approaches to SDM. Training is therefore a high priority. Facili-tators became more involved after being briefed thoroughly, with resulting increases in student engagement.

Regularity of sessions and consistency of support is essential for maximum student engagement. Staffing during the project remained problematic, which meant the session leader needed to work with individual students throughout each session. This compromised objective observation. However, the impact of this was minimised by the involvement of one of the consultants. Progress among students who had a consistent facilitator appeared to be greater than those who did not.

Student engagement in initial sessions also depended on their familiarity with their session peer group. Where the group came from a single class, earlier student engagement was noticed compared with groups in which students did not initially know their peers or facilitator group.

## Ideas for future research

As a result of research findings, areas for possible future research have been identified:

- *Creativity vs consistency in session delivery.* One of the key tenets of SDM is the opportunity for participants to be creative and, through recognition of their creativity, to increase self-esteem; however, for young people with ASD, this militates against their need for consistency and predictability. It would be interesting to explore the extent to which participant creativity could become a feature of an adapted SDM delivery.

- *The student voice.* While the findings relied mainly on facilitator/leader perspectives alongside other data collection methods, it would be valuable to explore the student voice on the effectiveness of the programme.

- *Resourcing one-to-one support through inclusive learning.* In a situation where One-to-one facilitator-to-student support is not possible, the dynamic has to be peer collaboration. At Sunfield, some preliminary work was done during this research project in training students with severe intellectual disabilities to support younger peers with ASD at Sunfield under rigorous supervision. There were some interesting indications – student facilitators who were usually distractible became more focused and developed a more sensitive and caring attitude towards their younger peers; their self-esteem appeared to improve, and their support staff reported that they had become more responsible in other areas of daily living

- *Exploration of engagement through SDM with other groups.* Extension work could be done with engagement-focused programmes for students with different disability profiles (e.g. students with emotional and behavioural difficulties). The emotions element of SDM could provide an appropriate way of providing managed and appropriate physical contact.

## Conclusion

The current philosophical climate and interest in supported interaction with young people with intellectual disabilities is providing a platform for the re-establishment of SDM and other reciprocal communication initiatives (Pauli, 2006; see also Chapters 3 and 9). There is also a growing realisation that these approaches can be set within the National Curriculum (Hill, 2006). SDM has the flexibility to accommodate the individual's learning needs and patterns within its philosophical approach, and this liberates teachers to modify the approach to meet the these on a day-by-day basis.

Within the scope of this research project, the main objective of enhancing the social engagement of students with ASD through SDM by implementing adapted teaching approaches has been achieved. The results indicated that students have improved levels of eye-contact, joint attention and shared experiences. In addition, facilitator/leader evaluation reports showed that participants' attention spans and turn-taking abilities had increased.

Many head teachers and staff from the participating schools acknowledged the effectiveness of the 'Sherborne @ Sunfield' programme and expressed their readiness to offer it to a wider student population in their schools. One head teacher, who was personally involved as a facilitator in the sessions at his school, said that he had never been involved in such a valuable piece of collaborative work. One of the Sherborne Association UK consultants involved with the project said that she felt that the 'Sherborne @ Sunfield' model would be tremendously important for the future of SDM – not only from the point of view of young people with ASD, but also in that the framework would give new leaders of traditional SDM confidence during their first sessions.

### The way forward

Prior to the development of an ASD-specific approach to SDM, the programme did not articulate a pathway for students with ASD. 'Sherborne @ Sunfield' is not a deviation from Sherborne's work, but a specific application within the spirit of Veronica Sherborne's own approach to 'Developmental Movement'. As she stated:

> *Each teacher or caregiver can make use of the materials described in this book in his or her own way. Teachers develop their own variations and ideas as do the children they teach.* (Sherborne, 2001)

### References

Aitken, K.J. and Trevarthen, C. (1997) 'Self/other organisation in human psychological development', *Development and Psychopathology,* 9, 653–677.

American Psychiatric Association (2000) *Diagnostic and Statistical Manual of Mental Disorders – Text revision (4th edn)*. Washington, DC: APA.

Autism National Committee (2003) *The Neurophysiology of Autism: Movement, sensory processing and relationships.* [Online at: http://www.autcom.org]

Bondy, A. and Frost, L. (2002) *A Picture's Worth: PECS and other visual communication strategies in autism.* Bethesda, MD: Woodbine House.

Cohen, L., Manion, L. and Morrison, K. (2000) *Research Methods in Education (5th edn).* London: RoutledgeFalmer.

Davis, K. (1997) 'The value of movement activities for young children'. [Online at: http://www.iidc.indiana.edu/IRCA/SocialLeisure/movementact.html]

Department for Education and Science (1991) *National Curriculum Physical Education for Ages 5 to 16*. London: HMSO.

Dibbo, J. and Gerry, S. (1994) *Developments in Sherborne Developmental Movement*. Paper presented at the PE International Conference, Plymouth, UK.

Filer, J. (2006) 'SDM and its role in family therapy'. In: C. Hill (2006) *Communicating through Movement: Sherborne Developmental Movement – towards a broadening perspective.* Clent: Sunfield Publications.

Foundation for People with Learning Disabilities (2002) *Report of the National Committee of Inquiry into the Mental Health Needs of Children and Young People with Learning Disabilities*. London: Mental Health Foundation.

Grandin, T. (1995) *Thinking in Pictures and Other Reports from My Life with Autism*. New York, NY: Doubleday.

Greenspan, S. (1995) *The Challenging Child*. New York: Addison-Wesley Publishing.

Guralnick, M. (2004) 'Early Intervention for children with intellectual disabilities: current knowledge and future prospects.' Keynote address to the 12th IASSID World Congress, Montpellier, France (15 June 2004).

Hycner, R.H. (1985) 'Some guidelines for the phenomenological analysis of interview data', *Human Studies*, 8, 279–303.

Jones, G. (2002) *Educational Provision for Children with Autism and Asperger Syndrome: Meeting their needs*. London: David Fulton.

Kellet, M. and Nind, M. (2003) *Implementing Intensive Interaction in Schools: Guidance for practitioners, managers and coordinators*. London: David Fulton.

Lord, C., Risi, S., Lambrecht, L., Cook, E.H., Jr., Leventhal, B.L., DiLavore, P.C., Pickles, A. and Rutter, M. (2000) 'The Autism Diagnostic Observation Schedule–Generic: a standard measure of social and communication deficits associated with the spectrum of autism', *Journal of Autism and Developmental Disorders*, 30 (3), 205–223.

Maurer, R. (2003) 'Autism and the cerebellum: a neurological basis for intervention'. [Online at: http://www.autcom.org]

Mesibov, G. and Howley, M. (2003) *Accessing the Curriculum for Pupils with Autistic Spectrum Disorders*. London: David Fulton.

Mesibov, G., Shea, V. and Schopler, E. (2005) *The TEACCH Approach to Autism Spectrum Disorders*. New York, NY: Kluwer Academic/Plenum.

National Research Council (2001) *Understanding Dropouts: Statistics, strategies and high-stakes testing*. Washington, DC: National Academy Press.

Pauli, D. (2006) 'Contact through colour', *Special Children,* June/July, 30–33.

Peter, M. (1997) *Making Dance Special.* London: David Fulton.

Piaget, J. (1969) *The Psychology of the Child*. New York, NY: Basic Books.

Porter, J. and Ashdown, R. (2002) *Pupils with Complex Learning Difficulties: Promoting learning using visual materials and methods*. London: National Association of Special Educational Needs.

Radnor, H.A. (1994) *Collecting and Analysing Interview Data*. London: Open University Press.

Robson, C. (2002) *Real World Research: A resource for social scientists and practitioner-researchers (2nd edn)*. Oxford: Blackwell.

Seach, D. (2006) *Interactive Play for Children with Autism*. London: Routledge.

Sheppard, S. (1996) 'The implementation of Sherborne based development with pupils on the autistic spectrum'. In: *Therapeutic Intervention in Autism: Perspectives from research and practice* (Conference proceedings). Durham: University of Durham.

Sherborne, V. (2001) *Developmental Movement for Children: Mainstream, special needs and pre-school (2nd edn)*. London: Worth Publishing.

Sugden, D. and Wright, H. (2001) 'Physical education'. In: B. Carpenter, R. Ashdown and K. Bovair (eds) *Enabling Access: Effective teaching and learning for pupils with learning difficulties*. London: David Fulton.

Stern, D.N. (1989) 'The representation of relational patterns: developmental considerations'. In: A.J. Sameroff and R.N. Emde (eds) *Relationship Disturbances in Early Childhood*. New York: Basic Books.

Teitelbaum, P., Teitelbaum, O., Nye, J., Fryman, J. and Maurer, R.G. (1998) 'Movement analysis in infancy may be useful for early diagnosis of autism', *Proceedings of the National Academy of Sciences of the United States of America,* 95 (23),13982–13987. [Online at: http://www.pnas.org]

Thornton, K. and Taylor, E. (2005) 'Play and the reduction of challenging behaviour in children with ASD and learning disabilities', *Good Autism Practice,* 6 (2), 75–80.

Werner, E., Dawson, G., Osterling, J. and Dinno, N. (2000) 'Recognition of autism spectrum disorder before one year of age: a retrospective study based on home videotapes', *Journal of Autism and Developmental Disorders,* 30 (2), 157–162.

Wing, L. (2002) *The Autistic Spectrum: a guide for parents and professionals.* London: Constable and Robinson.

Worth, S. (2005) *Autistic Spectrum Disorders.* London: Continuum.

## Endnotes

[1] Staff supporting students on a one-to-one basis during SDM sessions are referred to as facilitators throughout this summary.

[2] Sherborne-specific symbols were developed by the researcher and the Senior Occupational Therapist at Sunfield, Jackie Buscombe. These symbols were later adapted by Widgit Software and are now available as part of the Writing With Symbols computer programme (see http://www.widgit.com).

[3] Names in the chapter have been changed to protect identity.

# CHAPTER 5

# Why Do You Do That?

## Stories to Support Social Understanding for People with ASD

*Iain Chatwin*

Storytelling is a traditional method of teaching children within most cultures around the world. Stories are used to develop social and moral awareness, teach values and identify aspirational behaviour.

Story has also been used with a therapeutic objective in books created to engage the reader in exploring behaviour in specific situations. The stories are written with the intention of helping the reader to identify how their own behaviour may be unacceptable to others, and guide them toward more appropriate responses. Stories allow the storyteller to create scenarios involving characters with whom the reader is able to identify. The whole environment and its associated characters can be completely controlled to focus attention on the desired content.

This technique of bibliotherapy has been used as a focused intervention with children with intellectual disabilities and behaviour disorders (Sridhar and Vaughn, 2000). These stories are written about a specific issue, but for a general audience, assuming that the reader will be able to identify with the central character. This facet of storytelling has been further adapted and formalised into a specific approach for addressing difficulties with social understanding in people with autistic spectrum disorders (ASDs) and is known as 'social stories' (Gray, 1994a). Social stories are becoming widely used as a written intervention strategy to address difficulties with social interaction (Delano and Snell, 2006), written for specific individuals and typically being written in the first person featuring the individual concerned as the central character.

### Social skills and ASD

All ASDs are characterised by repetitive behaviour patterns, and impaired skills of communication and social interaction (Wing, 2002). However, these characteristics are manifested uniquely for each individual, and so each will need individualised interventions. Jordan (2001) maintains that these 'impairments' are more appropriately seen as differences rather than delays.

Social skills deficits partially represent diagnostic criteria for autism and other ASDs including Asperger syndrome (American Psychiatric Association, 2000; World Health Organisation, 2005). All ASDs are characterised by repetitive behaviour patterns, and impaired skills of communication and social interaction (Wing, 2002); however, individuals show differences in how these characteristics are manifested, and so will need individualised interventions. Typical difficulties in relation to social interaction include inattention to others, problems in understanding social rules and conventions, and moderating behaviour according to different social situations. The effect on social communication and understanding is therefore more than just a delay in acquiring language.

Social impairments in ASD have been linked to difficulties relating to theory of mind (Baron-Cohen, Tager-Flusberg and Cohen, 2000) and central coherence (Happé and Frith, 2006), resulting in problems understanding what other people may be thinking and feeling. The level of development of theory of mind appears to be independent of intelligence (Brent, Rios, Happé and Charman, 2004), but impairs the ability of the individual to predict how others may behave, and what their expectations may be, in social situations. The overall impact on individuals typically is that the world appears confusing and stressful (Birch, 2006).

In order to address deficits in social understanding a range of strategies have been used with people with ASD including social skills training, scripting, social rules, storytelling, peer tutoring and video modelling (Graetz, 2003).

In relation to learning styles and cognitive development, the ability of people with ASD to process and comprehend visual information more successfully than auditory input has been implied by research studies (*inter alia* Dettmer, Simpson, Smith Myles and Ganz, 2000; Quill, 1997) and described by authors who themselves have an ASD (Grandin, 1995; Sainsbury, 2000; Williams, 1996).

Scripts and rules provide a resource to support appropriate behaviour, but do not seek to address issues of understanding the process. Children's stories can be a useful tool in social skills training for children with intellectual disabilities but, for the individual with ASD, they may not be specific enough to a situation or the people involved for them to understand sufficiently what is going on, and how people may or should interact and behave. Addressing issues of expressing frustration or misunderstanding of social situations can have an effect on reducing anxiety, stress and problem behaviour. Stories can encourage the individual to divulge unexpressed feelings or elaborate on their understanding of a situation (Del Valle, McEachern and Chambers, 2001).

## Social stories

The social story is an attempt to help the individual understand interactions between, and the perspectives of, people in a particular social situation. The stories decipher the rules of social engagement which are typically mystifying for people with ASD, and are individualised around specific understanding, support needs, interests, and attention skills; making the story meaningful and motivating for the person it is written for.

People with ASDs show a strong affinity for routines and rules. Stories describe a routine that can be successfully applied in a given situation while allowing the individual to feel in control, and may therefore have strong appeal to people with ASD. They may provide a less confrontational format than rules.

Typically, stories are written to provide the person with ASD with new insights and perspective about what is happening in a specific context, in an attempt to help a person to modulate their behaviour in response to social expectations. This may be due to the person with ASD showing high anxiety in a specific situation, having difficulty expressing emotions, or displaying unacceptable behaviour.

Social stories address limitations in social functioning in a consistent, structured manner in a form that is available for reference at the individual's own pace of learning. Though verbal reading of the story to the individual may support initial understanding, presenting information in a permanent visual form enables the individual to refer to its content as often as they require, thus supporting their understanding. A purely verbal delivery may be too transient to support recall. The opportunity to access the story without the additional interference of social engagement may also be important in increasing receptiveness (Scattone, Wilczynski, Edwards and Rabian, 2002).

Stories created to address a range of problems related to social understanding are now a widely used intervention strategy. A set of defining criteria for writing such social stories, developed in 1991 by Carol Gray, has been revised over time as perceptions of the key elements of the approach have been informed by experience (Gray, 1994a; Gray, 2000; Gray and Garrand, 1993). The most recent criteria and guidance are referred to as 'Social Stories 10.0', and include suggestions about how each sentence type within the stories should be constructed, and how the overall story should be presented (Gray, 2004).

More than providing a product in the form of a factual story, Gray (1996) describes the use of social stories as a two-way process through which the understanding of the person with ASD is explored and respected. This is said to result in improved responses by the person with ASD to social situations, and to provide others with greater awareness of the experiences of people with ASD.

Social stories generally incorporate information as text and pictures, modes which are better suited to the preferred learning style of most people with ASD. This also provides a non-social way of learning about and rehearsing social rules. The story should accurately and factually describe key factors of the environment, the people involved, their thoughts and/or feelings and why a certain conduct of behaviour is preferred.

Social stories were developed to be written by people who work with, or look after, people with ASD. However, many stories are deliberately presented in a format that requires the person with ASD to contribute to some extent to the story content. The social story assimilates a range of special educational tools, such as modelling, visual cues, priming and task analysis (Barry and Burlew, 2004).

## Social story topics

The subject matter for social stories is unlimited, and the intended impact is also wide-ranging. They have been used to target a range of behaviour including precursors to tantrums (e.g. Adams, Aphroditi, Van Lue and Waldron, 2004; Lorimer, Simpson, Smith-Myles and Ganz, 2002), transition to pre-school settings (Briody and McGarry, 2005), social interaction problems (e.g. Delano and Snell, 2006; Rogers and Smith Myles, 2001; Sansosti and Powell-Smith, 2006), screaming in class (Agosta, Graetz, Mastropieri and Scruggs, 2004; Scattone, Wilczynski, Edwards and Rabian, 2002), fear of dental treatment (Bäckman and Pilebro, 1999) and outdoor activities (Chapman and Trowbridge, 2000), mealtime behaviour (e.g. Norris and

Dattilo, 1999; Toplis and Hadwin, 2006), bedtime behaviour (Burke, Kuhn and Peterson, 2004; Moore, 2004) and personal hygiene issues (Hagiwara and Smith Myles, 1999; Moffatt, 2001).

Gray (1994a) also identifies that recognising achievement is an equally significant purpose for social stories, as people with ASD typically find written praise more meaningful than verbal plaudits. Building self-esteem through developing a series of stories that are based upon achievements is recommended, with the initial story for each individual portraying a situation that is already known to be successful for them.

Social stories are constructed around identified sentence types which are used according to a ratio which defines their relative frequency. Guidelines are also provided on how each sentence type should be constructed, and how the overall story should be presented (Gray, 2004).

**Types of social story sentence**
Gray (1994a) provided a format for constructing social stories around three sentence types designed to carry out specific functions within the overall influence of the story.

*Descriptive sentences* are candid factual statements that clarify the critical features of the subject matter. They are used as the framework for developing the story, explaining 'who', 'what', 'why', 'when', 'where' and 'how'; for example, 'My teacher is called Mrs Jones'.

*Perspective sentences* offer the reader insight into the thoughts, feelings, attitudes, motivations, preferences and values of people described in the story. They generally explain the internal states of others, and refer to the person with an ASD only where that person has confirmed their perspective; for example, 'Mrs Jones likes children to sit quietly when she is talking.'

*Directive Sentences* provide guidance on an acceptable action that the person with an ASD should attempt to achieve in the described situation. Directive sentences may offer a choice of alternative responses that the individual may strive to make. Gray (1994a) emphasises the need for directive sentences to be phrased 'I will try to…' or 'I may…' rather than 'I will…', in order to avoid rigid expectations of compliance that may cause anxiety to the individual if they fail to achieve the outcome; for example, 'I will try to be quiet when Mrs Jones is talking to the class.'

Later, a fourth sentence type was defined for use in social stories (Gray, 1996). *Affirmative sentences* are included to reinforce or augment the significance of preceding sentences. They normally reflect the values and rules of the prevalent culture; or provide reassurance that events or feelings are safe, expected or common; for example, 'Being quiet in class is a good thing to do.'

Involving the person with an ASD in the writing process may increase the relevance of the story for them, and give them a greater feeling of ownership and agreement in respect of the desired outcome. Participation in the writing process may be achieved through the incorporation of partial sentences. These allow the individual to state their own responses in a given situation, or to anticipate the response of others. Partial sentences also allow the individual to identify their own interests and motivations, and ensure that stories are written in a way that is meaningful to them. Any of the sentence types may be written with the inclusion of a blank space where the individual can insert their own text; for example, 'If I stay quiet, Mrs Jones will be…'

Social stories that are initially presented to the individual in complete form may later be modified to include partial sentences in order to evaluate the individual's retention of key aspects, or to encourage on-going attention to significant parts of the story. More recently (Gray, 2000) two further sentence types have been incorporated into social stories with the intention of identifying self-determined responses for the person with an ASD, and what other people will do to support them.

*Control sentences* identify individual strategies, typically reflecting the person's interests, that help remind them how to apply information or behave; for example, 'Quiet is like my cat sitting by the fire.'

*Co-operative sentences* outline the possible role of other people in supporting the individual to complete the described action. They identify who can provide help, and how they can provide that help; for example, 'Mrs Jones will remind us all to be quiet at the beginning of the lesson'.

The above sentence types are not mutually exclusive, and some sentences may be constructed in a style that could be related to more than one type. For example, the sentence, 'If I talk to my friend, he may be embarrassed and remind me to be quiet,' includes elements of a perspective sentence and a co-operative sentence. It is important that combination sentences do not contain directive sentence statements in order to avoid confusion.

The construction of a story from these sentence types is governed by the *Complete Social Story Ratio* (Gray, 2000). A social story will always contain descriptive sentences, but not necessarily any of the other sentence types. The emphasis of a story should always be biased toward providing information and increasing understanding, rather than directing action. Too great an emphasis on directive sentences results in what Smith (2003) terms 'bossy' stories. The ratio of sentences that direct (partial or complete directive or control sentences) to any permutation of sentences that describe (partial or complete descriptive, perspective, affirmative or co-operative sentences) should not exceed 1:2 (Gray, 2004).

The *Social Story Sets* format was developed purposely for younger children with ASD (Gray and White, 2002). These are collections of short stories associated with a single topic. One picture is used to illustrate the overall theme, while each story in the set describes a self-contained part of the concept or skill. Sets typically contain an introductory story and a concluding story to reinforce the linking relationship between the different aspects of the subject. A high proportion of stories within sets contain only descriptive and perspective sentences.

Social Story Sets are designed to respond to the learning style of young children with ASD in that each story requires only a short period of attention, and new information is introduced in small steps, one skill or concept at a time. The child is able to familiarise themselves with, and become confident about, the detail of individual aspects before learning how they interrelate.

While social stories were originally developed to be used with school-aged children, their potential for people with ASD and other social communication difficulties of all ages has been acknowledged. In recognition that the use of the word 'story' may not be seen as age-appropriate in certain situations, Gray (2004) has introduced the concept of social articles for use with adults. Whereas social stories are typically written in the first-person, social articles are generally written in the third person, contain more detail, and are intended to meet the needs of more able individuals. The guidelines for social stories are also applied to social articles (Gray, 2004).

## Writing a social story

Social stories should be written with a specific goal in mind, and informed by gathering as much information as possible about the individual and the chosen situation (Gray, 2000). Padfield (2004) asserts that it is important that the goal is both relevant to a social story approach and important in the current situation that the individual is facing.

Gray (1994b) and Howley (2001) suggest the use of 'comic strip conversations' for assessing the perspective of an individual in order to inform the content and style of a story intervention. The reassessment of the individual's understanding following implementation, through a second comic strip conversation, could then indicate any alteration in their understanding (Howley and Arnold, 2005).

A comic strip conversation involves creating simple illustrative drawings contemporaneously with a conversation. The purpose of this strategy is to provide visual support to aid comprehension of transient verbal communication. They were developed specifically for use with children with autism and related developmental disabilities, based on feedback from pilot trials, and incorporating social cognition and theory of mind research findings (Gray, 1994b).

Comic strip conversations should give equivalent significance to the opinions, beliefs and feelings of others as they do to their speech and behaviour. Symbols are used to emphasise abstract social skills which people with an ASD have difficulty understanding, and colour may be used to represent emotional content (e.g. red for anger, blue for sadness)(see Figure 3.1 ).

**Figure 3.1. An example of a comic strip conversation**

Despite becoming a widely used technique for interpreting the understanding that people with ASD have of social interactions, comic strip conversations have not been a subject of published research. In descriptive accounts, Rogers and Smith Myles (2001) report beneficial outcomes of using comic strip conversations for a young man with Asperger syndrome, and Glaeser, Pierson and Fritschmann (2003) report a reduction in classroom and playground incidents for two children with language difficulties in a mainstream school. Hutchins and Prelock (2006) used social stories and comic strip conversations in combination with two children with ASD.

## Implementing social stories

Once the story has been created, the way in which it is introduced to the individual will influence the outcome of the intervention. A new story should be presented in a calm and reassuring manner and in relaxing surroundings where distraction is minimised. It is important to avoid times when the individual is anxious, in order to support positive learning. Joint attention to the story should be achieved through its medium of presentation, and face-to-face attention or gesturing avoided (Gray, 1998, 2000). The duration, frequency and mode of presentation of the story need to be appropriate to the individual. For some individuals, acceptance will be dependent on their attention to the story and avoidance of direct social interaction with a story-teller (Howley and Arnold, 2005).

The story should be read through with the young person, more than once if necessary, and their reactions observed. The presenter should also explain when the story will be read, and who will read it with the individual. It may then be necessary to rewrite the story to address any sections the individual has difficulty understanding. Subsequent readings should be used to review the story. It is desirable for these reviews to be conducted by more than one person, preferably including others involved in the story. This helps to emphasise shared understanding of the situation to the person with ASD. Reviewing must, however, avoid any punitive comments relating to failure to follow the guidance of the story (Gray, 2000). When the story is complete, it is necessary that the individual knows how to access it for reference.

Where a social story has been successful, recommendations for fading stories include reducing the number of sentences, rewriting sentences in partial form or extending the period between readings of the story (Howley and Arnold, 2005). However, Gray (2000) warns that in some instances 'experience indicates it may not be possible, or advisable, to fade a Social Story from use'.

## Evaluations of social story interventions

The available literature on social stories is limited though increasing, and is supportive of positive outcomes for the approach, though short on rigorous empirical data. The studies all have small sample sizes, ranging from single case to five subjects, with the exception of Smith (2001a,b) who evaluated stories for 19 children (15 with ASD, 2 with intellectual disabilities, 1 with Tourette syndrome and 1 with semantic pragmatic difficulties).

Several published studies on social stories used the format in conjunction with strategies such as behavioural social skills training (Swaggart et al., 1995), and verbal prompts with a token economy (Kuttler, Smith-Myles and Carlson, 1998). Crozier and Tincani (2005) employed modified social stories that did not adhere to the guidelines on sentence ratio and phrasing. Because of variations from the social story guidelines, many studies therefore fail to provide evidence to interpret the efficacy of the method due to the potential impact of these additional variables. In a study specifically designed to implement social stories adhering to Gray's (1998) guidelines, Scattone, Wilczynski, Edwards and Rabian (2002) investigated the extent to which social stories reduced disruptive behaviours of children with ASD. This study found that targeted behaviours decreased for all three participants; however, they noted that verbal prompting to refer to the story had been present within observed intervention sessions.

Different designs for intervention withdrawal have been trialled (e.g. Agosta, Graetz, Mastropieri and Scruggs, 2004; Brownell, 2002; Crozier and Tincani, 2005; Kuoch and Mirenda, 2003; Lorimer, Simpson, Smith-Myles and Ganz, 2002; Toplis and Hadwin, 2006), although here an ethical consideration arises since it represents the withdrawal in the final stage of an intervention with perceived effectiveness (Robson, 2002).

Multiple baseline studies across participants (e.g. Burke, Kuhn and Peterson, 2004; Delano and Snell, 2006), across settings (Hagiwara and Smith Myles, 1999; Soensken and Alper, 2006) and across skills/behaviour (Thiemann and Goldstein, 2001) provide more robust evidence. Rust and Smith (2006) offer a range of factors for consideration in designing future studies into the efficacy of social stories.

One particular characteristic of ASD is difficulty with generalising skills to new situations. The ability of social stories to support generalisation to a new environment has been explored by Delano and Snell (2006), Adams, Aphroditi, Van Lue and Waldron (2004), Thiemann and Goldstein (2001) and Hagiwara and Smith Myles (1999).

As mentioned above, social stories were originally devised for use with children, and studies have tended to focus on this population, mainly in education settings. Some applications have been in the home (e.g. Adams, Aphroditi, Van Lue and Waldron, 2004; Moore, 2004), and one relating to an adult in residential care in the community (Chalk, 2003).

While social stories are a technique developed for children with ASD, the technique has been used with a broader population. Soenksen and Alper's (2006) study involved a child with hyperlexia,[1] but no diagnosis of an ASD. Toplis and Hadwin (2006) and Burke, Kuhn and Peterson (2004) conducted studies on the effectiveness of social stories in addressing inappropriate behaviours in normally developing children with behavioural difficulties, and Briody and McGarry (2005) describe the use of social stories with two typically developing toddlers.

Very high success rates are reported across all studies. Where the intervention has been unsuccessful, specific reasons have been suggested. Erangey (2001) identifies that one unsuccessful story required the child to use a degree of perceptual judgement (i.e. to estimate vehicle speed while waiting to cross a road) which was beyond their ability. Graetz (2003) reports that the social stories effected no improvement for one of the five subjects, and relates this to the many years that the behaviour being targeted had pre-existed.

The study by Toplis and Hadwin (2006), involving five children who did not have a diagnosis of an ASD, found that the stories implemented were effective for three of the subjects. The two children for whom the intervention showed no effect were reported to show oppositional behaviour and had demonstrated age-appropriate perspective-taking in tests, whereas the other three children had below-age-range scores on these tests. The authors suggest that the pre-existent social awareness of these two children may explain why stories focusing on increasing the children's understanding of social expectations were not successful helping them to modify their behaviour.

Brownell (2002), using singing of stories, found that the stories had a significant effect on behaviour for all three subjects in his study, but that singing was only more effective than speaking the story for one of them.

Sansosti and Powell-Smith (2006) identify ineffectiveness of the intervention with one of the three subjects of their study. They propose four possible factors that may have contributed to this: weak adherence to the treatment protocol; inadequate story construction; low reward quality of the reinforcing activity; and no clear link between behaviour and reinforcement.

Social stories were devised to increase social understanding, with an aim to increase socially acceptable behaviour. Most studies, with the exception of Rowe (1999) and Howley (2001), focus on effects on behaviour rather than directly exploring changes in understanding. Additionally, many studies look at effecting a decrease in unacceptable behaviour as opposed to an increase in acceptable behaviour; in other words changing existing behaviour rather than creating new behaviour skills.

Effective use of social stories is related to their individualisation, and therefore relies on the person devising the story to adjust them to the comprehension level of the reader. This modification may include the format of presentation, such as written word, pictures and recorded voice. Variations in the medium of presentation used for social stories include music (Brownell, 2002) and ICT (Hagiwara and Smith Myles, 1999). Haggerty, Black, and Smith (2005) supported the use of a social story with a multi-sensory approach, in which a child with ASD acted out scenes from the story using an apron storyboard. The child wore a green canvas apron which had a large pocket containing felt pieces representing areas of the school. These could be attached to the apron, and provide a 'set' on to which pictures and photographs from the story could be placed as 'puppets'. Schlosser (2003) states that alternative and augmentative communication techniques need to have 'social validity'; that is, they need to be acceptable to those who will use them. If social stories are as successful as reported, then there may be value in further exploring their use with children who require adapted formats of presentation.

**Social stories and ICT**
Hagiwara and Smith Myles (1999) have successfully used computer-based presentation of social stories, although using software not commonly available in UK schools. Further exploration of this format, but using a software programme more readily available to teachers (and families or care settings), may help to extend knowledge of the range of children for whom stories can be effective, and help increase successful social participation for this population.

Theoretical understanding of ASD points to the phenomenon of weak central coherence, problems with determining overall contextual meaning, and difficulty filtering out superfluous information (Happé, 1994). In this respect, the amount of information presented via the computer can be regulated, and thereby help the person with ASD to concentrate on the significant content (Silver and Oakes, 2001), and so attune more closely to the subject of the story.

Murray (1997) suggests that computers interact co-tropically with the person with ASD, meeting the individual at their point of attention.

> *By presenting autistic individuals with outward manifestations of their thoughts, computers may potentiate reflection.* (Murray, 1997)

Computers can offer a controlled environment that provides predictability, and minimises the risk of overloading the individual with too much information. Alongside this, computers allow information to be available on demand, yet at a rate that may be controlled by the individual. They also support problems with memory retrieval. While presenting a bridge between abstract understanding and the real world, all of the resources needed are contained and integrated within a single-unit interface (Murray, 1997).

A significant difficulty in learning appropriate social behaviour is that the environment and interpersonal responses are inconsistent, possibly leading to extended periods of learning. Computers provide a means of ensuring consistent and predictable responses which may help learning of appropriate responses more quickly (Yamamoto and Miya, 1999). Another aspect of computer-supported learning is that it allows repetition without the risk of teacher fatigue which may give rise to paraphrasing and inconsistent presentation of the story content (Panyan, 1984).

Williams, Wright, Callaghan and Coughlan (2002), in the only published study to have compared computer-based reading programmes to book-based activities, found that children with ASD were less resistant to engaging in computer-based intervention, and spent more time on task with computer accessed reading material than with the traditional book format.

One software programme that has been used for story-telling with children with intellectual disabilities is Microsoft PowerPoint. Walter (2002) describes the use of Microsoft PowerPoint to create a special educational resource known as 'Talking Books'. These were developed to increase independent reading, and provide a motivating individualised story format. These presentations can include text supported by pictures, or line drawing symbols generated using programmes such as Widgit Software's Writing with Symbols.[2]

Lahm (1996) suggests that computer programmes using multi-media, including animation and sounds, increase the engagement of children with intellectual disabilities. Gray (2004) suggests that the use of computer technology has great promise as a learning tool for people with ASD. She proposes the use of Microsoft PowerPoint as a medium for presenting social stories, in particular making use of this software's animation features to support the individual's understanding. Using timed transitions between slides with animated text and pictures could 'hold promise for additional tailoring of information to a child's ability, learning style, and interests' (Gray, 2004). Crozier and Sileo (2005) suggest the need for further investigation into the effectiveness of multimedia-based social stories before they are used in preference to a traditional social story format.

**Figure 3.2. A student prepares to read his social story**

**Social stories at Sunfield**

Many of the studies cited have not been conducted with students with profound ASD, yet the potential is obvious to their teachers/carers. A pilot study conducted with three young people with ASD and intellectual disabilities at Sunfield have shown that they demonstrated a clear motivation to engage with stories presented using Power-Point. These stories were compiled to support the students in learning appropriate social conduct relating to events within the classroom. An understanding of the issues to be addressed was informed by conducting comic strip conversations with each of the young people and interviewing staff working with them. Stories were then written in accordance with Gray's (2004) guidelines before being produced as PowerPoint slide shows.

These slide shows consisted of between 12 and 19 slides, and the transition between slides was controlled by automated time settings. Each story was narrated. Slides consisted of plain coloured backgrounds with text, which for two of the subjects included line drawing symbols to support the key information carrying words. Devices such as speech bubbles, photographs and drawings were used, and on many of the slides these were animated to reinforce the content and link with the narration (Figures 5.3, 5.4 and 5.5).

The young people involved were given time to view their story prior to the relevant event occurring. For one young man, the story related to greeting his classroom staff (Figure 5.3), and so he viewed his story before leaving his residential house in the morning. The other two young men viewed their stories relating to Circle Time (Figure 5.4) and talking aloud in class (Figure 5.5) in their classrooms at the beginning of the school day.

An issue affecting intervention reinforced by this study is the need for stories to remain accurate and relevant. The stories created needed to be revised due to changes in classroom staffing and pupils. Such changes have an impact on measuring the effectiveness of stories as an intervention, as the influence of new variables is encountered following the collection of baseline data. However, in terms of evaluating the viability of this mode of intervention, there was still a high level of engagement shown by the young people participating. While not conducted as a comparative study between computer-based presentations and other modes of story

**Figure 5.3. A slide from a social story related to greeting people**

**Figure 5.4. A slide from a social story related to circle time**

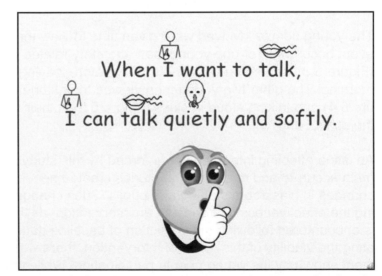

**Figure 5.3. A slide from a social story related to voice levels**

delivery, the potential of PowerPoint to engage the young people involved has stimulated further work in exploring this approach for a wider population.

## Conclusion

Stories represent one strategy in the toolkit available to those supporting people with ASD. They need not be used in isolation, nor should they be used as a stigmatising account which places the sole responsibility for change on people with ASD. Social interaction is a two-way process, and so, as Howley and Arnold (2005) acknowledge, from a social constructionist viewpoint it should also be considered how social partners can change their behaviour and understanding, rather than just looking at shaping change in the behaviour and understanding of the person with ASD. When inappropriate social behaviours are modulated, then the benefits are experienced not just by the individual, but also their social contacts and the wider community (Lynch and Simpson, 2005).

It is important that stories are implemented only after careful assessment of the given situation to ensure that they are the most suitable intervention tool. The goal should always be to develop an effective intervention, not just to develop the most effective social story (Padfield, 2004). Where stories have been written to address a particular misunderstanding, it is important to verify that the presenting problem is clearly addressed by the story.

The advantages of adapting communication styles to meet the needs of children with intellectual disabilities and ASD have long been recognised (Watson, Lord, Schaffer and Schopler, 1989; Weitz, Dexter and Moore, 1997). However, Schlosser (2003) also emphasises the need for communication that is acceptable to all the communication partners. Though stories may be effective, the means of presentation may need adjustment to attain this social validity for the individual. While the more typical formats for stories (e.g. written text with illustrations) can be effective for many individuals, using alternative modes such as ICT can provide this for children who would not accept more traditional formats.

Debate will continue as to whether it is appropriate to teach social skills in a social environment (Jordan, 2001), but the unique needs of children with ASD require novel strategies, and learning may be more effectively achieved within controlled environments, including 'virtual worlds'. However, the ultimate goal of the strategies discussed here is to increase social skills, and so they present opportunities for skill rehearsal activities rather than a substitute for real world experiences. Social understanding may be supported by such activities, but social interaction and engagement require real people.

## References

Adams, L., Aphroditi, G., Van Lue, M. and Waldron, C. (2004) 'Social story intervention: improving communication skills in a child with an autism spectrum disorder', *Focus on Autism and Other Developmental Disabilities*, 19 (2), 87–94.

Agosta, E., Graetz, J., Mastropieri, M. and Scruggs, T. (2004) 'Teacher–researcher partnerships to improve social behavior through social stories', *Intervention in School and Clinic*, 39 (5), 276–287.

American Psychiatric Association (2000) *Diagnostic and Statistical Manual of Mental Disorders (4th edn) (text revision) [DSM-IV-TR]*. Washington, DC: American Psychiatric Association.

Bäckman, B. and Pilebro, C. (1999) 'Augmentative communication in dental treatment of a nine-year-old boy with Asperger syndrome', *Journal of Dentistry for Children*, 66 (6), 419–420.

Baron-Cohen, S., Tager-Flusberg, H. and Cohen, D. (2000) *Understanding Other Minds: Perspectives from autism and developmental cognitive neuroscience (2nd edn)*. Oxford: Oxford University Press.

Barry, L. and Burlew, S. (2004) 'Using social stories to teach choice and play skills to children with autism', *Focus on Autism and Other Developmental Disabilities*, 19 (1), 45–51.

Birch, J. (2006) 'Insight into an autism spectrum disorder', *Kairaranga*, 7 (2), 16–19.

Brent, E., Rios, P., Happé, F. and Charman, T. (2004) 'Performance of children with autism spectrum disorder on advanced theory of mind tasks', *Autism*, 8, 283–299.

Briody, J. and McGarry, K. (2005) 'Using social stories to ease children's transitions', *Journal of the National Association for the Education of Young Children*, 60, 38–42.

Brownell, M. (2002) 'Musically adapted social stories to modify behaviors in students with autism: four case studies', *Journal of Music Therapy*, 39 (2), 117–144.

Burke, R., Kuhn, B. and Peterson, J. (2004) 'Brief report: a "storybook" ending to children's bedtime problems – the use of a rewarding social story to reduce bedtime resistance and frequent night walking', *Journal of Pediatric Psychology*, 29, 389–396.

Chalk, M. (2003) 'Social stories for adults with autism and learning difficulties', *Good Autism Practice*, 4 (2), 3–11.

Chapman, L. and Trowbridge, M. (2000) 'Social stories for reducing fear in the outdoors', *Horizons*, 121, 38–40.

Crozier, S. and Sileo, N. (2005) 'Encouraging positive behaviour with social stories: an intervention for children with autism spectrum disorders', *Teaching Exceptional Children*, 37 (6), 26–31.

Crozier, S. and Tincani, M. (2005) 'Using a modified social story to decrease disruptive behavior of a child with autism', *Focus on Autism and Other Developmental Disabilities*, 20, 150–157.

Delano, M. and Snell, M. (2006) 'The effects of social stories on the social engagement of children with autism', *Journal of Positive Behavior Interventions*, 8, 29–42.

Del Valle, P., McEachern, A. and Chambers, H. (2001) 'Using social stories with autistic children', *Journal of Poetry Therapy*, 14 (4), 187–197.

Dettmer, S., Simpson, R., Smith Myles, B. and Ganz, J. (2000) 'The use of visual supports to facilitate transitions of students with autism', *Focus on Autism and Other Developmental Disabilities,* 15, 163–169.

Erangey, K. (2001) 'Using social stories as a parent of a child with an ASD', *Good Autism Practice*, 2 (1), 26–28.

Glaeser, B., Pierson, M. and Fritschmann, N. (2003) 'Comic strip conversations: a positive behavioural support strategy', *Teaching Exceptional Children*, 36 (2), 14–19.

Graetz, J. (2003) 'Promoting social behaviour for adolescents with autism with social stories', *Dissertation Abstracts International*, 64 (2), 460–462.

Grandin, T. (1995) *Thinking in Pictures and Other Reports from My Life with Autism.* New York: Random House.

Gray, C. (1994a) *The New Social Story Book.* Arlington, TX: Future Horizons.

Gray, C. (1994b) *Comic Strip Conversations: Colorful, illustrated interactions with students with autism and related disorders.* Arlington, TX: Future Horizons.

Gray, C. (1996) *Social Stories and Comic Strip Conversations: Unique methods to improve social understanding.* Arlington, TX: Future Horizons.

Gray, C. (1998) 'Social stories and comic strip conversations with students with Asperger syndrome and high functioning autism'. In: E. Schopler, G. Mesibov and L. Kunce (eds) *Asperger Syndrome or High Functioning Autism?* New York: Plenum.

Gray, C. (2000) *The New Social Story Book (illustrated edn).* Arlington, TX: Future Horizons.

Gray, C. (2004) 'Social Stories 10: the new defining criteria and guidelines', *Jenison Autism Journal*, 15 (4), 2–21.

Gray, C. and Garand, J. (1993) 'Social stories: improving responses of individuals with autism with accurate social information', *Focus on Autistic Behaviour*, 8, 1–10.

Gray, C. and White, A. (2002) *My Social Stories Book.* London: Jessica Kingsley.

Haggerty, N., Black, R. and Smith, G. (2005) 'Increasing self-managed coping skills through social stories and apron storytelling', *Teaching Exceptional Children*, 37 (4), 40–47.

Hagiwara, T. and Smith Myles, B. (1999) 'A multimedia social story intervention: teaching skills to children with autism', *Focus on Autism and Other Developmental Disabilities*, 14, 82–95.

Happé, F. (1994) *Autism: An introduction to psychological theory.* London: University College London Press.

Happé, F. and Frith, U. (2006) 'The weak coherence account: detail-focused cognitive style in autism spectrum disorders', *Journal of Autism and Developmental Disorders*, 36 (1), 5–25.

Howley, M. (2001) 'An investigation into the impact of social stories on the behaviour and social understanding of four pupils with autistic spectrum disorder'. In: R. Rose and I. Grosvenor (eds) *Doing Research in Special Education.* London: David Fulton.

Howley, M. and Arnold, E. (2005) *Revealing the Hidden Social Code: Social stories for people with autistic spectrum disorders.* London: Jessica Kingsley.

Hutchins, T. and Prelock, P. (2006) 'Using social stories and comic strip conversations to promote socially valid outcomes for children with autism', *Seminars in Speech and Language*, 27, 47–59.

Jordan, R. (2001) *Autism with Severe Learning Difficulties.* London: Souvenir.

Kuoch, H. and Mirenda, P. (2003) 'Social story interventions for young children with autism spectrum disorders', *Focus on Autism and Other Developmental Disabilities,* 18, 219–227.

Kuttler, S., Smith-Myles, B. and Carlson, J. (1998) 'The use of social stories to reduce precursors to tantrum behaviour in a student with autism', *Focus on Autism and Other Developmental Disabilities*, 13, 176–182.

Lahm, E. (1996) 'Software that engages young children with disabilities: a study of design features', *Focus on Autism and Other Developmental Disabilities*, 11, 115–124.

Lorimer, P., Simpson, R., Smith-Myles, B. and Ganz, J. (2002) 'The use of social stories as a preventative behavioral intervention in a home setting with a child with autism', *Journal of Positive Behavior Interventions,* 4, 53–60.

Lynch, S. and Simpson, C. (2005) 'Social Stories: tools to teach positive behaviors', *Dimensions of Early Childhood*, 33, 32–36.

Moffatt, E. (2001) 'Writing social stories to improve students' social understanding', *Good Autism Practice*, 2 (1), 12–15.

Moore, P. (2004) 'The use of social stories in a psychology service for children with learning disabilities: a case study of a sleep problem', *British Journal of Learning Disabilities*, 32, 133–138.

Murray, D. (1997) 'Autism and information technology: therapy with computers'. In: S. Powell and R. Jordan (eds) *Autism and Learning: A guide to good practice*. London: David Fulton.

Norris, C. and Dattilo, J. (1999) 'Evaluating effects of a social story intervention on a young girl with autism', *Focus on Autism and Other Developmental Disabilities*, 14, 180–186.

Padfield, K. (2004) 'The use of social stories as a tool for problem analysis'. In: Autism Research Unit (ed.) *Current Issues for Research and Practice: Collected papers from the 2004 Durham International Research Conference on Autism held at Van Mildert College, University of Durham.* Sunderland: Autism Research Unit.

Panyan, M. (1984) 'Computer technology for autistic students', *Journal of Autism and Developmental Disorders*, 14 (4), 375–382.

Quill, K. (1997) 'Instructional considerations for young children with autism: the rationale for visually cued instruction', *Journal of Autism and Developmental Disorders*, 21, 697–714.

Robson, C. (2002) *Real World Research (2nd edn)*. Oxford: Blackwell.

Rogers, M. and Smith Myles, B. (2001) 'Using social stories and comic strip conversations to interpret social situations for an adolescent with Asperger's syndrome', *Intervention in School and Clinic*, 36, 310–313.

Rowe, C. (1999) 'Do social stories benefit children with autism in mainstream primary school?', *British Journal of Special Education*, 26, 12–14.

Rust, J. and Smith, A. (2006) 'How should the effectiveness of social stories to modify the behaviour of children on the autistic spectrum be tested?', *Autism*, 10 (2), 125–138.

Sainsbury, C. (2000) *The Martian in the Playground: Understanding the schoolchild with Asperger's syndrome.* Bristol: Lucky Duck.

Sansosti, F. and Powell-Smith, A. (2006) 'Using social stories to improve the social behaviour of children with Asperger syndrome', *Journal of Positive Behaviour Interventions*, 8, 43–57.

Scattone, D., Wilczynski, S., Edwards, R. and Rabian, B. (2002) 'Decreasing disruptive behaviors of children with autism using social stories', *Journal of Autism and Developmental Disorders*, 32, 535–543.

Schlosser, R. (2003) *The Efficacy of Augmentative and Alternative Communication: Toward evidence-based practice.* San Diego, CA: Academic Press.

Silver, M. and Oakes, P. (2001) 'Evaluation of a new computer intervention to teach people with autism or Asperger syndrome to recognize and predict emotions in others', *Autism*, 5, 299–316.

Smith, C. (2001a) 'Using social stories with children with autistic spectrum disorders: an evaluation', *Good Autism Practice*, 2 (1), 16–25.

Smith, C. (2001b) 'Using social stories to enhance behaviour in children with autistic spectrum difficulties', *Educational Psychology in Practice*, 17, 337–346.

Smith, C. (2003) *Writing and Developing Social Stories: Practical interventions in autism.* Bicester: Speechmark.

Soenksen, D. and Alper, S. (2006) 'Teaching a young child to appropriately gain attention of peers using a social story intervention', *Focus on Autism and Other Developmental Disabilities*, 21, 36–44.

Sridhar, D. and Vaughn, S. (2000) 'Bibliotherapy for all: enhancing reading comprehension, self-concept, and behavior', *Teaching Exceptional Children*, 33 (2), 74–82.

Swaggart, B., Gagnon, E., Jones-Bock, S., Earles, T., Quinn, C., Myles, B. and Simpson, R. (1995) 'Using social stories to teach social and behavioral skills to children with autism', *Focus on Autistic Behaviour*, 10, 1–16.

Thiemann, K. and Goldstein, H. (2001) 'Social stories, written text cues, and video feedback: effects on social communication of children with autism', *Journal of Applied Behavior Analysis*, 34, 425–446.

Toplis, R. and Hadwin, J. (2006) 'Using social stories to change problematic lunchtime behaviour in school', *Educational Psychology in Practice*, 22, 53–67.

Walter, R. (2002) *How to Create Talking Books in PowerPoint 97 and 2000* (3rd version). Oxford: ACE Centre Advisory Trust.

Watson, L., Lord, C., Schaffer, B. and Schopler, E. (1989) *Teaching Spontaneous Communication to Autistic and Developmentally Handicapped Children.* New York: Irvington.

Weitz, C., Dexter, M. and Moore, J. (1997) 'AAC and children with developmental disabilities'. In: S. Glennen and D. DeCoste (eds) *Handbook of Augmentative and Alternative Communication.* San Diego, CA: Singular.

Williams, C., Wright, B., Callaghan, G. and Coughlan, B. (2002) 'Do children with autism learn to read more readily by computer assisted instruction or traditional book methods?: a pilot study', *Autism*, 6 (1), 71–91.

Williams, D. (1996) *Autism: An inside-out approach.* London: Jessica Kingsley.

Wing, L. (2002) *The Autistic Spectrum: A guide for parents and professionals (updated edn).* London: Robinson.

World Health Organisation (2005) *International Classification of Diseases – Tenth Revision (ICD-10): Classification of mental and behavioral disorders diagnostic criteria for research (2nd edn).* Geneva: World Health Organisation.

Yamamoto, J. and Miya, T. (1999) 'Acquisition and transfer of sentence construction in autistic students: analysis by computer-based teaching', *Research in Developmental Disabilities*, 20 (5), 355–377.

**Endnotes**

[1] Hyperlexia is a fascination with words featuring a discrepancy between the ability to recognise words and comprehension of the ideas represented.

[2] http://www.widgit.com/

# PART 3

# Enhancing Health and Well-Being

CHAPTER 6

# Identifying and Responding to the Needs of Young People with ASD and Mental Health Problems

## Implications for Organisation, Research and Practice

*Barry Carpenter, Barry Coughlan, Nick Logan and Teresa Whitehurst*

### Introduction

Training, development and improved interconnection of services were outcomes of the BIOMED-MEROPE Project (Holt et al., 2000) which sought to compare services for adults with intellectual disability and mental health needs in Austria, England, Greece, Ireland and Spain. The Project identified that policy and legislation tends to separate the disability aspects of people with intellectual disability from their mental health need with the result that the needs of people with both an intellectual disability and a mental health issue remain 'largely invisible'. Consequently, 'the effects on the lives of people with intellectual disability and their families and carers are detrimental' (Holt et al., 2000). These problems are further compounded by diagnostic systems which are not fully compatible with assessing the mental health needs of people with an intellectual disability. The European Association for Mental Health in Mental Retardation is attempting to address some of these issues through the publication of Practice Guidelines which support the need for evidence-based practice (Deb, Matthews, Holt and Bouras, 2001). The *DC–LD: Diagnostic criteria for psychiatric disorders for use with adults with intellectual disabilities/mental retardation* has been developed by the Royal College of Psychiatrists (2001) in the United Kingdom. It reflects 'a consensus of current practice and opinion among learning disabilities psychiatrists in the United Kingdom and Republic of Ireland' (Royal College of Psychiatrists, 2001) and complements traditional methods of diagnosis by enhancing and expanding criteria to be more applicable and relevant to those individuals with intellectual disabilities.

It is important to recognise that young people with severe and complex intellectual disabilities are young people first: good mental health is their entitlement, as it is that of all young people. *Count Us In*, the report of the inquiry into the mental health of young people with learning disabilities (Foundation for People with Learning Disabilities (FPLD), 2002) put great emphasis on the need for schools and colleges to assume more responsibility in recognising their role in promoting and sustaining emotional well-being and positive mental health in young people with intellectual disabilities. Through their ethos and curriculum, schools and colleges need to take a holistic overview of the young person and their emotional well-being alongside meeting their academic requirements. Carpenter and Morgan (2003) have illustrated how schools should use the opportunities of the curriculum within subjects such as Citizenship and Personal Social and Health Education (PSHE) to enable young people to develop their self-esteem and self-awareness.

The purpose of this article is to describe the process of developing an in-service training course for staff working in an intellectual disability setting which would sensitise them to issues relating to the mental health of young people with intellectual disabilities. The article seeks to demonstrate how the challenge relating to workforce development set by the Inquiry (FPLD, 2002) could be resolved in a localised, within-organisation way and directly in response to student need.

## Background

Adolescents face a constant stream of challenging situations. This is part of the often exhilarating, sometimes troubled, journey from childhood to adulthood. They face challenges in personal, physical and emotional development, peer and family relationships, sexuality and learning. During this period, feelings about self-worth and self-esteem can change quite regularly and dramatically. Recent mental health studies have focused on the role of resilience and looking at what protects children against difficult life events, e.g. protective factors (Fuller, McGraw and Goodyear, 1999; Stevens, 1987). The task of health and education services is to help these young people build a realistic awareness of their personal strengths and abilities, as well as a better understanding of what their problem areas are and how they can use their abilities to compensate. A framework for development within schools has been advocated by Hornby and Atkinson (2002), and the broad goals of this approach are no different in a special school such as Sunfield.

The lack of differentiation in the adolescent population has been further emphasised by Emerson (2003), who has identified that there are no statistically significant differences between young people with intellectual disabilities and young people without intellectual disabilities with regard to depressive disorders, eating disorders or psychosis. However, there are additional burdens on families due to the 'triple jeopardy' of stress, disadvantage and disability (Mental Health Foundation, 1997). A major study by Meltzer, Gatwood, Goodman and Ford (2000) indicates that such families are more likely to suffer from poverty and deprivation thus compounding the emerging mental health problems that up to 40% of all young people with intellectual disabilities will experience between the ages of 13 and 25 years (FPLD, 2002).

The Committee of Inquiry (FPLD, 2002) noted that there was no set national standard for the amount of teaching about intellectual disability, and also mental health, in any pre-qualification professional training. Consequently, they recommended that attention should be given to the development of interdisciplinary training. In fact, de Ruiter et al. (2004) estimate that young people with intellectual disabilities are 3–4 times more at risk of developing emotional and behavioural problems compared to peers without intellectual disabilities (Carpenter, Emerson, Kerr and Turk, 2004). From the limited materials available, other researchers had indicated that training was crucial to effective professional practice (e.g. Bailey, Barr and Bunting, 2001), and others had put in place some useful materials as starting points for the development of such training (Holt and Bouras, 1997).

Sunfield, as an organisation with a transdisciplinary approach spanning education, social care, psychology, therapies and allied professions, was ideally poised to develop training that could ensure that all frontline staff had a clear and workable knowledge about the mental health needs of young people with intellectual disabilities. A clear goal would be that the training should lead to an awareness that people with intellectual disabilities can suffer from mental health problems, and also that not all challenging behaviour is associated with an intellectual disability. There is a need for staff to be able to monitor and record behaviour and mood. They should understand the range of interventions possible and how to obtain and work with specialised mental health services. In-house networks for staff support and development would also be a crucial feature of such training.

The report of the Committee of Inquiry (FPLD, 2002) acted as a spur to Sunfield School to explore more fully its staff training in relation to the mental health needs of its young people, the majority of whom have severe and complex learning needs arising from autistic spectrum disorders (ASD). The report had emphasised that staff need to be trained to identify the emergence of mental health problems of young people with intellectual disabilities, and that, within the professions supporting these young people, staff competence to support the young people was crucial. Sunfield School already had in place a high calibre staff development programme (as recognised by the National Training Award given to the school in 2003). Thus staff had many training opportunities in matters related to intellectual disability and ASD, but there had been no specific focus on mental health, and only minimal attention given to promoting emotional well-being.

**Aims of the Mental Health Training Package**
People with intellectual disability are a very diverse group with significant variations in the extent and nature of their intellectual impairments and functional disabilities, the presence of related sensory and physical disabilities and in their social and family backgrounds. Hence, emotional difficulties or persistent mental health problems can present in both typical and atypical ways. A partnership approach is required between those providing for the continuing support of people with intellectual disability and those with specialist health expertise that can address developmental, biological, psychological and social factors that may predispose to, precipitate or maintain the presence of mental health problems. Such a partnership is required in order to enhance or promote mental health and prevent occurrence of future mental health problems, and ensure that, if such problems arise, they are taken seriously so that effective and ethical treatments and supportive strategies are made available (Mental Health Special Interest Research Group, 2000).

While much knowledge on the area of mental health has been acquired from research studies undertaken in the general population, academics, researchers and professionals have become aware that such knowledge is not necessarily sufficient to understand the many complexities associated with the mental health problems faced by people with intellectual disability (Dosen and Day, 2001). There is now a growing awareness that those with intellectual disability do experience the full range of mental health problems in the general population (McCarthy and Boyd, 2002), but very often such mental health problems are exhibited in atypical ways, and so are not recognised by many health care professionals (Carpenter, Emerson, Kerr and Turk, 2004). Hence appropriate assessment, diagnosis and treatment cannot be routinely undertaken.

The 'Count Us In' inquiry report (FPLD, 2002) found that in many areas of the UK, appropriate services were not in place to deal with the mental health needs of young people with intellectual disability. This report states:

> *...we must face up to the fact that we often do not serve these young people well. There are pockets of good practice, worthy of replication...but...we do not have a cohesive, multi-disciplinary framework capable of delivering good mental health.'* (FPLD, 2002).

Through the placement of a clinical psychology student, it was possible to consider in-depth the development of a training course for staff at Sunfield School.

## Developing the Mental Health Training Package

Having identified a clinical psychology student with the right balance of interest and commitment to develop a training course for staff at Sunfield School, the next phase was to decide upon the practical issues that needed to be addressed.

The first challenge was how to provide a training model which would be accessible, and of interest, to a large staff group. Sunfield currently employs over 370 employees across its different departments. There was a need to make sure that both content and delivery of the training model were standardised, and, therefore, ensuring as much as possible that a consistent message was presented. It was agreed to create 'Day 1' and 'Day 2' of the package, as stand alone components that were interrelated. Day 1 would focus on general factors of intellectual disability and mental health, such as definitions and classification systems. On the other hand, Day 2 would focus more on specific conditions and treatment. The next step was to prioritise, from all the available literature, the main messages that needed to be conveyed (See Table 6.1).

**Table 6.1. Main messages to be conveyed**

| Main messages | Core points of interest |
|---|---|
| • Concept of dual diagnosis | • Mental health problems occur frequently in people with intellectual disability, but are often undiagnosed, due to the complexity of the intellectual disability. |
| • Presentation and discussion of main classification systems utilised in assessment and diagnosis of mental health problems | • DSM–IV ( American Psychiatric Association, 2000); ICD–10 (World Health Organisation, 2005), and the DC–LD (Royal College of Psychiatrists, 2001). |
| • 'Pathway' to mental health services for people with intellectual disability/special needs | • People with intellectual disabilities are at a distinct disadvantage with respect to referral for mental health assessment. There is a greater need for earlier identification of mental health problems, thus ensuring prompt referral for assessment |
| • Common symptoms of mental health problems | • An overview of the various mental health problems (and their symptoms) which occur most frequently in people with intellectual disabilities (depression, anxiety, schizophrenia, etc.) |

Dual diagnosis, was a term initially coined by Menolascino (cf. Menolascino and Mc-Cann, 1983) to refer to situations where both mental illness and intellectual disability co-exist (Szymanski et al., 1998). Many students come to Sunfield School with an established diagnosis, for example, of ASD or attention deficit hyperactive disorder (ADHD). It is easy to forget that over time the student's circumstances might change and that other complications may come to the surface. Clements and Zarkowska (2000) explore the relationship between ASD and mental health factors. They explain that many people with ASD appear to have difficulties sustaining a sense of positive well-being. Sometimes people with ASD experience marked cycles in their emotional well-being which is characterised by positive phases and negative phases. In practical terms, it is complicated for us to decipher with such complex students where the initial diagnosis ends and mental health problems take over. Jordan (2001) explains that dual diagnoses are difficult to obtain, since an adolescent or adult who develops mental health problems may have these problems simply attributed to their ASD or other disorders. Consequently, the onset of mental health problems may not be addressed. In a similar fashion, there is now a greater awareness that an individual, regardless of the presence of an intellectual disability, may suffer from more than one mental health problem, a term known as co-morbidity (Szymanski and Grossman, 1984).

## Common symptoms of mental health conditions

A further message to be conveyed was how some of the common symptoms of mental health conditions can present themselves in atypical ways among students with intellectual disabilities. Notably, many of the students that arrive at Sunfield do so because of their long histories of challenging behaviour. It is very easy for all concerned to be pre-occupied with these problem behaviours and overlook any mental health factors that might be contributing to their maintenance. Clements and Martin (2002) state that any assessment of intense and enduring behavioural difficulties must include an investigation into mental health issues. They suggest that life changes and losses can impact upon behavioural functioning over an extended period of time.

An example of how this can manifest itself was recently identified in an older student at Sunfield. The student was displaying a rise in classic challenging behaviours of aggression towards staff members. Through conversations with key people in the young man's life, it was discovered that the likely cause was this young man's experience of bereavement at the loss of his male key worker and his grandfather, the latter having played a very influential role in his life for many years. Following specialist counselling, a vast improvement in the young man's behaviour was noted. Had the factor of bereavement not been identified as influencing the student's behaviour, he would not have been given counselling support to assimilate this emotional experience, which may have then become a foundation for depression. Dwivedi and Harper (2004) cite the early experience of loss as a reason for the onset of depression in young people.

## Importance of assessment and diagnosis

It is important to convey to staff members that the assessment and identification of mental health problems is much more complex and subjective for students with intellectual disabilities compared to the general population.

Most of the assessment techniques for investigating mental health problems rely on self-reporting questionnaires and checklists as opposed to clinical interview. These techniques are apt for students with average intelligence or mild intellectual disabilities, but not for young people with severe intellectual disabilities such as those at Sunfield. Aside from the low levels of language and communication skills, there is the major factor of 'emotions'. As Jordan (2001) mentions, students on the autistic spectrum have to be taught about the emotions of others and themselves, because the concept does not come naturally. Consequently, students at Sunfield are not always capable of providing clues to any feelings of low self-esteem, stress, anxiety or other mental conditions.

## Implementing the Mental Health Training Package

With those messages in mind, a two-day training package was developed. As previously mentioned, Day 1 and Day 2 are stand-alone training sessions offered to all staff within Sunfield working with students with intellectual disabilities (See Table 6.2).

**Table 6.2. Main content of the Mental Health Training Package – Days One and Two**

| Content of Training Package: Day 1 | Content of Training Package: Day 2 |
| --- | --- |
| • Messages from the National Inquiry into the Mental Health of Young People with Learning Disabilities<br><br>• General introduction to mental health<br><br>• Mental health and intellectual disability<br><br>• Assessment and diagnosis of mental health problems: key issues<br><br>• Pathway to mental health services<br><br>• Mental health in children and adolescents<br><br>• Mental health in people with ASD<br><br>• Evidence-based treatment approaches<br><br>• Case study evidence<br><br>• Course evaluation | • Overview of key issues from Day 1<br><br>• Diagnostic issues in the principle mental health problems in people with intellectual disabilities and ASD:<br>  o Anxiety disorders<br>  o Affective disorders<br>  o Schizophrenia and delusional disorder<br>  o Attention and over-activity problems<br>  o Anorexia and bulimia nervosa<br><br>• Further assessment issues in intellectual disabilities and ASD<br><br>• Information on using the Mini PAS-ADD (Psychiatric Assessment Schedule for Adults with Developmental Disability; Moss, 2001a,b)<br><br>• Open forum discussion<br><br>• Course evaluation |

## Impact on the organisation

All staff attending mental health training are required to complete a training evaluation form, which may be anonymous. This has enabled the organisation to identify the extent to which training needs are being met, the suitability of the training for those attending and the impact on the organisation. A large number of staff, with representation from all disciplines, completed the training. As is usual with training courses, the participants were at varying stages in their knowledge and experience in this area. Over 90% of those staff rated the course as 'good' or 'very good' on a four-point rating scale, and felt that the course content was appropriate despite their differing knowledge base.

Further qualitative analysis of the Evaluation Forms, in relation to what participants said they found to be useful, can be broken down into aspects which were helpful with regard to delivery of the training and aspects which were useful within the content of the training. With regards to delivery of training, participants found that the opportunity to explore a case study which demonstrated the way in which mental health problems can present in young people with intellectual disabilities was particularly useful. This enabled them to relate the material delivered to their own practice. Similarly, they commented that the opportunity for group work enabling them to discuss issues with colleagues was beneficial. Several aspects of the course content were emphasised as particularly beneficial (see Table 6.3):

Participants commented particularly that had been able to gain an understanding of terms and definitions in relation to mental health problems and to expand upon these to consider specific diagnoses such as depression, anxiety and schizophrenia. Further, they felt they would now be able to differentiate between the symptoms representing mental health issues and those associated with ASD. Equally important to this process was the opportunity to gain an understanding not only of the tools involved in the assessment and diagnostic process but also an understanding of the different roles of professionals involved. One participant commented that they now realised what 'indications to look for in our students and who is involved' another commented that the training would lead to 'more discussions with the psychology and therapies team based at Sunfield'. Clearly, the ability to identify pathways of referral in addition to identification of mental health issues enable staff to feel confident and supported.

**Table 6.3. Beneficial aspects of course content**

| **Course content**<br>*What did Participants feel was beneficial?* |
|---|
| • Exploration of mental health in relation to intellectual disability and ASD |
| • Signs/symptoms to look for |
| • Assessment and diagnostic criteria |
| • Information on specific disorders |
| • Definitions and terminology |

Course evaluation forms also gave scope for participants to consider aspects of the course they would take further. Feedback from participants suggested that aspects they would follow up fell into two distinct categories – 'Future needs' and 'Immediate outcomes' (see Table 6.4).

**Table 6.4. Future needs and immediate outcomes**

| **Future needs** | **Immediate outcomes** |
|---|---|
| • Undertaking further training | • Raised awareness |
| • Attending Day 2 of mental health training | • Improved practice |
| • Learning more about diagnostic tools | • Dissemination of information to colleagues |

Participants felt that their knowledge base had expanded and that they were now in a better position to identify mental health issues. They felt this would have an impact upon their practice and would enable them to 'find ways for [students] to communicate what they feel'. The course also gave participants a 'better understanding of what [Sunfield] children face every day'. An awareness of the diagnostic tools used by the psychology and therapies team to assess mental health problems appeared to equip staff with a greater understanding. Importantly, participants felt that the knowledge gained from the course should be disseminated and they were in a position to 'make other people aware' and 'pass on information to my staff team'.

**Implications for the organisation**

Implications of the Mental Health Training Package have been identified in a wider organisational context in addition to course evaluation feedback. Provision of specific mental health training has led to an awareness of:

■ The need to teach young people with intellectual disabilities ways to identify and communicate their personal emotions and feelings

■ The importance of feedback on behaviours from significant people in the lives of those with intellectual disabilities.

Firstly, a greater emphasis has been placed upon teaching students at Sunfield about their personal emotions and feelings. This initiative is being spear-headed by the speech and language therapists at Sunfield, and is partially based on the work of Baron-Cohen, Golan, Wheelwright and Hill (2003) at the University of Cambridge on computer interactive approaches to emotions. Using the associated DVD-Rom or CD-Rom, individuals are helped to study emotions and improve their skill at recognising the expression of emotions in the faces and voices of other people.

Secondly, training has led to an extension of the existing transdisciplinary model of assessment and intervention. It is important to recognise that collation of assessment data relies on gaining responses from a range of individuals including key workers, teaching staff, parents and other professionals. There has been evidence of raised awareness among staff of routes of referral. Sunfield is in a fortunate position of having its own 'in-house' health team, consisting of four experienced and qualified nurses. The information gained can be discussed with the health team, and, if indicated, follow up referral made to Sunfield's visiting child psychiatrist, who specialises in children with intellectual disabilities. The psychiatrist has the sole professional responsibility for making mental health diagnoses. Diagnosis is based on a combination of information sources, including personal observations of the student, meeting with parents, and written reports submitted by the care, education and psychology staff involved with the student.

Finally, part-time counsellor has been appointed. The counsellor endeavours to adapt counselling approaches and skills to meet the needs of Sunfield's complex students, including those on the autistic spectrum. The counselling techniques currently employed include the use of life books, social stories (Gray and Leigh White, 2003) and relationship maps (see Table 6.5 for definitions).

**Table 6.5. Table of definitions**

| | |
|---|---|
| Relationship maps | The purpose of these 'maps' is to identify the extensiveness and overall quality of the individual's social network. A photograph of the person concerned is placed at the centre of a sheet of paper/computer screen. They are asked to draw lines ('roads') connecting this photograph to the photographs of people who are significant to them. |
| Social stories | These try to convey visually – through objects of reference, pictures, photographs, icons, written words, etc. – important day-to-day information, forthcoming events, behaviour and social expectations (Clements and Zarkowska, 2000). |
| Life books | These enable a person to trace, in sequence, the critical events in their life story including birthdays, school and special memories. The book may contain photographs of significant people and places in the person's life. It is used to enhance the person's self-identity and self-esteem. |

Within these approaches, the counsellor relies on photographs of adults and peers of the student, in order to identify a support network of individuals who might be able to provide the re-assurance and encouragement to help them cope with a phase of mental health difficulty.

**Moving forward**

The effectiveness of any training course will ultimately be reflected in changes in practice. This article reports the development of a training model, and evaluations based on six Day 1 trainings and five Day 2 trainings. The participant evaluations have been positive, corroborating the selected course content made by the first three

> **Case profile**
>
> A recent case for our counsellor concerned a male student who was presenting with aggressive behaviour, low self-esteem and anger management problems.
>
> This student found it difficult to self-reflect or have a positive and realistic self-image. In order to promote a more positive perception of self, the student's life book was utilised. This helped link his past, present and future by looking at photographs of past events, significant others and current experiences. This store of information enabled the student to experiment in verbalising feelings, emotions and opinions about others and self-reflect on past and current events.
>
> Specific anger management strategies were then introduced, including self-talk techniques. The strategies focused on situations where the student had experienced anger based on how he interpreted the situation, and the negative outcomes resulting from the consequences of his behaviour.

authors. Participant evaluation indicated that they felt that this model of training had met their needs, and that other than updating the content in line with other initiatives, research findings and national policy development (e.g. Department of Health (DH), 2004), the course content should remain largely unchanged.

However, the impact upon practice is the time test of the value of this training model. Literature identifies that 'the transfer of knowledge into clinical practice remains a relatively unresearched field' (Jordan, 2000). Clearly, it is important to ensure that staff are not only equipped with the information they need, but that this knowledge is used to inform and improve practice. In order to assess the impact upon practice, Sunfield's Staff Development Co-ordinator will look at the interface between training and interventions through sampling over a 12-month period. From this exercise, it is hoped that a clearer profile of extensive training on mental health for key staff will emerge. Already the topic of sexuality and mental health has been identified as one requiring further investigation.

## Conclusion

Various implications arise from the initial pilot evaluation of this training model. Its development is timely, particularly in the light of the White Paper (DH, 2004) emphasising the need for staff training in mental health, within the context of the *National Service Framework for Mental Health* (DH, 1999).

For schools there are curriculum implications. Right from early childhood educational provision, staff should be mindful of the emotional well-being of children with special needs. They are particularly vulnerable (Carpenter and Russell, 2005). Educational experiences that embed, in the framework of the curriculum, opportunities to explore the emotional dimension of self, as well as the dynamics of interactions with others, are to be valued. Such approaches can be seen as preventative, building up emotional resilience and strengthening the individual (DH, 2004).

Support networks, such as advocacy, peer mentoring, student councils (Ross, Kelly, Lee and Pearson, 2003) and counselling, all promote self-esteem and personal empowerment in young people with intellectual disabilities. Families, too, should have training opportunities to consider the mental health needs of their sons/daughters;

Sunfield has a well-developed families training model (Carpenter, Addenbrook, Attfield and Conway, 2004), and this topic is being incorporated into their next phase of training.

Further research around this training model is needed in a variety of multidisciplinary settings outside Sunfield. The psychology and therapies team at Sunfield continue to try to identify appropriate assessment techniques that focus specifically on adolescents with intellectual disabilities, and which can more accurately profile their emotional functioning.

For 40% or more of young people with ASD who also have an intellectual disability, it is suggested that during adolescence and young adulthood, fraught as it is with major transitions, their mental health will become fragile (Emerson, 2003; FPLD, 2002), and that they may experience significant difficulties which require support and intervention (Ghaziuddin, 2005). This will come from their main caregivers. The training programme described here has endeavoured to go some way to sensitising staff at Sunfield to these complex needs through increased knowledge levels and greater skill acquisition. Further monitoring is required, but the first wave analysis of this two-year trial is positive and encouraging, with possibilities for further dissemination to a wider audience.

## References

American Psychiatric Association (2000) *Diagnostic and Statistical Manual of Mental Disorders (4th edn)* (text revision) [DSM-IV-TR]. Washington, DC: American Psychiatric Association.

Bailey, A., Barr, O. and Bunting, B. (2001) 'Police attitudes towards people who have intellectual disabilities: an evaluation of awareness training', *Journal of Intellectual Disability Research,* 45 (4), 344–350.

Baron-Cohen, S., Golan, O., Wheelwright, S. and Hill, J. (2003) *Mind Reading: The interactive guide to emotions.* London: Jessica Kingsley.

Carpenter, B. and Morgan, H. (2003) 'Count us in: the role of schools and colleges in meeting the mental health needs of young people with learning disabilities', *British Journal of Special Education,* 30 (4), 202–206.

Carpenter, B. and Russell, P. (2005) 'Early intervention in the United Kingdom: current policy and practice'. In: M.J. Guralnick (ed.) *The Developmental Systems Approach to Early Intervention.* Baltimore, MD: Paul H. Brookes.

Carpenter, B., Addenbrooke, M., Attfield, E. and Conway, S. (2004) 'Celebrating families: an inclusive model of family-centred training', *British Journal of Special Education,* 31 (2), 75–80.

Carpenter, B., Emerson, E., Kerr, M. and Turk, J. (2004) 'Meeting the mental health needs of young people with intellectual disabilities', *Journal of Intellectual Disability Research,* 48 (4), 291–320.

Clements, J. and Martin, N. (2002) *Assessing Behaviours Regarded as Problematic for People with Developmental Disabilities.* London: Jessica Kingsley.

Clements, J. and Zarkowska, E. (2000) *Behavioural Concerns and Autistic Spectrum Disorders.* London: Jessica Kingsley.

Deb, S., Matthews T., Holt G. and Bouras, N. (2001) *Practice Guidelines for the Assessment and Diagnosis of Mental Health Problems in Adults with Intellectual Disability.* Brighton: Pavilion.

Department of Health (1999) *National Service Framework for Mental Health: Modern standards and service models.* London: DH. [Online at: http://www.dh.gov.uk/]

Department of Health (2004) *Choosing Health: Making healthier choices easier (White Paper in Public Health for England and Wales)*. London: DH.

de Ruiter, K.P., Douma, J.C., Dekker, M.C., Koot, J.M. and Verhulst, F.C. (2004) 'Psychopathology in young people with mild to moderate intellectual disabilities: stability, change and persistence'. Paper to the 12th IASSID World Congress, Montpellier, France (June).

Dosen, A., and Day, K. (eds) (2001) *Treating Mental Illness and Behaviour Disorders in Children and Adults with Mental Retardation*. Washington, DC: American Psychiatric Press.

Dwivedi, K.M. and Harper, P.B. (2004) *Promoting the Emotional Well Being of Children and Adolescents and Preventing their Mental Ill Health*. London: Jessica Kingsley.

Emerson, E. (2003) 'Prevalence of psychiatric disorders in children and adolescents with and without intellectual disability', *Journal of Intellectual Disability Research,* 47 (1), 51–58.

Foundation for People with Learning Disabilities (2002) *Count Us In: Report of the Committee of Inquiry into the Mental Health of Young People with Learning Disabilities.* London: Mental Health Foundation.

Fuller, A., McGraw, K. and Goodyear, M. (1999) 'Bungee-jumping through life: what young people say promotes well-being and resilience'*, Australian Journal of Guidance and Counselling*, 9 (1), 159–168.

Ghaziuddin, M. (2005) *Mental Health Aspects of Autism and Aspergers Syndrome*. London: Jessica Kingsley.

Gray, C. and Leigh White, A. (2003) *My Social Stories Book*. London: Jessica Kingsley.

Holt, G. and Bouras, N. (1997) *Mental Health in Learning Disabilities: A training pack for staff working with people who have a dual diagnosis of mental health and learning disabilities.* Brighton: Pavilion.

Holt, G., Costello, H., Bouras, N., Diareme, S., Hillery, J., Moss, S., Rodriguez-Blazquez, C., Salvador, L., Tsiantis, J., Weber, G. and Dimitrakaki, C. (2000) 'BIOMED-MEROPE project: service provision for adults with intellectual disability – a European comparison', *Journal of Intellectual Disability Research*, 44 (6), 685–696.

Hornby, G. and Atkinson, M. (2002) *Mental Health Handbook for Schools*. London: RoutledgeFalmer.

Jordan, S. (2000) 'Educational input in patient outcomes: exploring the gap', *Journal of Advanced Nursing,* 31 (2), 461–471.

Jordan, R. (2001) *Autism with Severe Learning Difficulties*. London: Souvenir Press.

McCarthy, J. and Boyd, J. (2002) 'Mental health services and young people with intellectual disability: is it time to do better?', *Journal of Intellectual Disability Research,* 46 (3), 250–256.

Meltzer, H., Gatward, R., Goodman, R. and Ford, T. (2000) *Mental Health of Children and Adolescents in Great Britain*. London: The Stationery Office.

Menolascino, F.J. and McCann, B.M. (eds) (1983) *Mental Health and Mental Retardation: Bridging the gap*. Baltimore, MD: University Park Press.

Mental Health Foundation (1997) *Don't Forget Us: Children with learning disabilities and severe challenging behaviour.* London: Mental Health Foundation.

Mental Health Special Interest Research Group (2000) *Mental Health and Intellectual Disabilities: Assessing the mental health needs of people with intellectual disabilities. Draft report by the Mental Health Special Interest Group of the International Association for the Scientific Study of Intellectual Disabilities to the World Health Organisation.* Geneva: World Health Organisation.

Moss, S. (2001a) *The Mini PAS-ADD Handbook: Psychiatric Assessments Schedules for Adults with Developmental Disabilities.* London: Pavilion.

Moss, S. (2001b) *The Mini PAS–ADD Checklists.* London: Pavilion.

Ross, L., Kelly, L., Lee, S. and Pearson, M. (2003) 'The student council at Sunfield', *The SLD Experience,* 36 (Summer), 27–30.

Royal College of Psychiatrists (2001) *DC–LD: Diagnostic criteria for psychiatric disorders for use with adults with learning disabilities/mental retardation.* London: Gaskell.

Stevens, R. (1987) 'The learning disabled adolescent', *Learning Disabilities Magazine,* 3 (2), 1–15.

Szymanski, L.S. and Grossman, H. (1984) Dual implications of 'dual diagnosis', *Mental Retardation,* 22, 155–156.

Szymanski, L.S., King, B., Goldberg, B., Reid, A., Tonge, B. and Cain, N. (1998) 'Diagnosis of mental disorders in people with mental retardation'. In: S. Reiss and M.G. Aman (eds) *Psychotropic Medication and Developmental Disabilities: The international consensus handbook.* Columbus, OH: Ohio State University Nisonger Centre.

World Health Organisation (2005) *International Classification of Diseases – Tenth Revision (ICD-10): Classification of mental and behavioral disorders diagnostic criteria for research (2nd edn).* Geneva: World Health Organisation.

# CHAPTER 7

# Mental Health Difficulties in People with Intellectual Disability

## Integrating Theory and Evidence-Based Practice

*Barry J. Coughlan, Brothers of Charity Services, Limerick, Ireland*

### Introduction

The mental health of people with intellectual disability has assumed increased importance over the past 15 to 20 years (Dykens, 2000; Moss, Bouras and Holt, 2000; Tonge, 1999;). There is now a growing international awareness of the need to respond more adequately to the mental health needs of individuals with intellectual disability, not only in terms of assessment and diagnosis, but also in terms of appropriate treatment and service provision (Day, 1994; Bouras, 1999; Jacobson, 1999). The two main reasons for this increased awareness largely stemmed from the idea of 'normalisation' (Wolfensberger, 1972), which advocated that people with intellectual disabilities should have a lifestyle and opportunities appropriate to their age, and from the practice of 'de-institutionalisation', which involved people with intellectual disabilities moving from large institutional-type settings to smaller community facilities. With de-institutionalisation and normalisation, there has arisen a greater need to recognise that those with all levels of intellectual disability are subject to the full range of mental health problems, and therefore should be in receipt of the full range of mental health services (Foundation for People with Learning Disabilities (FPLD), 2002, 2005; Simpson, 1997).

Children, adolescents and adults with all levels of intellectual disability have a greater risk of developing additional mental health problems. Such problems can go unrecognised, and have a major impact on the person's quality of life, productivity, personal independence and a range of other factors (Mental Health Special Interest Research Group (SIRG-MH), 2000). Hence, appropriate evidence-based interventions for mental health problems in this population are of the utmost importance, not only from a treatment perspective, but perhaps more significantly from a preventative perspective (Crocker, 2003).

It is with this in mind that the present chapter examines the current evidence-based literature on the topic of mental health difficulties for people with intellectual disability. Much has been written about this over the past 15 to 20 years, but it is only in more recent times that the literature has focused on interventions which are proving both appropriate and successful in treating mental health difficulties in this population.

### Towards a working definition of mental health

When considering mental health difficulties, professionals have tended to describe these conditions from a medicalised perspective, referring to them as 'mental disorders', 'psychiatric illnesses', etc. The American Psychiatric Association (APA) has generated a number of definitions since the 1950s. Now in its fourth edition, the DSM-IV defines a 'mental disorder' as:

> *...a clinically significant behavioural or psychological syndrome or pattern that occurs in an individual and that is associated with present distress (e.g. a painful symptom) or disability (i.e. impairment in one or more important areas of functioning) or with a significantly increased risk of suffering death, pain, disability, or an important loss of freedom.* (APA, 2000).

While useful in terms of classification, this definition does not recognise the entire range of factors associated with mental health difficulty, including their causes and reasons for continuation. Social, environmental, developmental and psychological influences also need to be taken into account (SIRG-MH, 2000).

In this chapter, the term 'mental health difficulty' is used. Simpson (1997) notes that it is far easier to recognise *health problems* than it is to recognise *health* itself. He suggests a possible definition of mental health, bearing in mind the difficulties surrounding this area, stating:

> *...persons who have good mental health are able to respond to their social situation and environment in a way that is expected for their level of development, and have no significant alteration of mental functioning associated with distress or disability.*

In a similar fashion, the SIRG-MH (2000) states:

> *...mental health...consists of more than the absence of mental disorder. It is a state of mental well-being that, together with other factors, enables children and adults to attain independence, be productive, and participate in personally fulfilling ways in society.*

The 'Count Us In' Inquiry (FPLD, 2002) also contains useful definitions, which further emphasise the importance of protective factors such as friendships, social supports and the notion of emotional resilience in terms of mental well-being.

### The prevalence and causes of mental health difficulties
#### Prevalence

It has been difficult to establish the prevalence of mental health difficulties among the population of people with intellectual disabilities, and researchers have arrived at different figures. There may be a number of reasons for this, including:

■ Researchers may define and describe intellectual disability in different ways

■ The participants in research studies may not be representative of the wider population of people with intellectual disabilities and mental health difficulties

■ Assessment and diagnosis often rely upon the people with intellectual disabilities being able to say how they feel

■ The criteria used to diagnose mental health difficulties may need to be modified for the intellectually disabled population.

These differences across research studies make direct comparisons between them extremely difficult. However, there is substantial evidence to support the idea that people with intellectual disability do experience high rates of the full range of mental health difficulties (Bregman, 1991; Holland, 1999).

From the literature to date, mental health difficulties appear to be more common in those with intellectual disability than the general population (Dosen and Day, 2001). Prevalence rates range from 20% to 74% (Bregman and Harris, 1996; Campbell and Malone, 1991; Corbett, 1979; Eaton and Menolascino, 1982; Einfeld and Tonge, 1996; Lund, 1985; Szymanski, 1994). These figures have depended on the diagnostic criteria employed, the type of disorder screened, the nature of the sample, the type of data collected and the level of intellectual disability, ages and gender of the populations studied (Jacobson, 1990). Studies of representative population samples indicate an overall prevalence of 30% to 40% in adults (Corbett, 1979; Gostason, 1985; Lund, 1985; Reiss, 1990) and 40% to 60% in children (Gillberg, Persson, Grufman and Themmer, 1986; Koller, Richardson, Katz and McLaren, 1983; Rutter, Tizard, Graham and Whitmore, 1976). Findings to date suggest that prevalence decreases with age, lowering to approximately 20% in those aged over 65 years (Corbett, 1979; Day 1985; Kiernan and Moss, 1990). Higher rates of mental health difficulties have been found in those with more severe intellectual disability in comparison to those with mild intellectual disability (Gillberg, Persson, Grufman and Themmer, 1986; Gostason, 1985; Koller, Richardson, Katz and McLaren, 1983).

Emerson (2003) notes that to date there have been few 'population-based' studies on prevalence. Some studies (e.g. Dykens, 2000) have indicated that children with an intellectual disability are at a far greater risk of developing a mental health difficulty than children without an intellectual disability. Emerson's study found an overall prevalence rate of 39% of mental health difficulties among children with an intellectual disability compared to just over 8% in children without intellectual disability – a finding in accordance with existing international literature (Cormack, Brown and Hastings, 2000; Dykens, 2000; Einfeld and Tonge, 1996; Stromme and Diseth, 2000).

Interestingly, Jacobson (2003) notes that as people with intellectual disability age, the rates of associated mental health difficulties tend to be higher, whereas the rates of many behavioural difficulties tend to decrease to levels seen in the general population. However, specific mental health difficulties, conditions such as depression, sleep difficulties and anxiety tend to increase in frequency with age (Weber, 2003).

### Causes
With regard to the causes of mental health difficulties, research has shown that higher prevalence rates of such difficulties among people with intellectual disabilities are associated with a range of neurological, social, psychological and personality risk factors including impaired cognition, organic brain damage, communication problems, physical disabilities, family dysfunction and psychosocial factors (Fraser and Nolan, 1994; Gualtieri, 1988; Reid, 1988; Szymanski, 1980). In essence, the causes can be said to be multifactorial.

In relation to this point, the authors Dosen and Day (2001) state:

*...singly or in combination, these factors increase the vulnerability...to psychiatric or behaviour disorders. Specific chromosomal abnormalities may also predispose to psychiatric illness or behaviour disorder.* (also see Crow, 1988; Day, 1983; Holland and Gosden, 1990)

### Evidence-based treatment interventions

The occurrence of mental health difficulties are best understood as the outcome of complex interactions between developmental, biological, psychological and socially determined risk and protective factors (SIRG-MH, 2000). These various risk and protective factors are important when examining evidence-based treatment interventions, as they give one an important starting point in terms of where to intervene in this population. Positive mental health may be reflected in appropriate social and coping skills and in resilience, and these factors are very necessary in order to enhance the chances that individuals with intellectual disability will be able to participate fully in society, in personally productive and satisfying ways.

Evidence-based treatment interventions for mental health difficulties can be understood in terms of psychotherapeutic approaches (various forms of psychological therapy) and psychopharmacological (drug-based) approaches. Included under the broad heading of psychotherapeutic approaches are behavioural interventions, cognitive-behavioural interventions or indeed a wide 'variety of highly specific therapeutic methods, each with its own theoretical and clinical basis, and its own extended training' (Hollins, 2001).

Drug-based approaches on the other hand have their origins in medicine and pharmacology and involve the use of drug treatment for a wide variety of conditions, including mental health difficulties, behavioural problems, reduction of aberrant sexual drive and treatment of epilepsy (Tyrer and Hill, 2001).

According to the SIRG-MH (2000) 'an important principle of assessment and case formulation is that it is a process with certain components including':

- The initial recognition that a mental health problem may be present

- A period of data collection involving the person and one or more key informants, including information on the onset and course of any observed changes, the developmental, personal and medical history, as well as direct observation, mental state and physical examination and structured assessments and investigations invariably involving medical and allied professionals

- The development of possible hypotheses to explain the observations, including diagnosis of any possible acquired mental health problem

- The synthesis of this information, frequently from different theoretical perspectives, to arrive at a formulation and treatment plan, which includes issues of consent.

It is perhaps this last point relating to the building of information and formulation (the process of 'putting it all together'), which is unique to evidence-based practice. More generally, it is central to appropriate interventions and practice, and these ranges of techniques are frequently employed within the practice of clinical psychology.

Throughout this discussion, the importance of multidisciplinary assessment, formulation and treatment will be highlighted because of the complexity of mental health difficulties which arise. In this respect, it is vitally important to have all relevant professionals involved in assessment, diagnosis and treatment. Such multidisciplinary assessments lead to a comprehensive and informed understanding of the presenting problems, and thus increase the opportunity for successful evidence-based interventions.

## Evidence-based psychotherapeutic approaches

For the purposes of the present chapter, psychotherapeutic approaches will encompass those approaches which are primarily psychologically orientated. Such approaches typically include psychodynamic psychotherapy, behavioural interventions, applied behaviour analysis, cognitive behaviour therapy, family therapy and rational emotive therapy, among others (Hollins, 2001). While it is beyond the scope of the present chapter to examine all of these approaches in detail, it will focus on a number of the more extensively used therapeutic approaches used for the treatment of mental health difficulties.

## Applied behaviour analysis and behaviour therapies

Terms such as applied behaviour analysis, behaviour modification, behaviour therapy, behaviour management, behavioural treatment, reinforcement therapy and, at times, cognitive-behavioural therapy are used to refer to specific groups of procedures which 'encompass the entire range of behaviour analysis and change procedures and their major conceptual foundations' (Gardner, Graeber-Whalen and Ford, 2001).

The Association for Behaviour Analysis (ABA) Task Force on the right to effective behavioural treatment stipulated that 'each individual has the right to the least restrictive effective treatment and to treatment that produces safe and meaningful behaviour change'. In this respect the application of behavioural procedures has improved the quality of life of people with intellectual disability in ways that range from the teaching of basic living skills to the elimination of behaviours which cause serious harm to the person, to others or to the environment.

While behavioural procedures have been applied to change specific behaviours, applied behavioural analysis, as a technique, places its emphasis on comprehensive lifestyle changes that improve all aspects of the person's life (Evans and Meyer, 1987; Lovaas and Smith, 1989). Hence applied behaviour analysis focuses on the development and strengthening of pro-social behaviour and the reduction of problematic or antisocial behaviour. It is a technique which is frequently used in the classroom setting by educators.

Reports on the successful application of behaviour therapies in the treatment of emotional and behavioural problems presented by those with intellectual disability began to appear with some regularity during the 1950s and 1960s. As far back as 1970, Gardner stated:

> *...results of the application of behaviour modification techniques described in the clinical and research literature provide illustration of behaviour change of a range, degree and rate that most psychiatric, psychological and rehabilitation professionals had not thought possible due to the presumed inherent limitations of those with mental retardation.*

Following this time, behavioural techniques and procedures have undergone significant advances. These include:

■ An increased emphasis on interventions which hypothesise instigating and maintaining factors (Carr, 1977; Carr and Durand, 1985)

■ The expansion of the unimodal (operant) behavioural model to include other psychological, biological and socioenvironmental contributions to aberrant behaviours (Bailey and Pyles, 1989; Carr, Reeve and Magito-McLoughlin, 1996; Gardner, Graeber and Cole, 1996; Griffiths, Gardner and Nugent, 1998)

■ Development of different models that systematically guide the diagnostic intervention formulation process to ensure appropriate integration of behavioural interventions with those addressing biomedical and socioenvironmental influences (Gardner and Sovner, 1994; Gardner and Whalen, 1996)

■ Adoption of a skill deficit perspective which places emphasis on teaching social and coping competency skills to replace aberrant responding (Gardner, 2000; Gardner, Graeber and Cole, 1996).

The initial step in the development of a behaviourally orientated programme is to identify the goal of the programme and to then go about defining target responses in terms of their frequency, duration, intensity and the environment in which they occur. Responses are defined as clearly and scientifically as possible, so that they can be reliably observed and recorded. The major assumption of using such techniques is that 'behavioural and emotional difficulties reflect the effects of faulty or deficient learning experiences' (Gardner, Graeber-Whalen and Lord, 2001).

To accomplish the above objective, the therapist selects specific therapeutic procedures from an array of those available. On the basis of each individual client, evidence-based treatments have looked at a range of specific therapy techniques in order to eliminate clinically significant fears and obsessive-compulsive behaviours (techniques such as systematic desensitisation) (Erfanian and Miltenberger, 1990; Hiss and Kozak, 1991), while others such as Bird, Dores and Moniz (1989) and Carr, Levin and McConnachie (1994) have looked at skills training programmes to teach alternative functional communication skills to replace self-injurious and aggressive symptoms. Such techniques would be typically used when working with people with significant anger issues, for example.

Interestingly, Matson and Stephens (1978) used a social skills programme to teach pro-social, interpersonal skills, as alternatives to aggressive and other disruptive responses, to adults with a dual diagnosis of psychosis and intellectual disability. From a cognitive-behavioural perspective, self-management programmes to teach coping alternatives to multiple behavioural and emotional symptoms for clients with chronic and severe behavioural problems have been shown to be an effective evidence-based intervention (Benson, 1992; Woods, Miltenberger and Lumley, 1996).

### Behavioural interventions and the multimodal contextual approach
Traditionally, mental health difficulties in people with intellectual disability were viewed from either a biomedical or a behavioural perspective. This view often led to behavioural problems being 'medicalised' and biomedical problems being 'behaviouralised' (Gardner, Graeber-Whalen and Lord, 2001) and the net result was that

evidence-based interventions were not utilised with good effect. Behavioural problems often tended to be treated with psychotropic medication without sufficient rationale (Coughlan, 2001), while mental health problems were often viewed solely in terms of a behaviour problem, and thus were not treated effectively. Dissatisfaction with such approaches has led to the development of a multimodal alternative to diagnosis and treatment. According to Gardner, Graeber-Whalen and Lord (2001):

> *...this multimodal alternative reflects a bio-psycho-social view of human behaviour in emphasising that behavioural and emotional difficulties represent the influences of a person with psychological and biomedical, including psychiatric and neuropsychiatric, characteristics as he or she interacts with physical and psychosocial environments.*

Following on from the multimodal, contextual approach comes the notion of a diagnosis-based treatment formulation. Diagnostic questions regarding the primary and contributing 'trigger' conditions, relevant vulnerabilities and the functionality of the symptoms form the basis for the development of a diagnostic-based intervention, which addresses each of the presumed contributing influences. Such evidence-based interventions are designed to:

1. Remove or minimise biomedical and psychological instigating and maintaining conditions

2. Teach pro-social coping alternatives and increase personal motivation to use the newly acquired skills

3. Reduce or eliminate pathological biomedical conditions.

In essence, then, the diagnostic intervention is a person-focused rather than a symptom-focused intervention (Gardner, Graeber and Cole, 1996), and this is central to the understanding and interpretation of behavioural interventions.

### Cognitive and social learning-based therapies

While behavioural interventions focus largely on stimulus–response or response–consequence relationships, cognitive and social learning interventions focus on thoughts, behaviours or a combination of the two (Benson and Valenti-Hein, 2001). It was largely due to dissatisfaction with behavioural principles and their lack of focus on important aspects of the individual (thought processes, for example) that more cognitively based interventions were developed. In more recent years in particular, significant advances have been made to integrate cognitive concepts into psychological interventions for those without intellectual disability, and such advances are increasingly utilised within the field of intellectual disability.

Traditionally, people with intellectual disabilities had little access to any form of 'talking' therapy or counselling. Many clinicians believed that such interventions were of little use to these people, and so, until recently, little research was available on their effectiveness (Willner, 2005). However, within the general population, Sturmey (2004) notes:

> *...as the debate over evidence-based practice continues the relatively strong evidence base of cognitive therapies continues to provoke reactions from supporters of other kinds of therapy...* (cf. Salkovskis, 2002)

Within present-day practice, psychotherapy for people with intellectual disabilities is increasingly being advocated (Willner, 2005). In fact, as the recent survey of Nagel and Leiper (1999) shows, 35% of clinical psychologists in the UK are now actively involved in using cognitive-behavioural approaches for people with intellectual disabilities, with the corresponding rates for psychodynamic psychotherapy being 17%, and the rates for humanistic and integrative therapy being 31%. Clearly, psychotherapeutic methods are being used with much greater frequency than was previously the case.

Any discussion regarding psychotherapeutic interventions in intellectual disabilities needs to focus on the general principles of appropriateness of therapy, regardless of the individual's level of ability. Issues of assessment remain of importance. One needs to be aware of the characteristics of therapy itself and the therapist characteristics, and to display an awareness of the individual being referred, as well as the specific nature of the presenting difficulty (Weber, 2003).

In terms of assessment for psychotherapy, this constitutes one of the most important pieces within the treatment framework. While there have been many problems associated with detection of mental health difficulties (Moss, 1999), once cases are detected and referred, the assessment process can then begin. When practising cognitive behavioural therapy in people with intellectual disabilities, a number of basic cognitive skills are required according to Willner (2006) and Whitehouse, Tudway, Look and Kroese (2006). In conjunction with having a reasonable level of communication skills and language, the skills required are as follows:

- An ability to distinguish between antecedent events and associated cognition and emotions

- An ability to recognise that cognitions mediate the effects of events on emotions

- A willingness to participate in a collaborative therapeutic relationship.

Once the above basic criteria are met, there is no reason why a psychotherapeutic technique such as cognitive behavioural therapy cannot be used with good effect.

Perhaps the three techniques which have attracted most interest for those with intellectual disability and mental health difficulties from a cognitive-behaviour perspective have been self-instruction, problem-solving and relaxation training.

It was initially Vygotsky in 1962 who noted that people direct their own behaviour by covert, self-directed statements. This was further elaborated upon, from a clinical perspective, by Meichenbaum (1969). Self-instruction involves using prompts and reinforcers to teach people to repeat statements that will help guide their behaviour. As self-statements become more automated, the prompts and reinforcers are gradually faded, and the client begins to speak covertly. While such techniques have proven useful for the general population, they have proven also to be successful in people with intellectual disability, but only in limited applications (Rusch, Morgan and Martin, 1985).

Problem-solving is a core feature of any form of psychotherapy. Problem-solving has been defined as:

> *...a cognitive and behavioural process that makes a variety of potentially effective response alternatives available and increases the probability of selecting the most effective response from these alternatives.* (D'Zurilla and Goldfried, 1971)

Problem-solving consists of several steps which include:

- Identifying the problem
- Identifying the solutions
- Evaluating the consequences of the solutions
- Choosing and enacting the best solution (Shure and Spivak, 1982).

Available evidence to date suggests that some studies do not in fact train all the components of problem-solving. Much of the research to date has focused on the tasks of generating or selecting the best alternative. Hence, in terms of specific studies on problem-solving in people with intellectual disability, the findings are limited, and further evidence is necessary in order to determine their true effectiveness.

Relaxation training is a general category of treatment which focuses on reducing anxiety. Research to date has shown that anxiety-related behaviours occur at a higher frequency in those with intellectual disability than in the general population (Donaldson and Menolascino, 1977). Hence, there is a great need for anxiety reducing techniques in this population. Two of the more common relaxation training techniques are deep diaphragm breathing and progressive muscular relaxation. Deep diaphragm breathing techniques are generally learned easily and provide immediate short-term benefits. Progressive muscular relaxation on the other hand requires some time to learn, while other approaches such as guided imagery can be quite pleasurable for the client.

While there is a strong evidence base for the use of relaxation techniques within the general population, and a large volume of literature to support its use and effectiveness, considerably less has been written on the use of this technique in people with intellectual disability. The majority of literature tends to focus on case studies where relaxation techniques have proven to be effective. Luiselli (1980) on reviewing 12 studies where relaxation was proven to be effective stated that:

> *...it seems effective in enhancing performance over that of no-treatment control subjects, but it was often no better than other 'placebo' treatments such as exercise.* (cited in Benson and Valenti-Hein, 2001)

Similarly, when looking at 'behavioural relaxation training' Lindsay, Baty and Michie (1989) noted that modelling and physical guidance greatly helped clients to discriminate between tense and relaxed states, while Lindsay and Morrison (1996) suggested that such techniques were particularly effective in clients with more severe forms of intellectual disability.

Additional evidence-based, cognitive-behavioural strategies can be found in a wide variety of treatment packages used for people with intellectual disability. Treatment packages such as those used for social skills training (Griffiths, 1995), assertiveness training (Nezu, Nezu and Arean, 1991), anger management training (Benson,1992) and sociosexual skills training (Valenti-Hein, 1989) have all been shown to be effective for people with intellectual disability and mental health problems. While it is beyond the scope of the present chapter to review such treatment packages in detail, the reader is referred to Benson and Valenti-Hein (2001).

On reviewing the use of cognitive-behavioural strategies for people with intellectual disability, these authors observe that:

> *...the present state of knowledge indicates that cognitively based interventions must be added to the treatment armamentaria of the clinician who works with people with mental retardation.*

### A note on psychotherapy and counselling-based therapies

While the recognition that people with intellectual disability are subject to the full range of emotional and mental health problems, there is considerable evidence that counselling and psychotherapy are often neglected as treatment modalities. This is largely due to the assumption that the presence of intellectual disability in some way 'precludes effective participation in the therapeutic process' (DesNoyers Hurley, Pfadt, Tomasulo and Gardner, 1996). There is considerable evidence from case reports and other writings to suggest that both individual and group psychotherapy is a effective means of treatment of mental health difficulties (Fletcher, 1993; Hurley, 1989, Nezu, Nezu and Gill-Weiss, 1992; Pfadt, 1991; Tomasulo, 1992).

There is now a considerable amount of evidence-gathering, suggesting that many forms of psychotherapy (when adapted) are effective in producing change in those with intellectual disabilities and mental health problems. Interestingly, much of this work has examined psychoanalytic approaches (Beail, 1998; Ruth, 2001; Sinason, 1992), and while many of the writings are still in case study and theoretical format, systematic controlled studies have been undertaken (Beail, 1998; Beail, 2002). While such techniques need adaptation in terms of simplification of material, language and session structure, Ruth (2001) notes that such changes are 'little different from other psychoanalytic therapies, the main differences deriving from the unique life experiences of the person with...intellectual disability'.

While still somewhat in their infancy, such approaches, in particular psychoanalytic approaches, have a considerable part to play in developing other forms of evidence-based interventions for people with intellectual disability. Not only is there a need for systematically controlled, psychoanalytic studies, there is a need to develop all forms of psychotherapeutic methods and to subject each to rigorous scientific evaluation to determine which may be most effective for this population.

### Drug-based therapies

The use of drug-based treatment approaches to mental health problems in people with intellectual disability has had an emotive history. Gualtieri (1991) cited in Crabbe (1994) notes 'the epidemic of neuroleptic overuse among people with mental retardation is one of those tragic experiments that nature, or history, will sometimes play'. In terms of a historical overview, several problems are evident. There are two beliefs in terms of drug treatment: firstly there are those who believe that pharmacological or drug-based interventions should be the technique of choice, and secondly, there are those who believe that the risks greatly outweigh the benefits in terms of prescribing medication. This is especially true of psychotropic medication in people with intellectual disability as the risk–benefit ratio can be difficult to determine at times.

In the USA in recent years, there has been much litigation around psychotropic medication. In general, there is a much greater awareness and interest by professionals who work with service users with intellectual disability in relation to the prescribing practices for these clients. The implementation of the multidisciplinary team in many organisations to review medication use is evidence of this heightened interest.

### Prevalence of psychotropic drug use
In one of the most widely documented drug prevalence studies cited in the literature, Lipman (1970) conducted a drug prevalence study involving 109 residential facilities in the USA. The results of this study were quite startling as 51% of clients were administered psychotropic medication. Resulting from the findings of this study, extreme concern was expressed by many professionals in the field that such a percentage was far too high a figure. In addition, Lipman's study acted as a catalyst for further research on the topic of prevalence of prescribing for this population. Due to the increased volume of studies published since Lipman's study in 1970, there have since been far more accurate and well-documented studies of this nature, which have inevitably lead to the heightened interest in this field.

Since the 1970s, a considerable amount of interest has been drawn to the rates of prescribing for clients with various forms of intellectual disability, in a variety of settings, most notably residential facilities (Aman, Field and Bridgman, 1985; Hughes, 1977; Jonas, 1980; Spencer, 1974). It is only relatively recently in the UK that any studies pertaining to the prescribing practices for clients in community facilities have been published – one of the first by Hemming (1984) and a subsequent study by Clarke, Kelley, Thinn and Corbett (1990).

As is noted by Aman and Singh (1991) people with intellectual disability 'are among the most medicated populations in our society'. In terms of the figures quoted for people living in residential or institutional facilities, the figures have ranged from 30 to 50% for psychotropic drugs and in terms of anticonvulsant or anti-epileptic medication, the figures have ranged from 25% to 35%. If one combines these totals, one is looking at an overall prevalence rate of between 50 and 70% (Aman and Singh, 1988).

When one looks to people living in the community, the typical prevalence rates of prescribing are within the range of 20 to 36%. For anticonvulsant medication, the figures have ranged from 20 to 25%. For a total combined prevalence rate, the figures published for community clients are 36 to 48%. The figures quoted above are for adults with various forms of intellectual disability ranging from mild to profound.

When it comes to children with intellectual disability, considerably less research has been undertaken. Earlier studies suggest that school-age children in the community are prescribed psychotropic medication within the range of 3 to 7%, the figures for anticonvulsants being 12 to 17%, with the combined rates falling within the 18 to 21% range (Aman, Field and Bridgman, 1985; Gadow and Kalachnik, 1981). Later studies, such as that undertaken by Hogg (1992), suggest the figure may be in the region of 33% and upwards, especially in those children with profound levels of intellectual disability.

### Evidence-based prescribing?

While there is no question regarding the frequency of prescribing of psychotropic medication, there remains widespread concern about the reasons for this prescribing (Coughlan, 2000a, 2000b, 2001). While those with intellectual disability do exhibit the entire range of mental health problems, a significant majority of those being administered such medication do not have a clearly defined mental health problem and are labelled more broadly as having 'behaviour disturbance' or challenging behaviour. The literature to date clearly suggests that efficacy and effectiveness of psychotropic medication for behavioural purposes, without the presence of a mental health difficulty, is as yet poorly understood and largely ineffective (Coughlan, 2001). In terms of the rationale for prescribing psychotropic medication, there have been clear guidelines developed from a theoretical perspective, but in practice such guidelines have not been enacted in many countries, and hence remain ineffective (Coughlan, 2000c).

As an example, Rivinus (1980) has stated:

> ...the same rules that apply to the use of psychotropic medications in adults and children of normal intelligence apply to [intellectually disabled] patients. Psychotropic drugs should be used to treat specific diagnoses, syndromes, or symptoms for which specific drug efficacy has been scientifically established.

In a similar fashion, Szymanski and Crocker (1989) state:

> ...psychotropic drugs work in the same manner and should be used in the same way whether the patients' intelligence is average, above average, or below average...psychiatric disorders, not specific symptoms, should be treated.

Specifically within an Irish context, research suggests that the most frequently prescribed classes of psychotropic medication are the antipsychotics, anticonvulsants, anxiolytics and the antidepressants. However, for each of these drug classes, there was a poor rationale for their widespread use and, in many cases, there was no available documentation to suggest reasons for use (Coughlan, 2001). Such a finding was in accordance with research undertaken by Aman, Sarphare and Burrow (1995) in the USA which found that there was a poor relationship between presence of a mental health difficulty and prescribing of psychotropic medication. Such research suggests that even when a mental health problem has been identified, there remains controversy regarding which drug should be the medication of choice.

Regarding the issue of evidence-based prescribing, there remains much controversy both from a theoretical and practical perspective. While there are numerous studies available from the general population suggesting the efficacy of specific medications in the treatment of specific mental health problems (disorder-specific prescribing), there is no compelling evidence to suggest this is the case in the field of intellectual disability. Resulting from this, the author suggests that evidence-based prescribing be based on a set of guidelines developed in the US by Kalachnik et al. (1998).

When prescribing for mental health problems, all practitioners should adhere to such guidelines in an attempt to ensure medication prescribing is as 'appropriate as possible'. If these guidelines are not adhered to, then evidence-based prescribing cannot be said to exist. Table 7.1 below synopsises the 14 guidelines as developed by

Kalachnik et al. (1998) and as discussed by Coughlan (2000b).

**Table 7.1. A table summarising Kalachnik et al. (1998) psychotropic medication guidelines**

| Synopsis of guidelines | Key elements |
|---|---|
| 1. Know the purpose of the drug being prescribed. | *Refer to all relevant literature.* |
| 2. Any medication prescribed should not be used in excess or in place of any other form of treatment for the purposes of convenience. | *Medication should not be used as a means of chemical restraint – utilise other treatment methods if appropriate and applicable.* |
| 3. Medication should only be prescribed as part of a multidisciplinary team approach. | *The multidisciplinary team of professionals should decide the best possible treatment plan for each individual.* |
| 4. Any prescription should arise from a thorough functional analysis and mental health assessment. | *A hypothesis should be generated as to the individual's condition and underlying causes.* |
| 5. Written informed consent must be obtained. | *Informed consent of the person or their family must be obtained prior to the use of any treatment.* |
| 6. The importance of index behaviours and quality of life measures should be reflected. | *Index of target behaviours needs to be specified and measured throughout treatment.* |
| 7. Side-effects need close monitoring. | *Importance of the use of a standardised rating tool to monitor any possible side-effects of medication.* |
| 8. Monitoring for tardive dyskinesia should take place. | *Tardive dyskinesia may develop in some individuals treated with older neuroleptic medication. This needs careful monitoring.* |
| 9. Systematic and regular review of all medications should take place. | *Regular reviews are essential to determine whether medication is having the desired effect.* |
| 10. Minimum effective dosage should always be used. | *The minimum effective dosage of any drug should be used – avoid excessive dosages.* |
| 11. Frequent changes in medication should be avoided. | *Frequent changes in medication should be avoided.* |
| 12. Polypharmacy should be avoided. | *Use of two or more medications should be avoided. Where add-on medication is necessary, a tapering off process for the initial drug should be implemented.* |
| 13. The aim should be a best-practice model of drug treatment. | *Avoid older medications where newer 'atypical' medications may be more effective. Avoid long-term use of 'Prescription Required as Needed' (PRN) medication.* |
| 14. External or peer review should take place via a 'clinical audit'. | *All prescribing should be subject to professional peer or external review so as to maximise effectiveness and avoid excessive prescribing.* |

## Concluding remarks and recommendations

Over the past 10 years, professional knowledge regarding mental health problems in people with intellectual disability has expanded significantly. Both mental health difficulties and behavioural problems can cause serious obstacles to their social integration (Deb, Matthews, Holt and Bouras, 2001).

Research studies and clinical experience have shown that existing diagnostic systems, such as ICD-10 (World Health Organisation, 2005) and DSM-IV (APA, 2000), are not fully compatible for people with intellectual disability, especially in terms of making a diagnosis. With respect to the present chapter, whose focus is evidence-based interventions, the lack of clarity with existing diagnostic systems may be one of the primary reasons why the evidence-based knowledge on assessment, diagnosis and treatment of mental health problems in this population is still relatively scarce.

While acknowledging that evidence-based interventions are still in their infancy for people with intellectual disability and mental health problems, the present chapter reviewed the principle approaches utilised in clinical practice for those people with mental health problems. Approaches such as applied behaviour analysis and behaviour therapy, cognitive and social learning therapies, psychotherapy and psychopharmacology were discussed, placing emphasis on evidence-based approaches drawn from the literature, where appropriate.

This said, however, the number of well-designed and systematically controlled studies are relatively few and there is now a need to develop appropriate methodologies in order to address this shortfall. Interestingly, a number of recent publications have begun to address this issue, and so guidelines are being developed regarding effective and appropriate assessment, diagnosis and treatment of mental health problems in this population. Aman et al. (2000) published consensus guidelines for the assessment and treatment of mental health problems, while more recently Deb, Matthews, Holt and Bouras (2001) published *Practice Guidelines for the Assessment and Diagnosis of Mental Health Problems in Adults with Intellectual Disability*. This latter publication in particular draws on current research evidence in conjunction with consensus opinion from expert clinicians working in this field in order to develop a set of guidelines and principles of good practice. It is a particularly useful document which places emphasis on the various features of mental health problems in a descriptive and practical manner, and outlines the inherent difficulties in the assessment and diagnostic process.

To conclude, the present chapter has discussed some of the available evidence-based approaches to treating mental health problems in people with intellectual disability. It is important to note that numerous therapeutic approaches are in use, but as yet are not subject to rigorous scientific exploration. In this sense the evidence-based literature is still in its infancy. With the development of consensus guidelines, however, and such guidelines being put into practice, there is no doubt that the next decade will be exciting in terms of research and development in this field.

## References

Aman, M.G. and Singh, N.N. (1988) 'Patterns of drug use, methodological considerations, measurement techniques and future trends'. In: M.G. Aman and N.N. Singh (eds) *Psychopharmacology of the Developmental Disabilities*. Berlin: Springer Verlag.

Aman, M.G. and Singh, N.N. (1991) 'Pharmacological intervention'. In: J.J. Matson and J.A. Mulick (eds) *Handbook of Mental Retardation (2nd edn)*. New York: Pergamon Press.

Aman, M.G., Field, C.J. and Bridgman, G.D. (1985) 'City-wide survey of drug patterns among non-institutionalised retarded persons', *Applied Research in Mental Retardation, 5,* 159–171.

Aman, M.G., Sarphare, G. and Burrow, W.H. (1995) 'Psychotropic drugs in group homes: prevalence and relation to demographic/psychiatric variables', *American Journal on Mental Retardation,* 99 (5), 500–509.

Aman, M.G., Alvarez, N., Benefield, W., Crismon, M.L., Green, G., King, B.H., Rojahn, J. and Szymanski, L. (eds) (2000) 'Diagnosis and assessment of psychiatric and behavioural problems in mental retardation', *American Journal on Mental Retardation, 105,* 159–227.

American Psychiatric Association (2000) *Diagnostic and Statistical Manual of Mental Disorders (4th edn) (text revision) [DSM-IV-TR]*. Washington, DC: American Psychiatric Association.

Bailey, J.S. and Pyles, D.A.M. (1989) 'Behavioural diagnostics'. In: E. Cipani (ed.) *The Treatment of Severe Behaviour Disorders*. Washington, DC: American Association on Mental Retardation.

Beail. N. (1998) 'Psychoanalytic psychotherapy with men with intellectual disabilities: a preliminary outcome study', *British Journal of Medical Psychology*, 71, 1–11.

Beail, N. (2002) 'Developing psychotherapy services for people with intellectual disabilities'. Paper given to Public Lecture Series 2002, University College Dublin: Centre for the Study of Developmental Disabilities.

Benson, B.A. (1992) *Teaching Anger Management to Persons with Mental Retardation*. Worthington, OH: IDS Publishing.

Benson, B.A. and Valenti-Hein, D. (2001) 'Cognitive and social learning treatments'. In: A. Dosen and K. Day (eds) *Treating Mental Illness and Behaviour Disorders in Children and Adults with Mental Retardation*. Washington, DC: American Psychiatric Press.

Bird, F., Dores, P.A. and Moniz, D. (1989) 'Reducing severe aggressive and self-injurious behaviours with functional communication training', *American Journal on Mental Retardation*, 94, 37–48.

Bouras, N. (1994) *Mental Retardation*. Cambridge: Cambridge University Press.

Bouras, N. (1999) *Psychiatric and Behavioural Disorders in Developmental Disabilities and Mental Retardation*. Cambridge: Cambridge University Press.

Bregman, J.D. (1991) 'Current developments in the understanding of mental retardation: II. psychopathology', *Journal of the American Academy of Child and Adolescent Psychiatry*, 30, 861–872.

Bregman, J.D. and Harris, J.C. (1996) 'Mental retardation'. In: H.L. Kaplan and B.J. Sadock (eds) *Comprehensive Textbook of Psychiatry*. Baltimore, MD: Williams and Wilkins.

Campbell, M. and Malone, R.P. (1991) 'Mental retardation and psychiatric disorders', *Hospital and Community Psychiatry*, 42, 374–379.

Carr, E.G. (1977) 'The motivation of self-injurious behaviour: a review of some hypotheses', *Psychological Bulletin*, 84, 800–816.

Carr, E.G. and Durand, V.M. (1985) 'Reducing behaviour problems through functional communication training', *Journal of Applied Behaviour Analysis*, 18, 111–126.

Carr, E.G., Levin, L. and McConnachie, G. (1994) *Communication-Based Intervention for Problem Behaviour*. Baltimore, MD: Paul H. Brookes.

Carr, E.G., Reeve, C.E. and Magito-McLoughlin, D. (1996) 'Contextual influences on problem behaviour in people with developmental disabilities'. In: L.K. Koegel and G. Dunlap (eds) *Positive Behavioural Supports: Including people with difficult behaviour in the community*. Baltimore, MD: Paul H. Brookes.

Clarke, D.J., Kelley, S., Thinn, K. and Corbett, J.A. (1990) 'Psychotropic drugs and mental retardation 1: disabilities and the prescription of drugs for behaviour and for epilepsy in three residential settings', *Journal of Mental Deficiency Research*, 34, 385–395.

Corbett, J.A. (1979) 'Psychiatric morbidity and mental retardation'. In: F.E. James and R.P. Snaith (eds) *Psychiatric Illness and Mental Handicap*. London: Gaskell Press.

Cormack, K.F.M., Brown, A.C. and Hastings, R.P. (2000) 'Behavioural and emotional difficulties in students attending schools for children and adolescents with severe intellectual disability', *Journal of Intellectual Disability Research*, 44, 124–129.

Coughlan, B.J. (2000a) 'Psychopharmacology in the treatment of people with learning disabilities: a review', *Mental Health Care*, 3 (9), 304–307.

Coughlan, B.J. (2000b) 'Issues in the assessment, classification and diagnosis of mental health problems in people with learning disability'. Paper presented to the 11th IASSID World Congress, Seattle, USA.

Coughlan, B.J. (2000c) 'Psychotropic medication and persons with learning disability: current perspectives and issues', *Frontline of Learning Disability*, 43, 24–26.

Coughlan, B.J. (2001) 'Issues in the prescribing of psychotropic and psychoactive medication for persons with learning disability: quantitative and qualitative perspectives' (Ph.D. Thesis). Cork, Ireland: University College Cork.

Crabbe, H.F. (1994) 'Pharmacotherapy in mental retardation'. In: N. Bouras (ed) *Mental Health in Mental Retardation: Recent advances and practices*. Cambridge: Cambridge University Press.

Crocker, A.C. (2003) 'Foreword'. In: P. W. Davidson, V.P. Prasher and M.P. Janicki (eds) *Mental Health, Intellectual Disabilities and the Aging Process*. Oxford: Blackwell.

Crow, T.J. (1988) 'Sex chromosomes and psychoses: a pseudoautosomal locus', *British Journal of Psychiatry*, 153, 675–683.

Day, K. (1983) 'Crime and mental retardation: a review'. In: K. Howells and C.R. Hollin (eds) *Clinical Approaches to the Mentally Disorders Offender*. Chichester: Wiley.

Day, K. (1985) 'Psychiatric disorder in the middle aged and elderly mentally handicapped', *British Journal of Psychiatry*, 147, 660–667.

Day, K. (1994) 'Psychiatric services in mental retardation: generic or specialized provision?'. In: N. Bouras (ed.) *Mental Health in Mental Retardation: Recent advances and practices*. Cambridge: Cambridge University Press.

Deb, S., Matthews, T., Holt, G. and Bouras, N. (2001) *Practice Guidelines for the Assessment and Diagnosis of Mental Health Problems in Adults with Intellectual Disability*. Brighton: Pavilion Press.

DesNoyers Hurley, A., Pfadt, A., Tomasulo, D. and Gardner, W.I. (1996) 'Counselling and psychotherapy'. In: J.W. Jacobson and J.A. Mulick (eds) *Manual of Diagnosis and Professional Practice in Mental Retardation*. Washington, DC: American Psychological Association.

Donaldson, J.Y. and Menolascino, F.J. (1977) 'Emotional disorders in the retarded', *International Journal of Mental Health*, 6, 73–95.

Dosen, A. and Day, K. (2001) *Treating Mental Illness and Behaviour Disorders in Children and Adults with Mental Retardation*. Washington, DC: American Psychiatric Press.

Dykens, E. (2000) 'Psychopathology in children with intellectual disability', *Journal of Child Psychology and Psychiatry*, 41, 407–417.

D'Zurilla, T.J. and Goldfried, M.R. (1971) 'Problem solving and behaviour modification', *Journal of Abnormal Psychology*, 78, 107–126.

Eaton, L.F. and Menolascino, F.J. (1982) 'Psychiatric disorders in the mentally retarded: types, problems and challenges', *American Journal of Psychiatry*, 139, 1297–1303.

Einfeld, S.L. and Tonge, B.J. (1996) *Manual for the Developmental Behaviour Checklist (DBC)*. Randwich, NSW, Australia: Prince of Wales Hospital, Department of Child and Adolescent Psychiatry.

Emerson, E. (2003) 'Prevalence of psychiatric disorders in children and adolescents with and without intellectual disability', *Journal of Intellectual Disability Research*, 47 (1), 51–58.

Erfanian, N. and Miltenberger, R.G. (1990) 'Brief report: contact desensitisation in the treatment of dog phobias in persons who have mental retardation', *Behav-*

*ioural Residential Treatment*, 5, 55–60.

Evans, I. and Meyer, L.H. (1987) 'Moving to educational validity: a reply to Test, Spooner and Cooke', *Journal of the Association for Persons with Severe Handicaps*, 12, 103–106.

Fletcher, R.J. (1993) 'Individual psychotherapy for persons with mental retardation'. In: R.J. Fletcher and A. Dosen (eds) *Mental Health Aspects of Mental Retardation: Progress in assessment and treatment*. Lexington, MA: Lexington Books.

Foundation for People with Learning Disabilities (2002) *Count Us In: The report of the committee of inquiry into meeting the mental health needs of young people with learning disabilities*. London: Mental Health Foundation.

Foundation for People with Learning Disabilities (2005) *Making Us Count: Identifying and improving mental health support for young people with learning disabilities*. London: Mental Health Foundation.

Fraser, W.I. and Nolan, M. (1994) 'Psychiatric disorders in mental retardation'. In N. Bouras (ed.) *Mental Health in Mental Retardation*. Cambridge: Cambridge University Press.

Gadow, K. and Kalachnik, J. (1981) 'Prevalence and patterns of drug treatment for behaviour and seizure disorders of TMR students', *American Journal of Mental Deficiency*, 85, 588–595.

Gardner, W.I. (1970) 'Use of behaviour therapy with the mentally retarded'. In: F.J. Menolascino (ed.) *Psychiatric Approaches to Mental Retardation*. New York: Basic Books.

Gardner, W.I. (2000) 'Behavioural therapies: using diagnostic formulation to individualise treatment for persons with developmental disabilities and mental health concerns'. In: R.J. Fletcher (ed.) *Therapy Approaches for Persons with Mental Retardation*. Kingston, NY: NADD Press.

Gardner, W.I. and Sovner, R. (1994) *Self-Injurious Behaviours: Diagnosis and treatment*. Willow Street, PA: Vida Publishing.

Gardner, W.I. and Whalen, J.P. (1996) 'A multimodal behaviour analytic model for evaluating the effects of medical problems on non-specific behavioural symptoms in persons with developmental disabilities', *Behavioural Interventions in Community Settings*, 11, 147–161.

Gardner, W.I., Graeber, J.L. and Cole, C.L. (1996) 'Behaviour therapies: a multimodal diagnostic and intervention model'. In: J. Jacobson and J.A. Mulick (eds) *Manual of Diagnosis and Professional Practice in Mental Retardation*. Washington, DC: American Psychological Association.

Gardner, W.I., Graeber-Whalen, J.L. and Ford, D.R. (2001) 'Behavioural therapies: individualising interventions through treatment formulations'. In: A. Dosen and K. Day (eds) *Treating Mental Illness and Behaviour Disorders in Children and Adults with Mental Retardation*. Washington, DC: American Psychiatric Press.

Gillberg, C., Persson, E., Grufman, M. and Themmer, U. (1986) 'Psychiatric disorders in mildly and severely mentally retarded urban children and adolescents: epidemiological aspects', *British Journal of Psychiatry*, 149, 68–74.

Gostason, R. (1985) 'Psychiatric illness among the mentally retarded: a Swedish population study', *Acta Psychiatrica Scandinavia*, 71 (suppl. 318), 1–117.

Griffiths, D.M. (1995) 'Teaching generalisation of several skills with persons who have developmental disabilities', *Developmental Disabilities Bulletin*, 23 (2), 43–58.

Griffiths, D.M., Gardner, W.I. and Nugent, J.A. (eds) (1998) *Behavioural Supports: Individual centred interventions*. Kingston, NY: NADD Press.

Gualtieri, C.T. (1988) 'Mental health of persons with mental retardation: a solution, obstacles to the solution and a resolution for the problem'. In: J.A. Stark, F.J.

Menolascino and M.H. Albarelli (eds) *Mental Retardation and Mental Health.* New York: Springer-Verlag.

Gualtieri, C.T. (1991) 'A system for prevention and control'. In: J.J. Ratey (ed.) *Mental Retardation: Developing pharmacotherapies.* Washington DC: American Psychiatric Press.

Hemming, H. (1984) 'Psychotropic medication needs of mentally retarded adults before and after transfer from institutions to new small units'. In: J.M. Berg (ed.) *Perspective and Progress in Mental Retardation: Volume 2.* Baltimore, MD: Baltimore Park Press.

Hiss, H. and Kozak, M.J. (1991) 'Exposure treatment of obsessive-compulsive disorders in the mentally retarded', *The Behaviour Therapist*, 14, 163–167.

Hogg, J. (1992) 'The administration of psychotropic and anticonvulsant drugs to children with profound intellectual disability and multiple impairments', *Journal of Intellectual Disability Research*, 36, 473–488.

Holland, A.J. (1999) 'Psychiatry and mental retardation', *International Review of Psychiatry*, 11, 76–82.

Holland, A.J. and Gosden, C. (1990) 'A balanced chromosomal transfication partially co-segregating with psychotic illness in a family', *Psychiatric Research*, 32, 1–8.

Hollins, S. (2001) 'Psychotherapeutic methods'. In: A. Dosen and K. Day (eds) *Treating Mental Illness and Behaviour Disorders in Children and Adults with Mental Retardation.* Washington, DC: American Psychiatric Press.

Hughes, P.S. (1977) 'Survey of medication in a subnormality hospital', *British Journal of Mental Subnormality*, 13, 88–94.

Hurley, A.D. (1989) 'Individual psychotherapy with mentally retarded individuals: a review and call for research', *Research in Developmental Disabilities*, 10, 261–275.

Jacobson, J.W. (1990) 'Do some mental disorders occur less frequently among persons with mental retardation?', *American Journal on Mental Retardation*, 94, 596–602.

Jacobson, J. (1999) 'Dual diagnosis services: history, progress and perspectives'. In: N. Bouras (ed.) *Psychiatric and Behavioural Disorders in Developmental Disabilities and Mental Retardation.* Cambridge: Cambridge University Press.

Jacobson, J.W. (2003) 'Prevalence of mental and behavioural disorders'. In: P.W. Davidson, V.P. Prasher and M.P. Janicki (eds) *Mental Health, Intellectual Disabilities and the Aging Process.* Oxford: Blackwell Publishing.

Jonas, O. (1980) 'Pattern of drug prescribing in a residential centre for the intellectually handicapped', *Australian Journal of Developmental Disabilities*, 142, 163–165.

Kalachnik, J.E., Harder, S.R., Kidd-Nielsen, P., Errickson, E., Doebler, M. and Sprague, R.L. (1998) 'Guidelines for the use of psychotropic medication'. In: S. Reiss and M.G. Aman (eds) *Psychotropic Medication and Developmental Disabilities: The international consensus handbook.* Columbus, OH: Ohio State University Nisonger Centre.

Kiernan, C. and Moss, S. (1990) 'Behavioural and other characteristics of the population of a mentally handicapped hospital,' *Mental Handicap Research*, 3, 3–20.

Koller, H., Richardson, S.A., Katz, M. and McLaren, J. (1983) 'Behaviour disturbance since childhood among a 5-year birth cohort of all mentally retarded young adults in a city', *American Journal of Mental Deficiency*, 87, 386–395.

Lindsay, W.R. and Morrison, F.M. (1996) 'The effect of behavioural relaxation on cognitive performance in adults with severe intellectual disabilities', *Journal of Intellectual Disability Research*, 40, 285–290.

Lindsay, W.R., Baty, F.J. and Michie, A.M. (1989) 'A comparison of anxiety treatments with adults who have moderate and severe mental retardation', *Research in Developmental Disability*, 10, 129–140.

Lipman, R.S. (1970) 'The use of psychopharmacological agents in residential facilities for the retarded'. In: F.J. Menolascino (ed.) *Psychiatric Approaches to Mental Retardation*. New York: Basic Books.

Lovaas, O.I. and Smith, T. (1989) 'A comprehensive behavioural theory of autistic children: paradigm for research and treatment', *Journal of Behaviour Therapy and Experimental Psychiatry*, 20, 17–29.

Luiselli, J.K. (1980) 'Relaxation training with the developmentally disabled: a reappraisal', *Behaviour Research of Severe Developmental Disabilities*, 1, 191–213.

Lund, J. (1985) 'The prevalence of psychiatric morbidity in mentally retarded adults', *Acta Psychiatrica Scandinavia*, 72, 563–570.

Matson, J.L. and Stephens, R.M. (1978) 'Increasing appropriate behaviour of explosive chronic psychiatric patients with a social skills training package', *Behaviour Modification*, 2, 61–76.

Meichenbaum, D. (1969) 'The effects of instructions and reinforcement on thinking and language behaviours of schizophrenics', *Behaviour Research and Therapy*, 7, 101–114.

Mental Health Special Interest Research Group (SIRG-MH) (2000) *Mental Health and Intellectual Disabilities: Assessing the mental health needs of people with intellectual disabilities. Draft report by the Mental Health Special Interest Group of the International Association for the Scientific Study of Intellectual Disabilities to the World Health Organisation.* Geneva: World Health Organisation.

Moss, S. (1999) 'Assessment: conceptual issues'. In: N. Bouras (ed.) *Psychiatric and Behavioural Disorders in Developmental Disabilities and Mental Retardation*. Cambridge: Cambridge University Press.

Moss, S., Bouras, N. and Holt, G. (2000) 'Mental health services for people with intellectual disability: a conceptual framework', *Journal of Intellectual Disability Research*, 44 (2), 97–107.

Nagel, B. and Leiper, R. (1999) 'A national survey of psychotherapy with people with learning disabilities', *Clinical Psychology Forum*, 129, 8–14.

Nezu, C.M., Nezu, A.M. and Arean, P. (1991) 'Assertiveness and problem-solving training for mildly mentally retarded persons with dual diagnosis', *Research in Developmental Disability*, 12, 371–386.

Nezu, C.M., Nezu, A.M. and Gill-Weiss, M.J. (1992) *Psychopathology in Persons with Mental Retardation: Clinical guidelines for assessment and treatment*. Champaign, IL: Research Press.

Pfadt, A. (1991) 'Group psychotherapy with mentally retarded adults: issues related to design, implementations, and evaluation', *Research in Developmental Disabilities,* 12, 261–286.

Reid, A.H. (1988) *The Psychiatry of Mental Handicap*. Oxford: Blackwell Scientific.

Reiss, S. (1990) 'Prevalence of dual diagnosis in community based day programs in the Chicago metropolitan area', *American Journal on Mental Retardation*, 94, 578–585.

Rivinus, T.M. (1980) 'Psychopharmacology and the mentally retarded patient'. In: L.S. Szymanski and P.E. Tanguay (eds) *Emotional Disorders of Mentally Retarded Persons: Assessment, treatment and consultation*. Baltimore, MD: University Park Press.

Rusch, F.R., Morgan, T.K. and Martin, J.E. (1985) 'Competitive employment: teaching mentally retarded employees self-instructional strategies', *Applied Research in Mental Retardation*, 6, 389–407.

Ruth, R. (2001) 'Psychoanalytic therapies'. In: A. Dosen and K. Day (eds) *Treating Mental Illness and Behaviour Disorders in Children and Adults with Mental Retardation*. Washington DC: American Psychiatric Press.

Rutter, M., Tizard, J., Graham, P. and Whitmore, K. (1976) 'Isle of Wight studies 1964–1974', *Psychological Medicine*, 6, 313–332.

Ryde, D. (1981) 'Prescribing – a controversial craft?', *Practitioner*, 225, 283–285.

Salkovskis, P. (2002) 'Empirically grounded clinical interventions: cognitive-behavioural therapy progresses through a multi-dimensional approach to clinical science', *Behavioural and Cognitive Psychotherapy*, 30, 3–9.

Shure, M.B. and Spivack, G. (1982) 'Interpersonal problem-solving in young children: a cognitive approach to prevention', *American Journal of Community Psychology*, 10, 341–356.

Simpson, N. (1997) 'Developing mental health services for people with learning disabilities in England', *Tizard Learning Disability Review*, 2 (2), 35–42.

Sinason, V. (1992) *Mental Handicap and the Human Condition*. London: Free Association Books.

Spencer, D. (1974) 'A survey of the medication in a hospital for the mentally handicapped', *British Journal of Psychiatry*, 124, 507–508.

Stromme, P. and Diseth, T.H. (2000) 'Prevalence of psychiatric diagnoses in children with mental retardation: data from a population-based study', *Developmental Medicine and Child Neurology*, 42, 266–270.

Sturmey, P. (2004) 'Cognitive therapy with people with intellectual disabilities: a selective review and critique', *Clinical Psychology and Psychotherapy*, 11, 222–232.

Szymanski, L.S. (1980) 'Psychiatric diagnosis of retarded persons'. In: L.S. Szymanski and P.E. Tangnay (eds) *Emotional Disorders of Mentally Retarded Persons*. Baltimore, MD: University Park Press.

Szymanski, L.S. and Crocker, A.C. (1989) 'Mental retardation'. In: H.I. Kaplan and B.J. Sadock (eds) *Comprehensive Textbook of Psychiatry: Volume 5*. Baltimore, MD: Williams and Williams.

Szymanski, L.W. (1994) 'Mental retardation and mental health: concepts, aetiology and incidence'. In N. Bouras (ed.) *Mental Health in Mental Retardation: Recent advances and practices*. Cambridge: Cambridge University Press.

Tomasulo, D. (1992) *Group Counselling for People with Mild to Moderate Mental Retardation/Developmental Disabilities: An interactive-behavioural model*. New York, NY: Young Adult Institute.

Tonge, B. (1999) 'Psychopathology of children with developmental disabilities'. In: N. Bouras (ed.) *Psychiatric and Behavioural Disorders in Developmental Disabilities and Mental Retardation*. Cambridge: Cambridge University Press.

Tyrer, S. and Hill, S. (2001) 'Psychopharmacological approaches'. In: A. Dosen and K. Day (eds) *Treating Mental Illness and Behaviour Disorders in Children and Adults with Mental Retardation*. Washington, DC: American Psychiatric Press.

Valenti-Hein, D. (1989) 'An evaluation of treatment approaches for romantic loneliness of mentally retarded adults' (Ph.D. thesis). Chicago, IL: University of Illinois at Chicago.

Van Houten, R., Axelrod, S., Bailey, J.S., Favell, J.E., Foxx, R.M., Iwata, B.A. and Lovaas, O.I. (1988) 'The right to effective behavioural treatment', *The Behaviour Analyst*, 11, 111–114.

Vygotsky, L.S. (1962) *Thought and Language*. Boston, MA: MIT Press.

Weber, G. (2003) 'Psychological interventions and psychotherapy'. In: P.W. Davidson, V.P. Prasher and M. P. Janicki (eds) *Mental Health, Intellectual Disabilities and the Aging Process.* Oxford: Blackwell Publishing.

Whitehouse, R.M., Tudway, J.A., Look, R. and Kroese, B.S. (2006) 'Adapting individual psychotherapy for adults with intellectual disabilities: a comparative review of the cognitive-behavioural and psychodynamic literature', *Journal of Applied Research in Intellectual Disabilities*, 19, 55–65.

Willner, P. (2005) 'The effectiveness of psychotherapeutic interventions for people with learning disabilities: a critical review', *Journal of Intellectual Disability Research,* 49 (1), 73–85.

Willner, P. (2006) 'Readiness for cognitive therapy in people with intellectual disabilities', *Journal of Applied Research in Intellectual Disabilities*, 19, 5–16.

Wolfensberger, W. (1972) *The Principle of Normalization in Human Services.* Toronto: National Institute of Mental Retardation.

Woods, D.W., Miltenberger, R.G. and Lumley, V.A. (1996) 'Sequential application of major habit-reversal components to treat motor tics in children', *Journal of Applied Behaviour Analysis*, 29, 483–493.

World Health Organisation (2005) *International Classification of Diseases – Tenth Revision (ICD-10): Classification of mental and behavioral disorders diagnostic criteria for research (2nd edn).* Geneva: World Health Organisation.

CHAPTER 8

# Zippy's Friends

## Developing Curriculum Resources to Support the Mental Health Needs of Young People with Special Educational Needs

*Gill Rowley and Jan Cook*

### Introduction

There is a dearth of autism-specific resources to promote the mental health and emotional well-being of children and young people with autistic spectrum disorders (ASD). These children and young people are at a much higher risk of developing mental health problems than other young people (Foundation for People with Learning Disabilities (FPLD), 2002). Three out of five are expected to suffer mental health problems at some stage in their lives, and these can adversely affect their education. A National Inquiry in 2001–2002 (FPLD, 2002) recommended the development of more curriculum resources to help schools for children with special educational needs, including ASD, to promote children's mental health and emotional well-being. However, six years on, there is still a serious lack of such resources nationwide.

### What is mental health?

Mental health is defined in many ways, often from the point of view of medical diagnosis (see Chapters 6 and 7). However, in its constitution, the World Health Organisation (WHO) emphasise the positive dimension of mental health:

> *Health is a state of complete physical, mental and social wellbeing and not merely the absence of a disease or infirmity.* (WHO, 1946)

The National Electronic Library for Health (NeLH) and Mentality (2004) describe it in the following terms:

> *Mental health is about maintaining a good level of personal and social functioning. For children and young people, this means getting on with others, both peers and adults, participating in educative and other social activities, and having a positive self-esteem. Mental health is about coping and adjusting to the demands of growing up.*

This description is very relevant to the aims of Personal Social and Health Education (PSHE) within the educational context and consequently the aims of this research project.

### The UK policy context

Recent literature has highlighted UK government concern with children's well-being and mental health. *The Future of Mental Health: A Vision for 2015* (Sainsbury Centre for Mental Health et al., 2006) states that by 2015 mental well-being should be promoted in all schools.

The UK government's initiative, Every Child Matters (Department for Education and Skills (DfES), 2003, 2004), addresses the well-being of children and young people from birth to age 19 years. Their aim is for every child, whatever their background or their circumstances, to have the support they need to be healthy, stay safe, enjoy and achieve, make a positive contribution, and achieve economic well-being (DfES, 2004). Within this remit, specifically referring to children's mental health, *Every Child Matters: Change for children* states the government's aim that:

> *All children and young people, from birth to their eighteenth birthday, who have mental health problems and disorders, have access to timely, integrated, high quality, multidisciplinary mental health services to ensure effective assessment, treatment and support, for them and their families.* (DfES, 2004)

In addition, the UK government's *National Service Framework for Children, Young People and Maternity Services* (Department of Health (DH)/DfES, 2004), also known as the Children's NSF, lays out the government's 10-year programme (launched in September 2004) to stimulate long-term and sustained improvement in children's health, and includes the mental health and psychological well-being of children and young people as one of its 11 standards. Standard 9 outlines the following vision for the future:

- *An improvement in the mental health of all children and young people*

- *That multi-agency services, working in partnership, promote the mental health of all children and young people, provide early intervention and also meet the needs of children and young people with established or complex problems*

- *That all children, young people and their families have access to mental health care based upon the best available evidence and provided by staff with an appropriate range of skills and competencies.* (DH/DfES, 2004)

In *Count Us In,* the report of the committee of inquiry into meeting the mental health needs of young people with intellectual disabilities in the UK, the FPLD (2002) found that:

> *Young people with learning disabilities are at a high risk of developing mental health problems – more so than young people who do not have learning disabilities. The committee therefore feels it is crucial to identify ways of promoting resilience and autonomy in this report. These include:*

- *Early intervention and support for children with learning disabilities and their families from the time of diagnosis of a learning disability*

- *Support for families (for example, providing appropriate information, skills teaching, emotional support, short-term breaks, adequate income and housing)*

- *Advocacy and circles of support, particularly for young people who are looked after*

- *Access to good care for physical health*

- *Support and training to enhance communication with the young person*

- *The implementation of anti-bullying and anti-abuse policies*

- *Support through times of loss and trauma*

- *Schools and colleges fostering a sense of achievement, developing emotional awareness and providing emotional support*

- *Young people being empowered to play a central role in plans for their futures*

- *A range of opportunities and support for a social life and respect for their friendships.*

The Foundation's message is that young people with intellectual disabilities can experience the same range of mental health problems as other young people; the only difference is that they are more prone to depression and anxiety. The more social interaction youngsters experience with non-disabled people the less likely they are to experience later mental health problems.

## Mental health in schools

A healthy school is recognised as one which is committed to improving physical and emotional health, and which invests in health to assist in the process of raising achievement and improving standards. The National Healthy Schools Status (DfES/DH, 2005), part of the Healthy Schools Programme led by the DfES and the DH, suggests that schools should adopt a whole-school approach, including identifying opportunities in the National Curriculum for healthy schools activities. Sunfield's commitment to develop a structured programme to support their students' mental and emotional health through their PSHE curriculum is in keeping with this recommendation.

## The situation at Sunfield

Sunfield has a population of 70 students with severe and complex learning needs, the majority of whom have a diagnosis of ASD. Most of these students regularly exhibit challenging behaviour.

There are inherent difficulties in teaching emotional literacy to young people with ASD. They have impairments in social understanding, which lead to problems with identifying and interpreting their own and others' emotions or how other people think (Baron-Cohen, 2000; Wing, 2002). Sunfield wanted to improve students' social understanding using a structured programme of learning which would give them access to a range of coping strategies to help them in their relationships with other people and when dealing with life's difficulties. It was also hoped that this learning would equip them to handle problems and crises in adolescence, and serve them well into their future adult lives.

Although emotional literacy was being taught at Sunfield as part of the PSHE curriculum, each teacher had developed their own way of approaching this, which meant that there was no coherent programme which could accommodate students' progression in learning. Without a systematic approach, there was a danger that not all areas of emotional literacy would be covered with the students as they moved up the school. However, 'Zippy's Friends', developed by Partnership for Children,[1] while originally developed for mainstream students offered a potential solution to this need.

**Zippy's Friends**

Zippy's Friends is a mainstream primary school PSHE resource that has been developed to teach coping skills while promoting the mental health and emotional well-being of six- and seven-year-old children. It is running in over 10 countries, and has been supported by HSBC Education in the UK, Brazil and Hong Kong. The programme has been thoroughly evaluated with mainstream children, with excellent results. The decision to use Zippy's Friends at Sunfield was made because the content within the programme matched the school's current plans for PSHE.

'Zippy's Friends' defines 'coping' as 'What we do to make a bad situation better, or to make us feel better about the situation'. They state that coping strategies should:

■ Improve the situation, or make us feel better, or both

■ Not harm you or anyone else.

The Zippy's Friends programme aims to teach children:

■ To identify and explore their own feelings, imagine how they might feel in different situations and to empathise with the feelings of other people

■ To communicate effectively with others (including listening, how to ask for help and to say what they want to say)

■ How to make and keep friends, and how to deal with loneliness and rejection

■ How to resolve conflicts (particularly the problem of bullying)

■ About coping with change and loss.

These aims are all *major* challenges for anyone with an ASD. The thinking behind Zippy's Friends is that if children can be taught how to cope with social situations and difficulties, this will equip them to be better able to handle problems and crises in the future.

However, the Zippy's Friends materials, being developed for mainstream children, needed to be adapted in various ways to make them cognitively and developmentally accessible for students at Sunfield. The purpose of the research was:

■ To develop adapted resources to support the implementation of the Zippy's Friends programme with students who had severe and complex intellectual difficulties

■ To find out how effectively the programme involved these students based upon the change in their levels of learning over a 3-month trial implementation period.

This chapter describes the pilot project which formed the first stage of the research.

**Methodology**

After considering the nature of the research question, it was decided that the enquiry would be best served by using the action research model. Action research is an applied research strategy involving a cycle of data collection, evaluation and reflection with the ultimate aim of improvement (McNiff, 2002). Action research allows practitioners not only to look at ways to improve their practice within the constraints in which they are working, but also to be critical of the constraints themselves (Zuber-Skerritt, 1992). By being reflective and analytical, practitioners can inform the cycle of research and development. This approach was suitable for the development of Zippy's Friends curriculum materials because it involved successive stages of trialling materials, assessing their appropriateness, adapting the materials based on that assessment, and then re-trialling them until the researchers and classes were satisfied that the adapted materials would accommodate the varied learning styles of the students at Sunfield.

A pilot project was planned in which Module 1 of the Zippy's Friends programme ('Full of Feelings') was adapted for Sunfield's student population. If this module provided successful learning experiences for the classes involved in the pilot project, then the programme would be extended across the whole school.

### The research participants

Following an introductory presentation to the school staff at Sunfield, classes were asked if, on a voluntary basis, they would like to trial Zippy's Friends. Staff from four classes came forward. These consisted of two Key Stage 3 classes (i.e. students aged 11–14 years), one Key Stage 4 class (i.e. students aged 14–16 years) and one post-16 class (i.e. students 16–19 years). These classes involved a total of 15 students in the trial.

As this was a new curriculum development, parents/guardians were sent full information about the project through letters and an enclosed booklet, *A Parents' Guide to Zippy's Friends* (Partnership for Children, 2003). They were also invited to fill in and return a questionnaire which asked them: for ideas about how best to adapt Zippy's Friends to meet their son/daughter's needs; to rank the modules in order of relevance to their son/daughter; and about any reservations they had with the programme. There was a 75% return rate of the questionnaires – all in favour of Zippy's Friends.

### Adapting the materials

The original Zippy's Friends resources included:

- Teachers notes
- Feedback sheet
- Zippy's rules
- Illustrations for the six modules

- Solution cards
- Situation cards
- Feelings cards
- Six story books (one for each module)

- Set of posters
- Puppet template
- Zippy's Friends pencil.

To make the programme accessible to Sunfield's population of students aged 6–19 years with ASD and/or severe and complex intellectual disabilities, many of whom had little or no verbal communication, it needed to be extensively adapted. It was decided that the school's current approach to accessible literacy, using objects, photographs and Widgit Software's 'Writing with Symbols 2000' program,[2] should be used to mediate the original Zippy's Friends materials for the students. The programme materials were made more concrete, and some activities were changed or replaced. Alternative lesson plans were developed (see Figure 8.1). The intended age range of the programme was extended to cover the needs of students across the whole Sunfield age range, and some additional activities were developed for adolescents.
It was important that the fundamental goals and ethos of the programme remained, and, to ensure this, the adaptations were overseen by a steering group, which included representatives of Partnership for Children.

**Sunfield Lesson Plan**

**Date:** 14.12.06     **Subject:** PSHE     **Key stage:** 3     **Time:** 10:45

**Duration:** 30 minutes     **Term:** Autumn 2006     **Unit title:** Module 1 –    Full of feelings

**Students:** John, Kevin[1]

**Staff:** Assistant Teacher, Senior Assistant

| Learning outcomes: | Assessment criteria: |
|---|---|
| • Turn-taking<br>• Talking about 'Angry' and how we can be angry and not shout at people. Students to observe staff role play. Highlighting the use of the word 'need' (John does not understand the word).<br>• To complete sheets depending on their level of ability (1:1 support) | Students will be assessed based on their progress towards achieving their 'small steps' targets (section on Personalised Learning path) |

| Teaching activity: | Resources: |
|---|---|
| 1. 'Zippy' and mat. Read out rules. Put name badge on.<br>2. 'Zippy' story.<br>3. How do we feel today? Choose the way we feel from 'face plates' (choice of 4).<br>4. Open discussion, including 'Angry'.<br>5. Role play about 'Angry' (shouting) and highlighting the word 'need'.<br>6. Emotion game. (Resource adapted from 'Listen Up!'.)[2]<br>7. Plenary: re-cap on emotions. (Face plates) | 1. 'Zippy'/rug/badge<br>2. Story book<br>3. Paper faces<br>4. Emotion pictures and symbols<br>5. Emotion game/mirror<br>6. Feedback sheets<br>7. Pens |

**Personalised learning paths:**

**John:** John is diagnosed with microcephaly, attention deficit hyperactivity disorder, autism and epilepsy. He needs a high degree of structure at all times, and an object of reference schedule to help him understand what is happening 'now' and 'next'. He is very verbal, but for him to understand what is required, it needs to be presented visually. He will not allow correction when doing work, so it is best to be as non-verbal as possible. John works better 1:1, but will occasionally join the group. He may remove himself from the group and sit on the periphery. However, he may still continue to listen and respond to questions. John can be very confrontational so he may be re-directed to the swing outside. John will be encouraged to join the group and take part to a full extent in all objectives of the lesson and demonstrate understanding by completing work.

**Statement objectives:**
1. To help John follow routines and expectations in a group setting [√ *Hard work for John!*]
2. To increase his attention to, and concentration on, tasks [√ *Hard work for John!*]
3. To develop his language and cognitive skills

**Individual Education and Care Plan target:**
Emotional and Behaviour: P6e
'I can trust and confide in an adult' (Joint-led between Education and Care staff)

**Literacy Priority Targets:**
Speaking and listening: NC1b
1. Communicates clearly about matters of interest to individuals [√ *to adults*]
2. Communicates clearly about matters of interest to a group

Reading
1. Comments on events in stories/poems/non-fiction
2. Comments on ideas in stories/words/non-fiction

*Continued.../*

**Figure 8.1. Page 1 of a lesson plan demonstrating adaptation of Zippy's Friends**

---

[1] Names have been changed to protect identity.
[2] 'Listen Up!' is a toolkit of multimedia resources available from Mencap (http://www.mencap.org.uk/).

## *The Role of ICT*

Symbols, photographs and objects, used to support communication, can enhance the participation of students with intellectual difficulties in a range of social and educational activities. They provide a conceptual bridge between the written or spoken word and what it refers to. Increased understanding brings a sense of achievement for the student, which is a precious tool in building self-esteem, and as such can make a valuable contribution to the lives and education of those with intellectual difficulties (Carpenter, 1995). Detheridge and Detheridge (2002) write:

> *Having a sense of what is happening, and what is going to happen, can make a big difference to an individual's feeling of control.*

To make a social impact on the world the student has to have some form of knowledge about themselves as a person. They need to recognise their own emotions and how they feel, in order that they can be given a tool to help them explain how they feel or how to ask for help. In their book, *Getting IT,* Murray and Aspinall (2006) write:

> *Unless and until people can find a way to make an impact on the discourse into which their lives are embedded they will be treated like children and they will be disempowered and de-skilled by being treated thus. That means we need to ensure people have – and recognise they have – access to ways of communicating which make the people on whose support they depend sit up and listen.*

Banes, Cole, Gossage and Thornett (2006) emphasise how information technology (IT) has a potentially enormous role to play in the development of early communication skills for students. For some students who are non-verbal, it may be possible to provide a means of expression, by using an IT switch to indicate a choice or to give an instruction. The development of information and communication technology (ICT) offers a student a means of communicating that is both accepted and understood by the wider community.

### Steps in the adaptation

At each stage in the adaptation of the Zippy's Friends materials, they were trialled, feedback was sought from teachers, modifications were made, and the revised materials retrialled. The first step was merely to re-create the story, 'Full of Feelings' from Module 1, in a symbol format, using 'Writing with Symbols 2000' (Widgit Software) and 'Communicate In Print 2'. This first attempt was called 'Level 1', and it soon became clear that for the majority of students this was inaccessible. The story was then re-written with fewer words with a main picture included (Level 2). A further level was developed (Level 3), this time with a large picture and just one or two lines of script. Level 4 became the base level comprising a large picture with 'stick on matching pictures' – an interactive book for students working at the lowest developmental levels. All books were printed in A4 and also in A3 (Big Books). The books relating to each module were then colour coded with a border to match those used in the mainstream Zippy's Friends resources (see Figure 8.2)

It was important to find the right level of symbolic representation to use with each student. An additional range of further differentiated resources was needed within each of the four pilot classes to meet the individual student's needs and levels of ability. These included photographs, and in some cases it proved very difficult to get suitable photographs depicting 'real life' expressions (students with ASD find it difficult to recognise facial expression) and feelings; for example, how can you capture a picture of jealousy?

Additional resources were devised because an even wider differentiated range of engaging materials were still required (see Table 8.1)

**Figure 8.2a. Original Zippy's Friend's resources**

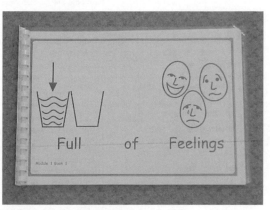

**Figure 8.2b. Module 1 Level 1**

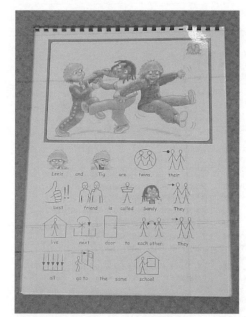

**Figure 8.2c. Module 1 Level 2**

**Figure 8.2d. Module 1 Level 3**

**Figure 8.2e. Module 1 Level 4**

**Table 8.1. Additional resources created for the adapted Zippy's Friends programme**

| Resource | Description | Aim |
|---|---|---|
| Emotion sheets – what do I do when I'm angry/sad/happy etc. | These are very simple 'comic strip conversations' which the teacher and student create together, using symbols or photos to show how the student usually reacts to an emotion, and alternative strategies the student might develop based upon what makes them feel happy/sad/angry, etc. | To enable students, when faced with emotional situations, to move away from behaviours which hurt either themselves or others and, in their place, develop positive ways of dealing with the situation |
| Work sheets – what should I do when I'm angry/sad/happy etc. | These are symbolled or photo work sheets at a level which reflects the students' abilities | To familiarise the student with behavioural options |
| Word searches | These are work sheets at a level which reflects the students' abilities. | To familiarise the student with words describing emotions, feelings and story characters<br><br>To help students to 'label' expressions |
| Crosswords | Using both word, symbol and picture clues | As above |
| Matching games | As above | As above |
| Interactive work sheets – using sound, picture, symbol | As above | As above |
| Picture dominoes | As above | As above |
| Feelings box | This is a box with a reflective surface on the inside of the lid. There are associated photos and symbols with this activity, so that students can either copy facial expressions (from a photo or another person) or initiate the expression in response to a word or symbol on a card | To increase students' awareness of their own and others' facial expressions |
| Emotions and feelings PowerPoint | An interactive, question and answer game | To familiarise students with labelling facial expressions |
| How would you feel if … | Using visual cards depicting an emotion word, symbol or photo, the students is asked to identify how a person in a photo might be feeling in the situation depicted. | To encourage students to predict how another person might feel in a particular situation |
| How do you feel today? | Depending on their ability, students are invited to choose a photographic, symbol or written representation of how they feel from an appropriate selection. | To encourage students to relate how they are feeling to photographs of facial expressions, symbols or words<br><br>To encourage students to tell another person how they are feeling |
| Concept Keyboard overlays | Allows students to input information into a computer using choices on a 'picture keyboard' instead of a letter keyboard. The keyboard can be programmed by a member of staff. The complexity of the overlay depends upon the student's ability, ranging from one large image to many smaller images, symbols or words | To enable students with limited computer, language and/or communication skills to contribute to a piece of computer work related to Zippy's Friends |

Following the adaptations to the Module 1 'Full of Feelings' materials, they were introduced to the research participants; further adaptations were made as required, and the effect of the intervention was evaluated regularly to ensure it was as accessible as possible to all students and that they could make progress.

### *Teacher assessment*

It was decided that students' progress would be monitored using teacher assessment. Teachers are used to carrying out assessment. It is a UK government requirement that they regularly assess the attainment levels of their students against National Curriculum levels. As most students at Sunfield work below Level 1 of the National Curriculum, the Qualifications and Curriculum Authority (QCA) performance descriptors or 'P' levels are used.[3] These eight 'P' levels (from P1 to P8) provide a means of assessing attainment and tracking progress over time, across a range of subjects, for students with intellectual disabilities. This information can be used to report to parents and also to the student's local authority. The 15 students involved in trialling Zippy's Friends were working at PSHE levels ranging from P3(ii) to P8.

Prior to using the adapted materials in March 2006, and again post-intervention in July 2006, teachers of the four classes were asked to make assessments about the individual students in their classes (see Figure 8.3) and to make 'best fit' judgements in respect of their students' knowledge, skills and understanding of the following feelings/emotions associated with Zippy's Friends Module 1:

■ Happy

■ Sad

■ Angry/annoyed

■ Jealous

■ Nervous.

These judgements were made using the following descriptions of students' relationship with learning, taken from *General Guidelines: Planning, teaching and assessing the curriculum for pupils with learning difficulties* (QCA/Department for Education and Employment (DfEE), 2001):[4]

1. *Encounter* (has experienced this emotion)

2. *Awareness* (shows a fleeting awareness or attention to this emotion)

3. *Attention and response* (begins to attend and respond to this emotion)

4. *Engagement* (demonstrates engagement by focused looking or listening)

5. *Participation* (engages in sharing, taking turns and anticipation)

6. *Involvement* (reaches out, joins in or comments in some way)

7. *Gaining skills and understanding* (strengthens or uses skills, concepts or understanding).

Positive self-esteem is fundamental to the success of the programme, and promoted at all times. The revised programme and the activities within it were presented in an appropriate, non-threatening manner so the students' confidence was not adversely affected. This was achieved through sensitive teaching by staff who knew each individual student's needs and personal learning pathways.

## Results

Of the 15 students, teachers assessed all except two as having demonstrated progression in at least two emotions. These two students were assessed at Step 1 (as having 'encountered' all five emotions) both in March and in July 2006, and it appeared their level of learning had not progressed.

To gain an overall perspective of the effectiveness of the programme in addressing students' learning styles, it is possible to make two observations by looking at the progression within Module 1 across the whole student group (see Figure 8.4):

■ Whereas in March 2006, there were no students assessed as being at the step of 'Gaining skills and understanding'; by July 2006, there were students judged to be reaching that step in four of the five emotions which had been worked on.

■ The number of students assessed by their teachers at the first step of 'Encounter' reduced between March and July 2006.

**Figure 8.3. Initial teacher assessment – recognition of attainment**

Thank you for volunteering to trial the adapted resource materials for the Zippy's Friends programme. Could you please indicate by placing a tick in the 'best fit' description of attainment recognition, and return to me **a.s.a.p. or by 22.3.06 at the latest.**

Before you introduced Zippy's Friends what was _____'s knowledge, skills and understanding of the following emotions/feelings?

|  | Learning steps | | | | | | |
|---|---|---|---|---|---|---|---|
| | **1**<br>**Encounter**<br>Has experienced this emotion | **2**<br>**Awareness**<br>Shows a fleeting awareness or attention to this emotion | **3**<br>**Attention and Response**<br>Begins to attend and respond to this emotion | **4**<br>**Engagement**<br>Demonstrates engagement by focused looking or listening | **5**<br>**Participation**<br>Engages in sharing, taking turns and anticipation | **6**<br>**Involvement**<br>Demonstrates involvement by reaching out, joining in or commenting in some way (e.g. speaking, signing, gesturing) | **7**<br>**Gaining skills and understanding**<br>Strengthens or uses skills, concepts or understanding |
| **ZF Module 1 emotions** | | | | | | | |
| Happy/sad | | | | | | | |
| Angry/ annoyed | | | | | | | |
| Jealous | | | | | | | |
| Nervous | | | | | | | |

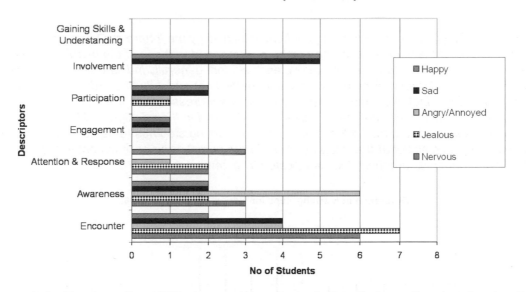

Figure 8.4a. Teachers 'best fit' judgements on students' level of emotional understanding (March 2006)

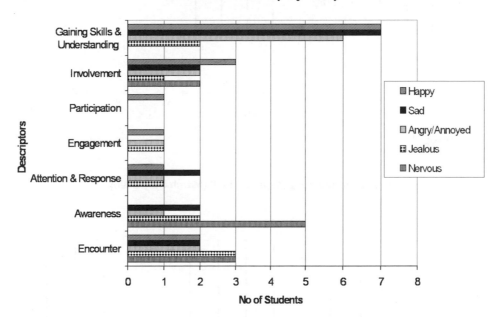

**Figure 8.4b. Teachers 'best fit' judgements on students' level of emotional understanding (July 2006)**

This suggests that there had been improvement within the student group. However, when the results of individual students' changes in learning steps between March and July 2006 are plotted by emotion (see Figure 8.5 a–e), this becomes even more obvious, and it is possible to see the extent to which most students' progressed over the period (see Table 8.2).

**Figure 8.5. Changes in learning steps between March and July 2006 for five emotions**

*Individual students are denoted along the horizontal axis by the letters A–O to preserve anonymity. Along the vertical axis, the numbers correspond to those of the learning steps outlined in Figure 8.3. The vertical lines above each student generally indicate progression between March 2006 (denoted by the lowest point of the line) and July 2006 (denoted by the upper point of the line). However, where a student has regressed, the line should be read in the opposite direction. An asterisk has been placed following their designated letter on the horizontal axis to indicate this. Where the student's learning step has remained the same, this is denoted by a small dot at that step number. Where partial or no assessment took place in respect of a particular emotion, this is indicated by a small dot at Step 0.*

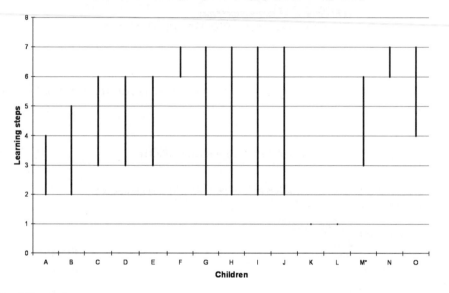

Difference in learning steps for 'Happy' (March-July 2006)

**Figure 8.5a. 'Happy'**

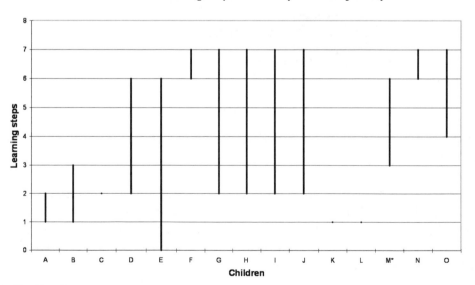

Difference in learning steps for 'Sad' (March-July 2006)

**Figure 8.5b. 'Sad'**

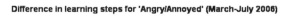

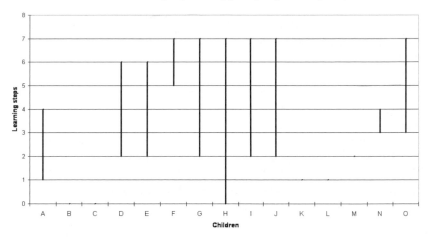

**Figure 8.5c. 'Angry/Annoyed'**

**Figure 8.5d. 'Jealous'**

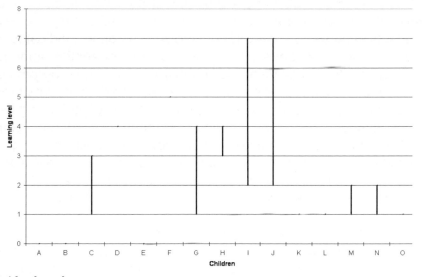

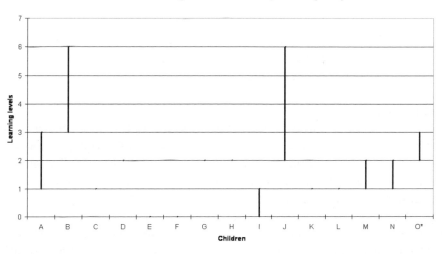

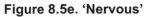

**Figure 8.5e. 'Nervous'**

| | | Emotion ( n = number of students) | | | | |
|---|---|---|---|---|---|---|
| | | Happy | Sad | Angry/ Annoyed | Jealous | Nervous |
| **Level of learning** | Achieved learning step 7 | 7 | 7 | 6 | 2 | – |
| | Progressed below learning step 7 | 5 | 4 | 3 | 5 | 6 |
| | Learning step unchanged | 2 | 3 | 3 | 3 | 4 |
| | Regression[1] | 1 | 1 | – | – | 1 |
| | No assessment in March and/or July | – | – | 2 | 5 | 4 |

[1] Students who have regressed are indicated in Figure 8.5 by an asterisk by their letter designation.

**Table 8.2. Changes in learning steps of students by emotion**

## Discussion

The results showed that there had been an increase in the steps of learning about different emotions through the adapted Zippy's Friends Module 1 materials for most students. This suggested that, for other students at Sunfield, the adapted Zippy's Friends may be a useful programme for learning emotional literacy. However, the fact that two students showed no improvement across all emotions, indicated that the programme materials would have to be further adapted, or another approach used, for these young people. Subsequently, an Intensive Interaction programme (Nind and Hewett, 2001) was introduced for them. The student who demonstrated regression in learning steps for 'Happy', 'Sad' and 'Angry/Annoyed' was experiencing personal difficulties which related to this negative change, although they did make some progress in learning steps for 'Jealous' and 'Nervous'. It is unclear why another student regressed in learning step for 'Nervous'. This could have been due to disengagement by the student at the time of assessment or perhaps an initial over-estimation of their understanding related to this particular emotion.

As expected, greater improvement by higher numbers of students was shown in the primary emotions – 'Happy', 'Sad' and 'Angry' – with generally less improvement made by fewer students in the more complex emotions of 'Jealous' and 'Nervous'. However, two students increased their learning by five steps for 'Jealous', and one student by four steps for 'Nervous'. It is clear that fewer students had reached the point of working on these more complex emotions.

Where the data indicated that there was no progression in learning steps for certain students in particular emotions, it may be that although students were assessed in both March and July, that the teaching had not focused on these emotions. This will be clarified in the next research phase.

## The next phase

The initial assessments carried out by teachers during the pilot phase have produced useful data; however, as individual teachers carried out the assessments, it is likely that they used differing criteria when making their assessments. For example, how much had their assessments related to the materials themselves, and how much to their perceptions of students' levels of emotional literacy. During the next phase, it would be interesting, in addition to collecting data, to interview teachers to gain more in-depth information about: students' progress; the teaching strategies and the way the materials were used; the criteria used to make assessment judgements; and further ideas for adaptation of the Zippy's Friends programme.

Research is always constrained by time and staffing resources. Ideally, it would have been useful for assessment to have been carried out also by independent observers as well as the teachers participating; however, staffing resources precluded this, although occasional tests of inter-rater reliability will be made during the next phase. It would also have been useful to carry out multiple assessments in March and July to reduce the possibility of atypical assessment results.

## Conclusions from the pilot study

Initially, the best outcome hoped for from the trial of Zippy's Friends materials was that the resources could be made visually interesting enough to 'Engage' the students and for them to be involved in some 'Active participation' in some of the activities (QCA/DfEE, 2001). At this early stage of the research, the indications are that some students are making progress in emotional learning as a result of being taught via the Zippy's Friends programme of study. Some of the students have made significant progress in PSHE, with one student moving up two 'P' levels from P6 to P8 and another student moving up three 'P' levels, from P5 to P8.

Evaluation has been central to the development and expansion of Zippy's Friends, and this will continue as the programme is adapted. In collaboration with Partnership for Children, Sunfield aims to develop and trial a resource that can be used with young people across the full spectrum of ASD. If the results are positive – and after any amendments or improvements have been made – the programme will be made available nationally, and Sunfield Professional Development Centre will provide teacher training.

Sunfield's aim, as expressed in their Mission Statement, is to develop each student's abilities so that they may come to experience life as worthwhile, and live as independently as possible. It is hoped that by accessing the revised Zippy's Friends programme, the students will achieve this aim more easily, through having learned a range of coping strategies that will help them in their relationships with other people and when dealing with life's difficulties. It is also hoped that they should be better able to handle problems and crises in adolescence, which may serve them well into their future adult lives beyond Sunfield.

## References

Banes, D., Coles, C., Gossage, P. and Thornett, C. (2006) *IT for All (Entitlement for All)*. London: David Fulton.

Baron-Cohen, S. (2000) 'Theory of mind and autism: a fifteen year review'. In: S. Baron-Cohen, H. Tager-Flusberg and D. Cohen (eds) *Understanding Other Minds: Perspectives from developmental cognitive neuroscience*. New York: Oxford University Press.

Carpenter, B. (1995) 'Foreword'. In T. Detheridge (ed.) *Communicating through Symbols*. London: David Fulton.

Department for Education and Skills (2003) *Every Child Matters (Green Paper)*. Nottingham: DfES.

Department for Education and Skills (2004) *Every Child Matters: Change for children*. Nottingham: DfES.

Department for Education and Skills/Department of Health (2005) *National Healthy Schools Status: A guide for schools*. London: DH Publications.

Department of Health/Department for Education and Skills (2004) *National Service Framework for Children, Young People and Maternity Services*. London: DH Publications [Online at: http://www.dh.gov.uk/]

Detheridge, T. and Detheridge, M. (2002) *Literacy through Symbols (2nd edn)*. London: David Fulton.

Foundation for People with Learning Disabilities (2002) *Count Us In: The report of the committee of inquiry into meeting the mental health needs of young people with learning disabilities.* London: Mental Health Foundation.

McNiff, J. (2002) *Action Research: Principles and practice.* London: Routledge-Falmer.

Murray, D. and Aspinall, A. (2006) *Getting IT: Using information technology to empower people with communication difficulties.* London: Jessica Kingsley.

National Electronic Library for Health/Mentality (2004) 'Mental Health Promotion: young people'. [Online at: http://www.library.nhs.uk/SpecialistLibrarySearch/Download.aspx?resID=111328]

Nind, M. and Hewett, D. (2001) *A Practical Guide to Intensive Interaction.* Kidderminster: British Institute of Learning Disabilities.

Partnership for Children (2003) *Zippy's Friends.* Kingston upon Thames: Partnership for Children.

Qualifications and Curriculum Authority/Department for Education and Employment (2001) *General Guidelines: Planning, teaching and assessing the curriculum for pupils with learning difficulties.* Sudbury: QCA Publications [Online at: http://www.nc.uk.net/ld/GG_content.html].

Sainsbury Centre for Mental Health, Local Government Association, The NHS Confederation and Leaders in Social Care (2006) *The Future of Mental Health: A vision for 2015.* London: The Sainsbury Centre for Mental Health [Online at: http://www.scmh.org.uk/80256FBD004F3555/vWeb/flKHAL6KPEKD/$file/mental+health+futures+policy+paper.pdf].

Wing, L. (2002) *The Autistic Spectrum: a guide for parents and professionals.* London: Constable and Robinson.

World Health Organisation (1946) 'The constitution of the World Health Organization'. [Online at: http://www.searo.who.int/]

Zuber-Skerritt, O. (1992) *Action Research in Higher Education: Examples and reflections.* London: Kogan Page.

**Endnotes**

[1] Online at: http://www.partnershipforchildren.org.uk/zippy/zippy.html

[2] Available online at: http://www.widgit.com/products/wws2000/index.htm

[3] Information available online at: http://www.qca.org.uk/8798.html

[4] Extended descriptions of these levels are available online at: http://www.nc.uk.net/ld/GG_content.html.

# CHAPTER 9

# Reconnecting Thinking, Feeling and Willing

## Children with Autism in a Colour Light Environment

*Diana Pauli*

### Introduction

The purpose of this chapter is to introduce an on-going research project, which is developing an innovative intervention for children at the profound end of the autistic spectrum (Pauli, 2004, 2006). There are two fundamental strands to the work. Firstly, it is proposed that in autism there is a malfunction in the co-ordination of the three psychological faculties of thinking, feeling and willing (Steiner, 1981, 1993) so that to some degree they function separately; and that it might be possible to 'reconnect' them through engaging with the feelings and will, as well as the intellect. Secondly, it is proposed that colour, particularly changing colours, can have a direct effect on the life of feelings and will, and can therefore be used to augment this engagement. 'Therapy' sessions take the form of interactive engagement between an adult and one child in changing colours of light. The project has been running for about eight years during which time the underlying hypotheses have been developed and methodologies refined. The research methods have evolved out of the practical processes of working with the children, and are a combination of case study and action research in that a methodology for each individual child has been developed and changed in response to individual behaviour over the course of time. Each child has generally been with the project for two to three years.

Firstly, the hypothesis concerning separated thinking, feeling and willing will be introduced. This will be followed by a discussion on the use of colour. Room design, staffing and the rationale behind 'therapy' sessions will then be described, followed by case notes for three children.

### Thinking, feeling and willing

The Austrian philosopher, Rudolf Steiner (1861–1925), advanced the idea that thinking, feeling and willing form a fundamental basis for human psychological functioning. Steiner was one of the earliest pioneers in the field of special education, and his ideas have been taken up all over the world. The Camphill Movement sprang from his work. His insights are a result of research methods, which he called 'spiritual science'. Although autism had not been described during his lifetime, his ideas have been found useful in explaining many of the characteristics of autistic behaviour.

To set the scene for this work, a brief review of some of the current views on the role of feeling and willing in autism, and how it might relate to the above, will be undertaken.

## The role of feeling

To begin with, the use of the two words 'feeling' and 'emotion' need consideration. For some authors (e.g. Damasio, 1994), 'feeling' is used to denote something that is more conscious, whereas 'emotion' is thought to be more instinctive. However, they are often used interchangeably, and in the context of most of the examples below they can be taken to mean more or less the same thing.

There is much in the recent literature that would suggest that the impairment in autism might lie to some extent in the realm of the feelings. For example, Hobson (2002) argues that normal development is largely dependent on emotional engagement with other people. He suggests that the root of the problem with autism might be the failure of this emotional engagement to take place in the earliest years of infancy:

> *Centrally and critically, autism reveals what it means to have mutual engagement with someone else. It reveals this by presenting us with the tragic picture of human beings for whom such engagement is partial or missing. The autistic child's lack of emotional connectedness with others is devastating in its own right, but also it has quite startling implications for the child's ability to think. These implications are what enable us to see how thinking itself is born out of interpersonal relations.*

He thus sees feelings as the lynchpin in the development of human relationships, and this in turn as the foundation for the development of thinking.

Two authors, Temple Grandin and Donna Williams, who themselves have autism give a fascinating insight into their views about feelings. In explaining in an interview how she believed she functioned differently from others, Temple Grandin said she had not originally realised that for most people 'thoughts are usually connected to feelings' (Grandin, 1997). Donna Williams expresses similar views in the following: '…I could say what I thought, but the problem was that I could not say what I felt.' And, concerning children with autism: 'All thought begins with feeling. Such children, I believe, have feeling but it has developed in isolation and can't be verbalized in the usual way…' (Williams, 1992). It appears, therefore, that both these authors consider that in autism feelings may in some way be separated or disconnected from thinking.

There are many other writers who also consider a problem in the feeling realm as a fundamental impairment in autism. These include: Frith (1989), Wing (1996) and Trevarthan, Aitken, Papoudi and Robarts (1998).

## The role of willing

Willing, as the third faculty, is probably not so widely discussed in the literature. It could be described as the 'drive' involved in carrying out an action. A conscious or deliberate act of will is often referred to as 'agency'. Jordan (1996) considers the role of all three psychological faculties, and describes them as cognitive, affective (emotional) and conative (will) factors.

The 'experience of agency' is discussed in some detail by Russell (1996). By this, he means 'the immediate knowledge that one has acted' and the recognition that these actions have had an effect on the outer world. He argues that it is necessary to perceive the action of one's own will to develop a sense of self or 'I'. He then discusses the relationship of a sense of agency to autism. Briefly, if the direct knowledge of one's own will or agency is impaired in some way, then the development of self-awareness or 'ego development' will also be affected. Without ego development, he argues, the acquisition of a theory of mind will also be impaired. He relates this to a possible 'disconnection' between thinking and willing in the following:

> *If there is an early impairment in the ability to determine what one does and how one's attention is directed then there will develop an inadequate sense of oneself – given that, at this primitive pre-theoretical level, first person-experience is an experience of the flowing together of apprehension and willing.*

Of typical development, he says that, '…the relation between the willing and knowing components must be in a relation, if not of identity, then at least of complete integration'.

In summary, he appears to be suggesting that in autism there is an inadequate consciousness of personal willing which leads to a lack of a sense of agency and hence a lack of a sense of self. This inadequacy could be viewed as lying in the area of thinking and willing.

Powell (2000) also expresses the view that in order to have a sense of self or 'I', it is necessary to be able to see the effect of one's will (actions) in the world. He goes on to connect this to autism in the following way:

> *In autism it seems that awareness of being an 'I who wills' is somehow impaired and therefore the conceptions of 'I knowing' and 'I believing' and 'I perceiving' are consequently difficult.*

Other authors who consider the role of willing or agency in autism include Damasio (2000), Wing (1996) and Nind and Hewett (2001). Thus, there is some level of acceptance that part of the impairment in autism may lie in the functioning of the will.

### Thinking, feeling and willing

According to Steiner (e.g. 1981, 1993), the three psychological faculties of thinking, feeling and willing are automatically co-ordinated by the body in typical development (see Figure 9.1), so that the individual human being functions effectively. For example, in normal circumstances a feeling would be recognised through thinking, and then the appropriate action taken. He indicated that this automatic co-ordination might sometimes break down so that thinking, feeling and willing could somehow become separated.

A simple example of how this might work is illustrated by the following: we feel cold (feeling); we think, 'I am cold so I need a coat' (thinking); we feel okay with this idea (feeling); and we put the coat on (willing). This all happens more or less automatically and, in the ordinary course of events, we do not have to make any deliberate effort to ensure that one follows the other in a logical and practical sequence.

Similarly, we see or hear something, and there is an immediate and usually unconscious drive (will) to know what it is because we are uncomfortable (feeling) at not knowing. We then form a concept (thinking) and find the significance in the sense

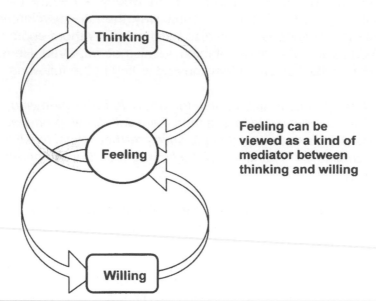

**Figure 9.1. A diagram showing in a simplified form how in typical development the three faculties of thinking, feeling and willing might function together**

perception. This would normally take place automatically and usually unconsciously. We become aware of the process only when we are unable to make sense of something, and failure to find the right concept often induces fear. We all know about unexplained things that go bump in the night!

There are numerous ways in which thinking, feeling and willing can work together, and normal human functioning can be thought of as a continuous, cyclical intermingling of 'currents' between the three. However, it should be noted that this idea represents psychological functioning, and the 'currents' should not necessarily be envisaged as actual neurological pathways.

### Separated thinking, feeling and willing and autism

With the premise that thinking, feeling and willing might in varying degrees become separated in autism, and that the 'disconnection' might manifest in different parts of the system, some examples of characteristic behaviours will now be examined.

### A disconnection from thinking to willing

It has often been observed that individuals with autism do not respond in the expected way to a range of different situations. Jordan and Powell (1995) describe unusual reactions such as putting up with extremes of cold or pain. Gerland (1996), an individual with autism, could not connect the discomfort of a full bladder with the action of going to the toilet. Caldwell (2000) describes how individuals attempting to follow instructions have apparently got stuck, and have been unable to move or to complete a task.

The circumstances described above would normally start with some kind of sense perception that leads to a feeling. This would then reach the thinking to produce meaning. In the normal course of events, this would lead via the feelings to the will, and the appropriate action would be taken. If there is no automatic 'current' to the will, then the action does not take place; hence the behaviours described above. Able individuals have been able to describe how the sense perception is felt and recognised, showing a connection from feelings to thinking, but their inability to act appropriately suggests that the 'block' appears to lie in the path to the will. This can be thought of as a disconnection, in this case, from thinking to willing. Another individual with autism, Wendy Lawson, describes this disconnection in the following:

> *I could tell the difference between a comfortable feeling and an uncomfortable one, but I didn't know what to do with it. I often felt so disconnected from the world around me and was completely unaware of expected or appropriate ways of responding.* (Lawson, 1998)

## A disconnection from willing to thinking

The need for 'sameness' has often been observed for individuals with autism (e.g. Frith, 1989; Wing, 1996); that is, there is a surprising degree of distress when, for example, objects or routines do not conform to the expected pattern. Examples are re-arranged furniture or possessions, or changes to bedtime routines, etc. The apparent lack of recognition of familiar faces, particularly if in unusual circumstances, is also a well-recognised characteristic of autism. In order to understand this in terms of thinking, feeling and willing, it is necessary to examine how we become familiar with the world around us. Steiner (1964) pointed out how sense perceptions, that is the pure sensations of, for example, colour, shape, movement, temperature, sound, etc., that reach the sense organs and then as nerve-impulses reach the brain, do not of themselves have meaning. Only when we begin to use our thinking to form the appropriate concepts, which give recognition and order, do we find meaning. This thinking process is normally instantaneous and unnoticed so that we usually have the concept immediately following the sense perception. This is often described as 'information processing'. Imagine what it would be like if this automatic thinking process did not take place – that is, if the natural drive to think and form concepts were not there. The world would simply be a mass of disjointed, random, chaotic and meaningless sensations. This lack of drive to find meaning could be attributed to a disconnection from willing to thinking, and could explain some of the features of autism.

Such a situation is beautifully described by Donna Williams in the following:

> *My experience of a total temporary systems shutdown on a visual channel means that even though the eyes continue to see form, colour, pattern and movement clearly, the brain does not process any meaning or significance of anything that is being seen (i.e. people, faces, objects, places, even parts of one's own body).* (Williams, 1996a)

Holtzapfel (1995) considers this to be significant in autism, and puts it in the following way:

> *We only become aware of the role of the concept-forming activity when it is lacking and as a result the world becomes an incomprehensible chaos. This is the central point of the disturbance manifested by the autistic child.*

It is described by Janert (2000) as 'dismantling' of the senses. Though it seems unlikely that there is normally a total lack of concept formation in autism, a partial or temporary lack could explain many of the observed phenomena.

Some of the behaviours described earlier may now begin to make more sense. To take the example of the moved furniture: if, as non-autistic individuals, we work on the sensations of form, colour and texture, etc. to form the concept 'furniture', and then the changed sensations to form 'moved furniture', we do not have a problem – someone has moved the furniture. If however, without the drive to form concepts, we have become used to a particular arrangement of visual but meaningless sensations, and then suddenly they are all different, we would be confronted by something entirely new and bewildering – little wonder we would become distressed. A similar situation might apply to the recognition of faces. To learn to recognise a face, we must be able to form a concept of the individual from the visual clues. It is this concept which can be remembered and transferred to different situations, not the detail of the sense perceptions. Again, without the drive to form concepts (willing into thinking), this would be difficult.

The whole question of symbolism and autism may also be related to this, for in symbolising we choose the symbol to represent the concept of something. This might apply to things like spoken or written words, gestures, toys (such as dolls or cars), etc. Similar reasoning can be applied to the difficulties with pretend play and imagination, since these also involve symbolising. Furthermore, the impaired understanding of feelings may also relate to a lack of appropriate concept formation from the raw sensations of, for example, fear, anger, joy, etc.

### A disconnection from feeling to thinking to willing

The lack of development of emotional connectedness described earlier can now be examined in terms of a disconnection between all three faculties. For an individual with autism, a disconnection from feeling to thinking will affect engagement with another person. If feelings are not recognised or understood, neither their own nor those of the other person, then there will be no recognition of the mutual emotional effects the two are having on one another. The subtle signs of pleasure or displeasure, interest or boredom, comprehension or otherwise, etc. will simply not be picked up, and the consequent lack of feedback will impede the progress of the interaction. Furthermore, the sudden explosion of temper so often seen could be explained as the result of a direct 'current' from feeling to will, without the normal restraining effect of the thinking.

The possibility should also be considered that the emotional content of an interaction is picked up and understood, but that the disconnection lies in the path to the will so that no appropriate action takes place. With no outer sign to indicate comprehension of the other's emotion, there is nothing recognisable on which to build for the next response. The consequent restriction in the mutual to and fro of normal human interaction could then be seen as characteristic of a lack of emotional connectedness.

Hobson's (2002) description of autism below can be seen as including an impairment in both the understanding of feelings and the lack of an appropriate response in the will. He describes autism in the following way:

> *One is tempted to say that children with autism are almost blind to the feelings of others. This is largely true, but the problem goes deeper than this. They are not moved by people's feelings. As I have stressed before, the business of being moved by others is vitally important for thinking as well as for refinement of feeling with our fellow humans.*

Not being 'moved' by people's feelings implies the lack of a visible and appropriate (or other sense-perceptible) response through the will. The fact that a characteristic of autism is the lack of such visible responses to personal feelings may have resulted in the early view that in people with autism feelings were actually absent.

There may be other possibilities, but is hoped that the above arguments go some way towards showing that a number autistic behaviours might be explained by a separation between thinking, feeling and willing.

### The effects of colour

Changing colours of light are used to augment the mood and atmosphere during an interaction. Various researchers have indicated that colour has an effect on mood, and have used it therapeutically (e.g. Verner-Bonds, 2002). Wilson (1966) used electrical skin conductance measurements to measure the effect of viewing red and green slides, and found that red is a more arousing colour than green. Hamid and Newport (1989) obtained similar findings when measuring physical strength and mood in that pink was more stimulating than blue. In general, research has shown that the red end of the spectrum is more stimulating than the blue, though not all results are consistent with this (e.g. Schauss, 1979; Pellegrini, Schauss and Miller, 1981). Donna Williams describes how red light made her feel alert whereas in blue light she felt mesmerised (Williams, 1996b).

### Design of the colour room

Sessions take place in a specially designed room (see Figure 9.2) in which the whole interior colour can be changed by altering the colour stage lights mounted round the top of the walls. The walls and floor are grey in colour so that they take up the colour of the light. Dimmer control from an observation booth allows the colour combinations and rates of change to be altered at will.

To begin with the child is observed in different colours to determine their response to different hues so that this knowledge can be used to enhance the mood during an interaction.

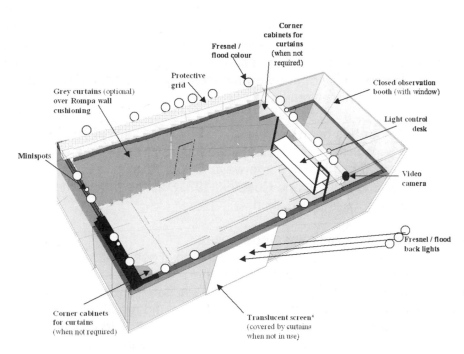

**Figure 9.2. Design of the colour room**

Figure 9.3 illustrates a quantitative analysis of the reaction to the three main additive primary colours. For this particular child, the more tense and excited he became the more he flicked his fingers in front of his eyes. This could therefore be measured as an assessment of his state of arousal. Mean flicking rates taken over four sessions are shown.

This shows that red appears to arouse, and green to calm, and this reaction has

**Figure 9.3. Comparison of % time flicking in red, blue and green light**

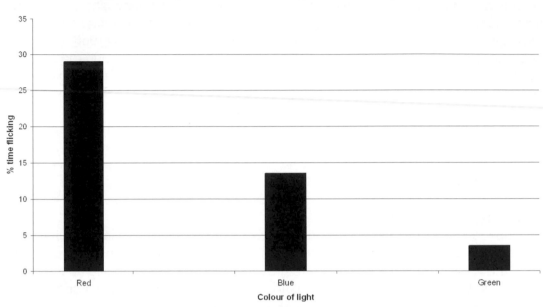

been found to be fairly typical. However, the effect is often quite subtle, and in many cases prolonged exposure to any one strong colour eventually produces discomfort. In general, the findings are that although colour can modify behaviour for short periods of time, the overall effect depends on mood and circumstances. For many children, soft pink and blue colours have been found to encourage a mood of calm concentration. The next stage is for the light operator to respond using the dimmers to the reactions of the child to build up a sort of 'dialogue'. The response to this stage has been found to vary, with some children becoming engaged and animated, while with others there was minimal interest.

In this research, colour has been used as a dynamic facilitator of changing moods, and it is up to the sensitivity and skill of the light operator to follow the interaction with the appropriate colour changes. In some ways, colour is used in the same way as music in music therapy (Nordoff and Robbins, 1971), as the artistic medium in a creative and spontaneous improvisation.

**Rationale behind the therapy sessions**
The first priority in interactive sessions is that the child gets to know the adult and to develop a feeling of confidence and trust. For this reason, sessions begin with exchanges based on the principles of Intensive Interaction (Nind and Hewett, 1994). Mirroring the child's behaviours, and then enhancing and modifying them 'in reply', builds up a sort of 'dialogue' in movement and sound. The child initiates the exchange so that what happens is at an appropriate level, and is therefore meaningful. Because of this, sessions are generally fun. Emphasis is laid right from the beginning

on picking up and augmenting the emotional mood of the child, while at the same time encouraging movement or vocalisations to engage the will. Many of the movements are similar to those used in Sherborne Developmental Movement (Hill, 2006). As is always the case with Intensive Interaction, it is the process of the interaction that counts, rather than the content, and it is essential that it becomes fun and creative for the child.

Once a good relationship has been established, the next stage is gradually phased in. Exactly what form this takes will depend on the child and what has already been built up during Intensive Interaction. However, the general principle is that the child's thinking, feeling and willing are not functioning together properly, and the adult ego must attempt to 'reconnect' them for the child.

The sense in which the word 'ego' is used will now be explained. It is described by Steiner (e.g.1954, 1969) as that part of the human psyche that is responsible for self-consciousness and which enables us to recognise our own 'I'. It is difficult to describe the use of the ego, but if we imagine what is required when we say to ourselves, 'I will make myself do such and such…' then this is the ego at work. Similarly, the conscious attempt to empathise with another's feelings is the work of the ego. These essentially human qualities of inner striving are dependent on a developed ego. It may be that the ego of the child with autism is not deeply embedded in the body, and this is why they are considered 'hard to reach', and probably why they often have difficulty in saying 'I' to express themselves. It may also explain why they have little self-directed will. According to Steiner (1969), separated thinking, feeling and willing is one of the characteristics of the ego not being fully engaged in the body, and the postulate in this research is that the adult ego can be used in the service of the child to reconnect them, with the aim of facilitating the engagement of the child's own ego.

To begin with, some general examples will be described; later they will be put in the context of real events in the case notes that follow. Although total separation is unlikely in real cases, this will be assumed for the sake of explanation. Firstly, we will look at feelings, and describe what would happen if they were disconnected from the thinking and will. If the child has, for example, a feeling of fear or anger, there would be neither comprehension of the sensation nor the possibility of deliberately expressing it. This would cause further distress that again could not be dealt with so producing a kind of vicious circle. Rather than trying to subdue the feelings, the attempt is made first to bring them into consciousness (feeling to thinking), and then to direct them so that they can be expressed by suitable actions (thinking to willing).

The adult will start by mirroring the actions of the child while at the same time using their ego consciously to imbue them with the appropriate feelings. Where emotional states result in undesirable actions such as self-harm or violence, the adult will lead the child towards a more suitable mode of expression such as stamping or shouting an appropriate word. In this way, emotions and actions are shared so that not only do they become more conscious for the child, but also they are acknowledged by an empathetic response from the adult. In the case of anger, strong red light is used to enhance the atmosphere, and also so that it acts as a sense-perceptible reflection of the feeling. It has often been found that in the case of anger, 'going with' the child through a crescendo, and then 'coming down' together is in fact an effective calming strategy. The lights would change from red to soft blues and greens as the tension reduces. Of course, this technique is equally applicable to feelings of happiness and joy, and learning how simply to 'have fun' with someone else is a fundamental part of the intervention. Yellows and blues (imitating sunlight) have been found appropriate for a mood of lightness and fun.

Secondly, we will look at problems with the will, and what might happen when there is a disconnection from thinking to willing. In this case, it may be that the child does not make the desired response to a stimulus; for example, an instruction. The adult must now direct their ego strength to 'will' the child into the required action. This will demand firmness and resolution in the asking – a sort of directed assertive support – but the attitude must be one of enabling rather than of power and coercion. As soon as the task is achieved, the atmosphere is immediately lightened with much praise. It has consistently been found that where a child has been 'willed' into an action in this way, the result is a clear sense of release and joy.

Red colours are usually associated with the engagement of the will, followed by a lightening once the task has been achieved. It must be assumed that, in cases where this approach works, the child would have wanted to carry out the action, but the path to the will was somehow 'blocked' so nothing could happen. The action of the adult ego as it were 'breaks the dam', the current flows, and the system works again. This is invariably the feeling one gets when the child succeeds. Sometimes, such difficulties are compounded by a will that appears to be in a sense 'overactive', and seems to work independently of the thinking. In this case, the child may show signs of hyperactivity or make uncontrolled movements or sounds (as with Tourette syndrome). Again, it has been found that when a strong adult ego can redirect the will of the child, relief and joy results.

There are numerous different possibilities for the engagement and nurturing of the feelings and will, and it will always be necessary to be spontaneously creative in developing responses and strategies that are suitable for individual children.

Once a relationship has been built up where feelings and will can be meaningfully shared in a productive way, the emphasis can be directed towards thinking. According to Steiner's (e.g.1988) educational philosophy, it is only once the will and the feelings are developed and in harmony that attention should be directed to the intellect (thinking). Although the children involved in this project have severe intellectual difficulties, it has usually been possible to include the meaningful use of speech once a sufficient level of rapport has been built up. Words are connected to actions by encouraging the use of the word while actually carrying out the action, as in 'pull,' 'push,' 'run,' 'jump,' etc. This brings a connection from will to thinking. Similarly, it is sometimes possible to direct an emotional situation towards the use of the appropriate word. For those who remain non-verbal, it is still possible to continue to develop meaningful communication by other means – for example, through gesture, movement and vocalisation – depending on the child's aptitudes.

As the child becomes more able to engage freely with the adult, so the colours become less important. Their main function is to help the child to connect with their own feelings and will so that once this is achieved the interaction can take place effectively in normal lighting. There is no reason why this style of interaction should not be attempted without coloured lights or perhaps with music as a background instead.

As the therapy progresses, simple participative stories with an emotional content can be introduced where speech is associated with actions, so that thinking, feeling and willing are connected. Poetry, nursery rhymes and other games are also used. Thus the learning process leads through will and feelings to speech and thinking. In this way, an attempt is made to enable the child to experience their humanity through social relationships. The practical details of how this might take place will be made clearer by the case notes described later.

## Evaluation

Evaluation is continuous, with alterations and improvements in the methodology being made regularly according to each child's needs and abilities. Assessment of progress is from notes and video recordings together with periodic comments from teachers and carers. Records are analysed for changes in, for example:

- Eye-contact
- Engagement, body posture, touch
- Signs of affection
- Imitation of movements
- Reciprocal responses
- Sense of fun, laughing
- Initiation of movements or games, etc.
- Sharing of affective states in exercises
- Learning of words through action
- Symbolising, pretending and acting
- Imitation of words
- Expression of emotion through gesture/language
- Use of words independently and appropriately
- General progress in school and at home.

## Case notes for three children

In all three cases, the children had a diagnosis of autism with severe intellectual difficulties. The cases will be reported as narratives, picking out important moments and showing general trends over a period of time.

## James

James was nine years old. Although his autism manifested in many different ways, his main problem centred on his difficulty in coping with feelings, particularly of fear, anger and irritation. He did not play or interact with other children, and did not communicate through language, though he would occasionally imitate words. He would easily become very distressed: crying out, punching and banging his head against any available object. Noise, altered routines or dislike of a task could easily trigger this behaviour. It occurred regularly in class and around the school.

To begin with, James showed only moderate interest in the colours, and made only minimal responses to changing shades. He seemed to be calmest in the blues and greens. Intensive Interaction was not particularly successful, and for some weeks the sessions did not really seem to be leading anywhere. He would reluctantly make some simple eurythmy movements (Steiner 1983, 1984) if the adult actually directed his arms, but he would not imitate speech sounds. His tantrums were becoming very regular in class, and also started in the colour room. It was at this point, when things were not going well, that a change in approach was tried. It was decided to join in with and share his frustration and anger, rather than trying to suppress it. As his anger level was seen to rise, the lights changed to strong red, and the adult copied his movements, shouting, stamping and gesticulating with the arms. He was directed to stamp his feet instead of banging his head, and this he quickly began to do. At the same time, he was encouraged to shout the word, 'cross'. The important thing was to feel and share his anger, not directed against him, but experienced with him. The effect was immediate and dramatic. The anger seemed to 'melt away', the frantic movements stopped, and James quickly became malleable and content. A similar but milder episode was repeated only once more in another session shortly afterwards, after which his whole outlook improved with no further outbursts.

James continued to make progress. He would carry out eurythmy movements, and would also imitate many speech sounds and words. He was also able to give answers to simple questions and to recite short sections of poetry. He would take part willingly in simple participative stories in which he could finish sentences and act in familiar scenes (e.g. drinking). Above all, there was now laughter and fun.

To return to the tantrum episode, this could retrospectively be seen as a turning point. Through the adult's mirroring his emotional state and showing him how to express it, he was able to be 'in touch' with his feelings (to become aware of them), and then able to channel them effectively into his will through a more appropriate action (stamping and shouting rather than head-banging) This could be seen as connecting the feelings to the thinking, and then to the will. After this, James was altogether happier, and the relationship with the adult greatly improved, with regular signs of affection. Also, from this time on, reports from school, other therapies and home became far more positive. James was becoming someone who was a pleasure to be with!

### Anna
Anna was 10 years old, and stayed with the project for about three years. She had no meaningful speech though she would occasionally imitate words; she avoided eye-contact, and play would always be on her own terms. She enjoyed 'rough and tumble', but could be quite rough and aggressive.

To begin with, Anna was observed in the different colours. She would sit cross-legged and make intermittent babbling sounds while rocking from side to side. In red, these would be animated and fast, whereas in blue and green she tended to be quieter and calmer. If the reds were flashing in response to her vocalisations, she would become more aroused, and her sounds quite 'fractious'.

Anna's natural tendency to rock from side to side was the starting point for Intensive Interaction. The adult would take her hands and rock gently accompanied by up-fading and down-fading of pink over blue in time to the movement. Sessions usually started in this way. When she got excited and began to run about, the adult would also join in with strong reds following the crescendo of the excitement, and subsiding again as the mood calmed. To begin with, Anna could often be belligerent in her behaviour: slapping, biting or head-butting. For some weeks, although she would take part in the interactions, there was little fun and no laughter. A simple exercise was then introduced called 'In and Out' where she and the adult came together in the middle of the room with the lights changing to red, and then moving apart again in blue. It had a 'breathing in, breathing out' rhythm. It took several attempts for Anna to grasp the exercise, and required a great effort from the adult to 'will' her into action, but once she achieved it there was an enormous burst of joy, and she quite sponta-neously used the word 'out'. The pleasure in the achievement was unmistakable. Over the next few months, this exercise continued to be fun. This could be thought of as an example of 'unblocking' the pathway to the will, thus enabling the child to carry out something new. Similar progress was made with jumping, pulling and pushing, and some simple eurythmy exercises. Laughter was now a consistent feature, and Anna was showing more and more signs of affection.

The next major change came unexpectedly. Anna was sitting down cross-legged with the adult facing her. For no apparent reason, she suddenly started to shake her head from side to side and make a sort of 'Brrr....Brrr...' noise. When this was mirrored, she began to laugh, and this strange exchange continued for several minutes, all the time with Anna becoming more amused and animated. This was accompanied with yellow and pink colours, following the tempo of the exchange. Once the principle of a vocal dialogue had been established, Anna was encouraged (again with consider-able 'will' from the adult) to make some of the simple speech sounds, accompanied by the appropriate eurythmy gestures and colours. These she picked up very quickly, all the time with laughter and joy. Gradually words and short sentences were intro-duced, wherever possible accompanied with the appropriate actions or moods, until after about three years she was able to use several words appropriately, and to answer simple one-word-answer questions. In the Reynell Developmental Language Scale (Reynell and Huntley, 1977), she progressed from below the lowest score to two years developmental equivalence.

Another interesting point was that, during the course of this intervention, her playing style altered considerably. At the start, she was inclined to be rough, get over-excited and then start biting, kicking, slapping, etc. However, after the first year, and with no particular instruction, she somehow 'knew' the bounds of reasonable behaviour, and was able to take part in rough and tumble games with no fear on the part of the adult of getting hurt. This has been noticed in other children, and since it seems just to 'happen', it would appear to come through the feelings. Perhaps the will is now guided through the feelings, which have now become more sensitive to those of the other person. Anna was also far happier and more sociable in the company of oth-ers. A delightful and charming personality was beginning to shine through.

### Tim

Tim was seven years old when he joined the project. He was hyperactive, unable to concentrate and always on the move. He was rarely affectionate, and would often bite, scratch and kick, sometimes for no apparent reason. He was non-verbal, and any progress in school was severely curtailed by his inability to stay in one place for more than a few moments. It could be thought of as a case of the will acting inde-pendently of thinking and feeling.

At first Tim was nervous in the unfamiliar surroundings, running about, watching the lights momentarily, and then lying on the floor. He appeared to be slightly more active in the reds and pinks, and on several occasions calmed considerably in blue/green. During Intensive Interaction, it was difficult to sustain engagement for any length of time, so the 'to and fro' of social encounter was rarely attained; added to which was the problem of biting and scratching. He was, however, able to enjoy rough and tumble play.

He sometimes could take part in simple games such as clapping, and he liked to have his arms or legs stroked, but generally Intensive Interaction was unsuccessful, and would often break down with outbursts of temper, crying or simply running off. After some months, a similar technique was used, as with James, where with strong red lights the adult would share his frustration by imitating his distress. Joining in with his shouting and crying, and imitating his expression of anguish, seemed to dissipate the temper. It would normally take less than a minute before he regained his composure. His mood after such an episode was consistently warm, friendly and relaxed with no residual feeling of resentment. Interestingly, this technique never had the effect of making him retaliate with violence against the adult. Perhaps there was some sort of inner recognition that this exchange was not actually adversarial. Such episodes were quite common at first, but gradually diminished in frequency over the course of a few weeks. In the same proportion as his tantrums decreased, his affection towards the adult increased. He could now sometimes repeat back simple one-syllable sounds.

The types of interaction and exercises over the next few months will not be described in detail, but the relationship with the adult was continually improving, and sessions were now often fun. Tim was always keen to attend. Teachers reported that he was usually calmer on returning from a colour session. His behaviour generally was improving, incidents of aggression were infrequent, and he was beginning to show an unexpected level of understanding in school tasks. However, concentration remained poor, and he could not keep still for long, often fidgeting, running away or climbing on furniture. He continued not to use words.

The next important step forward was achieved when it was decided to tackle the problem of his constant over-activity. With the assumption that his will was acting independently and that his restlessness was not intentional, it was decided that the adult would now use their ego to direct Tim's will so that he could keep on task. This meant persistently and firmly bringing him back when he ran away, and not giving in until he had completed the required exercise. This had to be repeated many times, and required considerable patience and determination on the part of the adult. The breakthrough came when one day he suddenly understood how to do the 'In and Out' exercise. He performed it many times with smiles and laughter, and there was no mistaking his feeling of joy in the achievement. The proposition is that the adult had helped him to control his will; so that he could now make his body do what he wanted; that is, his thinking was now more connected to his will. This strategy was continued for several months, and also followed through in class with the result that his behaviour and concentration improved significantly. This enabled him to succeed in many new school tasks, and he was clearly delighted with his newfound accomplishments. It was becoming increasingly clear how high his level of understanding was, and how his previous lack of achievement had not been due just to intellectual impairment. Attention to his uncontrolled will appears to have been the prerequisite for general progress. During this time (about 12 months), his 'P' level[1] in literacy improved by two (P3 to P5) and numeracy by one (P4 to P5). This was above average for the class, and a considerable step forward from his previous rate of progress.

In summary, although the details were different for each individual child, these cases demonstrate that this approach of interacting directly with the feelings and the will has helped to some extent to bring these children out of their autistic isolation and to improve their ability to learn. When they are able to communicate with others, even if not at the level of complex language, life becomes easier, happier and more fulfilling.

The ability to communicate with other human beings is also seen by Nind and Hewett (2001) as not only essential to the well-being of people, but also as something in the nature of a 'human right'. They state (2001):

> *Communicating seems to be central to being human. Being able to communicate gives us the ability to have relationships, friendships, to know the joy and fulfilment of human interaction. It is that important. When people have communication difficulties, it frequently has a negative effect on their well-being and behaviour. We would say that for people with SLD [severe learning disabilities], developing their communication ability is the most important issue in their lives. It is so important that we can view it virtually as a human right.*

It is hoped that this chapter will give encouragement to the idea that the efforts and commitment of another human being can do much to bring the child who is lonely and isolated through autism back into the human social organism.

## References

Caldwell, P. (2000) *You Don't Know What It's Like.* Brighton: Pavilion.

Damasio, A.R. (1994) *Descartes' Error.* London: Macmillan.

Damasio, A.R. (2000) *The Feeling of What Happens.* London: Vintage.

Frith, U. (1989) *Autism: Explaining the enigma.* Oxford: Blackwell.

Gerland, G. (1997) *A Real Person.* London: Souvenir Press.

Grandin, T. (1997) *'Mind Readers'.* An 'All Illuminations' production for Channel 4.

Hamid, P. and Newport, A. (1989) 'Effect of colour on physical strength and mood in children', *Perceptual and Motor Skills,* 69, 179–185.

Hill, C. (2006) *Communicating through Movement: Sherborne Developmental Movement – towards a broadening perspective.* Clent: Sunfield Publications.

Hobson, R.P. (2002) *The Cradle of Thought.* London: Macmillan.

Holtzapfel, W. (1995) *Children with a Difference.* East Grinstead: Lanthorn Press.

Janert, S. (2000) *Reaching the Young Autistic Child: Reclaiming non-autistic potential through communicative strategies and games.* London: Free Association Books.

Jordan, R. (1996) *Autism: An introductory handbook for practitioners.* Birmingham: University of Birmingham.

Jordan, R. and Powell, S. (1995) *Understanding and Teaching Children with Autism.* Chichester: Wiley.

Lawson, W. (1998) *Life behind Glass.* Lissmore, Australia: Southern Cross University Press.

Nind, M. and Hewett, D. (1994) *Access to Communication.* London: David Fulton.

Nind, M. and Hewett, D. (2001) *A Practical Guide to Intensive Interaction.* Kidderminster: British Institute of Learning Disabilities.

Nordoff, P. and Robbins, C. (1971) *Therapy in Music for Handicapped Children.* New York, NY: Macmillan.

Pauli, P. (2004) *Engaging the Feeling and Will of Children with Autism through the Medium of Colour (Unpublished Ph.D. Thesis).* Birmingham: University of Birmingham.

Pauli, D. (2006) 'Contact through Colour', *Special Children,* 173, 30–33.

Pellegrini, R.J., Schauss, A.G. and Miller, M.E. (1981) 'Room colour and aggression in a criminal detention holding cell: a test of the "tranquillizing pink" hypothesis', *Journal of Orthomolecular Psychiatry,* 1981, 10 (3), 174–181.

Powell, S. (2000) 'Learning about life asocially: the autistic perspective on education'. In: S. Powell (ed.) *Helping Children with Autism to Learn.* London: David Fulton.

Reynell, J.K. and Huntley, M. (1977) *Developmental Language Scales (3).* Windsor: NFER– Nelson.

Russell, J. (1996) *Agency: its role in mental development.* Hove: Erlbaum.

Schauss, A.G. (1979) 'Tranquillising effect of colour reduces aggressive behaviour and potential violence', *Journal of Orthomolecular Psychiatry,* 8, 218–220.

Steiner, R. (1954) *Theosophy.* London: Anthroposophical Publishing Co.

Steiner, R. (1964) *The Philosophy of Freedom.* London: Rudolf Steiner Press.

Steiner, R. (1969) *Knowledge of the Higher Worlds: How is it achieved?* London: Rudolf Steiner Press.

Steiner, R. (1981) *The Renewal of Education.* Forest Row: Steiner Schools Fellowship Publications.

Steiner, R. (1983) *Curative Eurythmy.* London: Rudolf Steiner Press.

Steiner, R. (1984) *Eurythmy as Visible Speech.* London: Rudolf Steiner Press.

Steiner, R. (1988) *The Child's Changing Consciousness and Waldorf Education.* London: Rudolf Steiner Press.

Steiner, R. (1993) *Curative Education.* Bristol: Rudolf Steiner Press.

Trevarthen, C., Aitken, K., Papoudi, D. and Robarts, J. (1998) *Children with Autism: Diagnosis and interventions to meet their needs.* London: Jessica Kingsley.

Verner-Bonds, L. (2002) *New Colour Healing.* London: Vermillion.

Wilson, G.D. (1966) 'Arousal properties of red versus green', *Perceptual and Motor Skills,* 23, 947–949.

Williams, D. (1992) *Nobody Nowhere.* London: Jessica Kingsley.

Williams, D. (1996a) *Autism. An inside-out approach.* London: Jessica Kingsley.

Williams, D. (1996b) *Like Colour to the Blind.* Toronto, Canada: Doubleday.

Wing, L. (1996) *The Autistic Spectrum.* London: Constable.

**Endnote**

[1] Most students at Sunfield work below Level 1 of the National Curriculum, so Qualifications and Curriculum Authority (QCA) performance descriptors or 'P' levels (P1 to P8) are used to assess students' levels of attainment and track their progress over time across a range of subjects. Information about 'P' levels is available online at: http://www.qca.org.uk/8798.html.

# PART 4

# Inclusion in the Community

## CHAPTER 10

# Journeys of Enquiry

## Working with Families in a Research Context

*Barry Carpenter, Sally Conway, Teresa Whitehurst and Elizabeth Attfield*

### The self-defining family

The stereotypical notion of 'the family' (two married parents of the opposite sex, with two children, who rely on the father's income) is a reality for only one family in seven in the European Union at the turn of the millennium (Roll, 1991). Nevertheless, research indicates that, despite anxieties about the destruction of the family, it is the form rather than the function that has changed (Barnett, Clements, Kaplan-Estrin and Fialka, 2003; Blacher and Hatton, 2001). The patriarchal model of the family, which comprised blood relatives and included safety nets for the aged, infirm or other dependent kin, is far less a feature of modern life than it was at the beginning of the last century.

Following the birth of a child with disabilities, the need for the family and the implicit emotional and practical means of support it can offer becomes very great. But does that family have to comprise blood relatives? In our modern mobile society, is this the reality for many families? Demographic trends – for example, the ever-increasing breakdown in marriages – can lead to many reconstituted families. For any of these families, the reality of support may be derived from a 'self-defined family': a flexible family comprising non-blood relatives carrying out the functions traditionally associated with the patriarchal, blood-related family (Carpenter, 2000; see Figure 2.1).

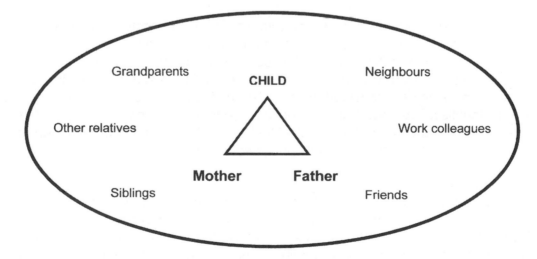

**Figure 10.1. A model of an extended family support network**

Figure 10.1 suggests an extended family-support network that reflects a more appropriate reality for many families than the traditional nuclear model. Patterns of interaction may vary within this group. Some may revolve around the triad of primary support – child, mother, father. They may also centre on a lone parent with a child with a disability, who seeks and receives various types of support from any of the identified groups.

In order to provide effective services for our families, we must understand and respect them. Roles in families differ according to situation and culture, and they may not fit stereotypical assumptions. The key to providing support is to listen to the families themselves.

A family-focused organisation should aim to work in partnership with its families, and nurture the bonds between them and their child rather than creating barriers. In order to facilitate a positive and productive relationship, the organisation must first identify the needs of its families and establish a reciprocal partnership that both parties contribute to equally. Sunfield adopted this approach to working with its families in 1998, and has gone on to develop a family services department to facilitate the work.

**The Family Charter**
A Family Charter was developed in 1998 to provide families with a tangible statement of expectation from the organisation. The Charter provides a list of expectations that parents are invited to have of staff at Sunfield – respect; honesty and integrity; confidentiality; regular communication; empathy; supportive listening; information and advice; partnership and a safe environment for their child – and goes on to illustrate the practical ways in which each of these will be delivered. The document is the basis of all work with families at Sunfield, and aims to demonstrate to families Sunfield's commitment to understanding and supporting their needs.

**Family surveys**
In order to develop effective ways of delivering services, Sunfield had to gain an insight into the needs of its families. In 1998, a postal questionnaire was commissioned to obtain the family view on all aspects of Sunfield's practices, including the potential development of a Family Services department. It was carried out by an independent research consultant to ensure anonymity and encourage families to be honest and open in their responses.

The feedback provided the organisation with a blend of quantitative and qualitative data with which to work. The quantitative data provided statistical evidence such as where families lived and the distance they travelled to visit their son or daughter, how often they visited, how many phone calls they received from staff at Sunfield, etc., while the qualitative data provided the story behind the statistics – the experiences of individual families. Together, both sets of data suggested the contents of an action plan that would address the deficits, identified by families, of the approach then used at Sunfield and develop services that could meet families' needs.

**Family Services**
As a result of the survey work, Sunfield developed a new department that focused on the co-ordination and monitoring of family support across the organisation. It began in 1999 with the appointment of a family liaison worker and the opening of a Family Centre (a self-contained flat where families could stay with their Sunfield-based son or daughter). It has now developed into a department that employs three staff who have a dedicated role in supporting the specific needs of all family members.

Siblings were identified as having specific needs that differed from parents, and as such needed a tailored programme of support. The Sibling Support Project entitled 'Getting Connected' was developed to offer activities and events that would provide them with a framework of support from both staff and fellow siblings.

In response to the feedback from the initial survey, a focus group of parents were invited to join Family Services staff and senior managers to design a staff training package to address the deficits identified by families. This produced a course entitled 'Talking to families; listening to families' which focused on developing staff skills in communicating with families, and increasing their understanding of the needs of the whole family, including siblings, grandparents, friends, etc. This has become an integral part of the foundation training for all new staff. The training has enabled Sunfield to deliver the organisational aims for working with families which are rooted in a specific family perspective. It has nurtured a family-focused ethos throughout the organisation by enabling staff to share the experiences and needs of families via messages from each of the family surveys.

## Partnership through 'experiential enquiry'

The journey that families take with their son or daughter with special needs is often fraught with difficulties and battles. In order to support them to navigate their life's path, it is important to understand their experiences and expectations. 'Experiential enquiry' roots the research process in the family perspective, and alters the balance between researcher and family, thus developing an empowering research partnership. A family-focused research model demands active participation by family members to reflect truly the essence of partnership.

The following are a series of case studies which illuminate how partnership has developed through experiential enquiry.

## Case Study 1: 'Celebrating families': an inclusive model of family-centred training

Whalley and Chandler (2001) point out that many parent education programmes have traditionally been based on a deficit model ('disabled families', for instance), and have over-emphasised professionalism, thus disempowering parents. These approaches were not sensitive to the family context, the ebb and flow of family dynamics, the need for families to 'have a life'. Such expert approaches have been widely condemned (McConachie, 1997), and a position of 'equivalent expertise' between parent and professional has been advocated (e.g. Beveridge, 2000, 2005).

Thus the notion of 'Celebrating families' was conceived at Sunfield: a week of training days not solely for parents, but for grandparents, aunts and uncles, younger brothers and sisters, and older siblings. There was a true recognition that, while bonded in a common, self-defined family, each family member had their own perspective, their own set of needs.

### *The training model*

The training model was therefore underpinned by a deep-seated commitment to families, manifested in five key themes which ran through the entire week:

- The notion of the self-defined family

- Recognition of family diversity and family uniqueness

- Awareness of the needs and contributions of *all* family members

■ Celebration of the resources that families find within themselves

■ The vital role that families play in educating professionals.

In response to these five key themes, the detail of the training model was developed. The following features were seen as critical to the model:

■ The week would include something for every family member, no matter how the family defined itself

■ The emphasis of the week would be on sharing and celebrating families' strengths

■ The programme would be led by a facilitator experienced in supporting families and committed to family-focused work

■ Family members themselves would be invited to host the events and present their perspectives

■ The programme would include a conference for professionals, at which family members would have the opportunity to be the educators.

### The role of family members

One of the most important and most powerful aspects of the training model was the role that family members played in hosting and presenting the events. Given the five key themes, this emphasis on family involvement was seen as a critical feature of the programme. Finding at least 10 family members willing to host and/or speak during the week might have been a challenge. In the event, however, parents, grand-parents and siblings showed an eagerness to participate that clearly validates the basic assumptions underpinning the week of events: families want to be involved and listened to. They want to have the opportunity to tell their stories, to be recognised for their resourcefulness and commitment, and to share with others some of their wisdom and experience.

### Format of the week

The programme took place over eight days to include two Saturdays: one dedicated to young siblings and one to fathers. The days in between offered events for other family members and a conference day for professionals.

The format for each day was broadly similar, with the keynote speaker setting the theme for the selected audience in an opening address. That theme was then expanded upon by additional speakers and in discussion groups and workshop sessions. The days for family members were constructed to fit within the school day. In this way, they acknowledged family responsibilities that had to be met, while giving ample opportunity both for formal discussion of key issues and a chance to chat more informally over a lunch.

Taking the week as a whole, each day could stand alone as an opportunity to explore family-related issues from a variety of perspectives. But the cumulative effect for those lucky enough to be attending the whole week was that of adding layer on layer to the complexity of family life. One mother who had participated in the week said how much she had enjoyed getting together with others, and finding out how much they had in common. She had experienced the week as a truly empowering event for parents. It was intensive and inclusive, fulfilling the family-oriented philosophy and aims outlined earlier in this chapter.

### Conclusion to Case Study 1

The outcomes and successes of 'Celebrating families' suggested that our traditional role-definitions of the family are no longer valid and can hinder professional interactions. The quality of dialogue between families and professionals during the week profoundly reshaped and refocused attitudes, particularly for the professionals. It enabled them to shift their thinking away from just 'parents' to 'families', and to realise the inherent and lifelong power for support that a family has towards a person with a disability. For as Winton (1990; cited in Carpenter, 2001) states:

> *Families are big, small, extended, nuclear, multigenerational, with one parent, two parents and grand parents. We live under one roof or many. A family can be as temporary as a few weeks, as permanent as forever. We become part of a family by birth, adoption, marriage, or from a desire for mutual support. A family is a culture unto itself, with different values and unique ways of realising its dreams. Together our families become the source of our rich cultural heritage and spiritual diversity. Our families create a neighbourhoods, communities, states and nations.*

And families are to be celebrated!

### Case Study 2: The experiences of siblings who have a brother or sister with special needs living away from the family home

Traditional views have portrayed parents as the 'family' while excluding wider family members such as siblings, grandparents, etc. Siblings are often known as the 'forgotten' family member, and as such their contributions and opinions largely remain unheard.

The relationship between siblings can be understated, but will often span their lifetime. It is therefore extremely important that these young people are made to feel valued during their childhood, so that they can journey into adulthood alongside their sibling with special needs with confidence and pride. Many siblings can find themselves as the key advocate for their brother or sister at the point that their parents are no longer able to carry out this role. This may not be a role that they would have chosen for themselves, and certainly it is one that many are not prepared for.

Sunfield values the positive contribution that siblings can and do make to the life of their brother or sister with special needs. It recognises the need for the sibling to be acknowledged and places great emphasis on understanding the sibling experience in order to develop services that will support them.

A project was undertaken to investigate the specific experiences and feelings of siblings who have a brother or sister with special needs living in a residential school (Conway and O'Neill, 2004). The study explored their recollection of life at home with their sibling, their perspective of their life since their brother or sister had moved to Sunfield, and their perceptions of the future.

All siblings of Sunfield students up to the age of 19 were invited to take part in the study. An introductory letter was sent to parents who were required to provide written consent for their son or daughter to be interviewed. Semi-structured interviews took place within the family home to enable siblings to feel more comfortable and relaxed within their own environment. All interviews were tape-recorded following verbal agreement from the participants, who received reassurance regarding anonymity, confidentiality and the opportunity to withdraw from the study at any point. Interviews were transcribed and analysed for themes.

Key themes informed the planning of future services and support for siblings with a focus on promoting involvement in all areas of their brother or sister's life at Sunfield, specifically by encouraging them to contribute to their brother or sister's review meeting, developing the existing Sibling Support Project and inviting them to engage in Sunfield's family-focused training programme.

**Case Study 3: Families as research partners: working together to explore family experiences of their induction to a residential setting**
Sunfield continued to seek the views of its families using survey as a tool and conducted a further two surveys in 2000 and 2002. This provided a measure for the effectiveness of the action plans and evaluated the changes that had been made and the new services that had been developed.

By 2002, the survey had become a consolidatory tool for the rapid developments that had taken place within the organisation and had become the catalyst for exploring future issues in greater depth using an alternative methodology.

In 2004, a research project to look at a specific aspect of Family Services was devised in place of the usual survey. The focus of the research was to explore the experiences of families at the point their son or daughter came to the residential setting.

*Model*
The research used as its basis a model developed by Dr Fran Russell (2004) which adopted a parent participatory approach. A parent advisory group (PAG) was formed which comprised three parents who had been invited to ensure every aspect of the research was rooted in the family perspective. The three parents forming the PAG were selected on the basis of their availability and their proximity to Sunfield. As a national provision, it was felt that too great a burden would be placed upon families who resided any great distance from school. This approach fostered collaboration with parents as research partners ensuring that parents led the focus of this family-based research.

*Transdisciplinary approach*
A whole-organisation approach was adopted in order to encourage staff participation from all departments. Eleven staff volunteered and were recruited as researchers. Training was provided in the form of a workshop which delivered a session on appropriate research methods, role play to provide an opportunity for practising interview techniques, and an afternoon seminar with Fran Russell illustrating the application of the model proposed.

*Structure of the Project Team*
The three core elements of the project structure involved: a project management team, comprising the chief executive, research officer and head of Family Services; the PAG; and the staff researchers. These three groups undertook specific roles in the project within a framework for design implementation and analysis (see Figure 10.2).

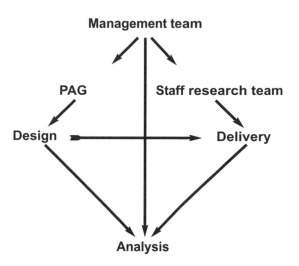

**Figure 10.2. Framework for design implementation and analysis**

### Design

The question posed by the organisation was: 'How is the induction process for families?' The PAG was then charged with the task of designing open-ended questions that probed specific areas of the developing induction process. The areas identified were:

- Families' most powerful memory of the time of their induction to Sunfield
- The most helpful aspect of the induction
- The least helpful aspect of the induction
- What gave parents the most confidence
- The process in the context of the needs of the whole family
- The appropriateness and usefulness of the 'Link family system'
- Suggested alterations/amendments to the process.

A decision was taken to undertake face-to-face, semi-structured interviews as opposed to telephone interviews due to the emotional nature of the subject and to capture the depth of individual experiences. Although this is a labour-intensive and time-consuming method of collecting data, it was felt that families should be allowed time to process their thoughts and feelings in a relaxed environment, enabling them to articulate a more detailed account of their personal recollections.

### Delivery

All families were invited to participate in the research project. Twenty families agreed to take part in the project and were matched with a research pair. Each research pair comprised an experienced researcher and a newly trained member of staff. Although this process seemed relatively straightforward, the logistics and practicalities, linked with the geographical constraints, made this extremely complex.

### Data collection

All interviews were tape-recorded, with permission from the family, and then transcribed. Transcripts were returned to the families for validation.

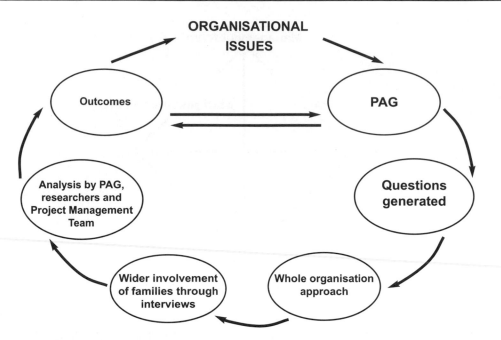

**Figure 10.3. Cycle of the research partnership**

## *Analysis*

A framework for analysing the transcripts was developed by the management team to ensure the cohesion of analysis between the stakeholder groups (management team, PAG and researchers). Each group identified consistent themes emerging from the family voice. The validity of this data was strengthened not only by the triangulation method employed, but further through external scrutiny via an independent research consultant. These themes then informed outcomes and action points.

A final meeting with the PAG corroborated the outcomes and action points ensuring that the whole process remained rooted in the family perspective, while answering an organisational need (see Figure 10.3)

## *Outcomes and action points*

Following on from the previous survey work an action plan was designed to ensure that organisational activity was influenced by family need. Key points from this project were incorporated into a half-day, training seminar to articulate the organisational response to the family voice.

## *Conclusion to Case Study 3*

This piece of research clearly demonstrated the capacity for parents as researchers (Carpenter, 1997). They not only contributed to the research process but led, analysed and evaluated, thus making them true and equal research partners. The approach was liberating and enabled the family voice, views and aspirations to be heard and listened to, and their outlooks to broaden the traditional research perspective.

## The family experience as research partners

The principle of equal partnership had been the cornerstone of the development of Family Services from the outset, with the involvement of Sunfield's families in all aspects of their son or daughter's life and the life of the school as the pivotal theme.

Creating a family-based research model, in order to illuminate partnership through experiential enquiry, represents a further step in ensuring that the family voice is heard in all areas of service development at Sunfield.

It is important that all family members have opportunities to be involved in training and research in order to share the diverse perspectives of mothers, fathers and siblings, and the family training provided under the banner of 'Celebrating families' created just those opportunities. Mothers talked and listened to other mothers, giving each other emotional support and understanding. Fathers were able to share their concerns away from the gaze of their female partners, enabling them to say more than they ever would in other circumstances and having their opinions valued by other men in a similar situation. Adult siblings were enabled to voice their unique concerns regarding the very special and long-lasting role they have to play in the lives of their disabled brothers and sisters, and grandparents, other relatives, friends and neighbours were offered a chance to play a part in the wider definition of family life touched by disability.

Another vital aspect to be considered in involving families is the recognition that all families are different, and that the level of involvement they are able and willing to undertake also differs. Not everyone has the time, confidence or inclination to give their views by attending family training. In recognition of this, family surveys and transition questionnaires were sent through the post, and the semi-structured interviews were home-based. The aim was for everyone to be able to participate at the level that suited them, which was greatly valued by families.

The PAG which guided the research process on induction, and was also involved in consultation on reviewing the Family Charter, comprised three parents who all lived close enough to Sunfield to be actively involved at all stages of the project, who had the required level of understanding of the process not to feel overwhelmed by the idea of themselves as research partners and welcomed that degree of involvement, whereas other parents might feel daunted by that level of participation.

## Conclusion

While many family members have had the opportunity to articulate their thoughts and feelings, and contribute to the service that Sunfield offers to families, there are some whose voices have not yet been heard. Sunfield constantly tries to find new ways of enabling all families and family members to contribute, while acknowledging their right to choose how and if they become involved. Empowering families to have a voice, and ensuring this voice is heard, respected and responded to, keeps our organisational process rooted in the continual changing needs of our families.

## References

Barnett D., Clements M., Kaplan-Estrin, M. and Fialka J. (2003) 'Building new dreams: supporting parents' adaptation to their child with special needs', *Infants and Young Children*, 16, (3), 184–200.

Beveridge, S. (2000) 'Implementing partnership with parents in schools'. In: S. Wolfendale (ed.) *Working with Parents of SEN Children after the Code of Practice*. London: David Fulton.

Beveridge, S. (2005) *Children, Families and Schools: Developing partnerships for inclusive education*. London: RoutledgeFalmer.

Blacher, J. and Hatton, C. (2001) 'Current perspectives on family research in mental retardation', *Current Opinion in Psychiatry*, 14, 477–482.

Carpenter, B. (ed.) (1997) *Families in Context: Emerging trends in family support and early intervention*. London: David Fulton.

Carpenter, B. (2000) 'Sustaining the family: meeting the needs of families of children with disabilities', *British Journal of Special Education*, 27 (3), 135–144.

Carpenter, B. (2001) 'Enabling partnerships: families and school'. In: B. Carpenter, R. Ashdown and K. Bovair (eds) *Enabling Access: Effective teaching and learning for pupils with learning difficulties*. London: David Fulton.

Conway, S. and O'Neill, K. (2004) 'Home and away', *Learning Disability Practice*, 7 (7), 34–38.

McConachie, H. (1977) 'Do UK services really support parents?', *Opportunity*, 15, 1–2.

Roll, J. (1991) *What is a Family?: Benefit models and social realities*. London: Family Policy Studies Centre.

Russell, F. (2004) 'Partnership with parents of disabled children in research?', *Journal of Research in Special Educational Needs*, 4 (2), 74–81.

Whalley, M. and Chandler, T. (2001) 'Parents and staff as co-educators: "parents" means fathers too'. In: M. Whalley and the Pen Green Centre Team (eds) *Involving Parents in their Children's Learning*. London: Paul Chapman.

Winton, R. (1990) *Report of the New Mexico Home Memorial 5 Task Force on Young Children and Families: Report 1*. New Mexico: New Mexico Home Memorial 5 Task Force on Young Children and Families.

# CHAPTER 11

# Changing Perspectives on Disability and Inclusion

## 'The Monkey King' Arts Project

*Teresa Whitehurst*

### Introduction

There will always be young people for whom the experience of education in a mainstream environment is not an option. Young people with special learning needs may require a range of expertise and tailored teaching approaches to enable them to participate in school life. However, mainstream and special education should not be seen as mutually exclusive, and there is much that both parties can gain through working inclusively.

Social inclusion has been incorporated into our everyday vocabulary, and refers to 'an array of strategies and initiatives designed to improve the life chances of disadvantaged groups in our society' (Kinder and Harland, 2004). Initially, the educational focus of inclusion centred on the benefits afforded to young people with intellectual disabilities through working with their mainstream peers (Department of Education and Science (DES), 1978). A more balanced approach is now taken, recognising that 'all children, wherever they are educated, need to be able to learn, play and develop alongside each other within their local community of schools' (Department for Education and Skills (DfES), 2004). Experiences of inclusive situations play a major role in the education of Sunfield's students. However:

> ...inclusion is about much more than the type of school that children attend: it is about the quality of their experience; how they are helped to learn, achieve and participate fully in the life of the school. (DfES, 2004)

### Listening to all the voices

Creating an inclusive society is not only a goal of policy-makers, but also of practitioners who seek to ensure that all children and young people, whatever their circumstances, are afforded the same life chances as their peers. It remains the case, however, that those with severe and complex intellectual disabilities pose challenges to inclusion. The voices of many stakeholders in this process, particularly within the world of education, can clearly be heard. Many studies which explore effective educational inclusion choose as their primary focus the views of head teachers, class teachers, teaching assistants, student teachers and parents of pupils (Fox, Farrell and Davis, 2004; Hastings and Oakford, 2003). A number of studies focus upon the views, attitudes and changing perceptions of mainstream pupils (Beveridge, 1996; Shevlin and O'Moore, 2000; Yazbeck, McVilly and Parmenter, 2004), but silent among these accounts of inclusion are the voices of those with profound disabilities.

## The research project

Sunfield is privileged to be set within a supportive and involved community and has enjoyed a close working relationship with its local mainstream schools for a number of years. A two-year, Arts-based, inclusion project enabled young people from Sunfield and one of the schools to work together. This project took the form of a musical performance based upon the tale of 'The Monkey King', an ancient story from Sri Lanka. The project involved six students from Sunfield supported on a one-to-one basis by a range of staff from the residential care, education and psychology departments, and 24 mainstream pupils accompanied by their teachers.

The production was led by professionals from a theatre company for actors with mild/moderate intellectual disabilities. While the concept of the performance remained true to the original tale, the young people were encouraged to develop their own ideas about how the story should be portrayed and to use their own skills to depict the scene. This played to the strengths of the differing abilities of the group as a whole. Rehearsals took place on a weekly basis, with both schools being utilised as venues. Initially, rehearsals focused on 'ice-breakers' and large group work to enable all the young people to familiarise themselves with their new surroundings and their peers. As time progressed, the large group was separated into smaller units consisting of one student from Sunfield, with their support worker, and three pupils from the mainstream school. At the end of the two-year period, the project culminated in a major production presented at the Hippodrome Theatre in Birmingham, attracting large audiences at each of its five performances.

## Research design

The research aimed to evaluate the mechanisms which were important in enabling young people, both with and without disabilities, to work collaboratively on the Arts-based project and to enable professionals to achieve a greater understanding of what it means to work inclusively. A qualitative approach was adopted, involving semi-structured interviews with the young people involved.

The aims of the evaluation were articulated in three research questions:

- How were perceptions held by mainstream pupils changed as a result of working alongside peers with autistic spectrum disorder (ASD) and severe and complex intellectual disabilities

- What impact did the project have upon the young people with ASD and severe and complex intellectual disabilities

- What did pupils think is important when working on an inclusion project?

Questions reflected epistemological and ontological assumptions that knowledge is constructed and can be known only within the reality of those who have lived those experiences. The questions did not seek to measure but to understand.

## Phases of the evaluation

There were three phases of data collection and evaluation.

*Phase 1*: Individual interviews were conducted with each of the mainstream pupils, within their own school. Pupils had been working on the project at this stage for approximately 14 months. This phase was designed to explore mainstream pupils' perceptions of, and attitudes towards, students with severe and complex intellectual disabilities and to explore the extent to which these had altered as a result of working collaboratively.

*Phase 2*: Once the collection of data from the initial interviews had been completed and the project concluded, mainstream pupils were revisited to investigate what they thought had been important in facilitating a change in their perceptions. Building upon the outcomes of Phase 1, they were also asked to explore the elements they thought were important to working inclusively.

*Phase 3*: Individual interviews with students from Sunfield were conducted, within their own school, with assistance from the speech and language department. This phase focused on finding out what students with intellectual disabilities had felt was important to them about working on the project.

Care was taken at each stage of the process to ensure that stringent criteria in relation to access to participants, informed consent, context/environment for interviews, and interpretation and analysis of data were adopted and complied with (Robson, 2002).

## Obtaining the views of young people

Eliciting the views of participants, particularly those of young people and more specifically young people with intellectual disabilities, warrants extra consideration (Lewis and Porter, 2004). Beveridge (1996) encourages caution in the interpretation of responses of young people to questioning by adults 'particularly when school is both the context for and the focus of the questions which are asked'. Separate issues are pertinent in relation to eliciting the views of students with severe intellectual disabilities. Generally speaking, resources to undertake such a task are limited. Porter (2003) points out that:

> *...although the policy literature in particular draws attention to the vital importance of eliciting the opinions of service users, it is mainly silent on how this can be meaningfully undertaken with those individuals who have limited language.*

Similarly, Lewis (2002 in Lewis, 2004) suggests that: 'we lack evidence concerning the authenticity, credibility and reliability of particular methods for exploring the views of children with learning difficulties'. Previous research warns that students with intellectual disabilities may have a tendency to acquiesce to the suggestions of others (Stalker, 1998).

In light of these challenges, it is important to seek methods of eliciting views which have been demonstrated as generating genuine responses.

### Resources used to obtain the views of young people with disabilities

Organisationally, Sunfield is in an ideal position to gain insight into the experiences of inclusion from students with profound and complex intellectual disabilities through the on-site speech and language team, who work in a variety of modalities to encourage and enhance communication. The team work to assess each student, finding and developing the best method of communication for the individual. This may be based on objects of reference, photographs, symbols or, indeed, a combination of all three. Communication is approached in its broadest sense using all modalities encompassing information which is generated verbally, through gesture, through body language, facial expression and behaviours. Students' capabilities in terms of their expressive and receptive language skills differ, and these variances are acknowledged and responded to by the speech and language team.

Essential to the process of eliciting responses and in order to communicate, 'a researcher must understand the child's communication capabilities and provide mechanisms in which the communicative exchange can take place' (Martinsen and Von Tetzchner, 1996, in Detheridge, 2000). This guidance provided a framework consisting of two key elements: that speech and language support was central to this phase of the research with therapists' expertise in each student's unique communication system, and that a mechanism to facilitate this level of complex communication exchange should be in place.

In order to maximise the reliability of the students' responses, interviews were facilitated by the speech and language department, conducted by members of staff who knew the students well and, equally, who were known to the student, and took place in an environment which was familiar. Mechanisms used to facilitate the complex communication exchange were individually dependent upon the student's preferred method of engaging and communicating. Through liaison with the speech and language team, the interview schedule was carefully negotiated to ensure that the young people would be fully supported by the correct communication method for their needs, the correct supporting photographic material and, most importantly, that the questions were posed in a way that the student could understand. The skills of the speech and language team were crucial at this stage.

Based upon these negotiations, it was decided that all students would benefit from having photographs to help them understand the context of the questions and identify their feelings. All interviews were therefore supported by photographs of the drama production, including pictures of all the adults and young people involved, taken during both rehearsals and performance. They were taken at a variety of locations including Sunfield, the mainstream middle school and the theatre.

In response to the students' differing needs, one interview was dependent upon verbal questioning supported by the photographs and Makaton, one interview was purely verbal and the remaining interviews were conducted using a selection of photographs and 'Talking Mats' (Murphy, 1997).

*Talking Mats*
'Talking Mats' were designed as a resource which was not intended to replace someone's communication aid, but to be used in conjunction with their normal mode of communication, together with other non-verbal methods such as facial expression and gesture (Cameron, Watson and Murphy, 2004). The aim of the resource is to enable those with communication difficulties to select concrete responses (e.g. in the form of pictures) and place them on a 'mat' in a way which demonstrates their preferences and feelings, using categories of 'Like' and 'Dislike'. This is a particularly useful tool for students with a diagnosis of ASD who rely on visual clues and concrete symbolism. This resource had been utilised by both the speech and language therapist and the resident counsellor at Sunfield for some time with a range of students. Therefore, in addition to its inherent benefits, it was both reliable and familiar as a technique to enable students to express ideas, feelings and emotions.

## Evaluation findings

### Phase 1: Did mainstream pupils' perceptions change during 'The Monkey King' project?

Initial interviews held with mainstream pupils were conducted as individual interviews, with one researcher paired with one pupil. It was anticipated that this would enable the pupil to respond in a more relaxed and open way, not being judged by other peers present. The areas explored within the initial interviews aimed to differentiate between *knowledge* and *perception* both prior to working collaboratively and as a result of working collaboratively. They also sought to explore the extent of internalised learning. The reason for this distinction being incorporated into the project was to enable the research to explore not only the extent to which attitudes towards people with disabilities may change, but further to consider what elements are important to making inclusion work for young people. What information do mainstream pupils need before embarking on such a venture? Is it necessary to have knowledge/facts regarding disability, or is the success of an inclusion project functionally more reliant upon perceptions held by the young people?

**Table 11.1. Interview questions for Phase 1: mainstream pupils**

| |
|---|
| • What was your knowledge-base regarding disability/ASD? |
| • What do you think of people who are disabled? |
| • Do you know any more about these disabilities now? |
| • Have your feelings towards people with disabilities changed? |
| • How has this project helped you develop as an individual? |

*Analysis of interview data*

Analysis needed to be grounded in the participants' own accounts. It was decided that it would be based primarily upon the discovery of regularities: themes which emerged from the data in a regular pattern and which could be identified within all of the texts. This analysis was conducted in a similar style to that of a grounded theory approach. The aim of grounded theory is to generate a theory to explain what is central to the data (Robson, 2002). In this way, the theory is allowed to emerge from the texts. This enabled the accounts produced by the mainstream pupils to construct knowledge, and any theories relating to their construction of disability were allowed to emerge.

The text was broken down into manageable units by considering each of the answers as one set of data; for example, all answers to Question 3 were analysed to identify regularly occurring themes.

Example: Question 3: 'What did you think about these people?'

This question aimed to elicit mainstream pupils' perceptions of people with intellectual disabilities and ASD prior to the inclusion project – investigating what pupils *thought* of people with disabilities rather than what they *knew.*

The following are an example of responses from mainstream pupils:

- *I thought they were strange and different – they were strangers and I wasn't used to them, but they were different to normal strangers*

- *They are completely different to us*

- *Normal. They need more help than others, but they are the same as you*

- *They are normal people who need extra help.*

Initially, this data was coded for 'Perceptions of difference' (PD) and 'Perceptions of normality' (PN). These were clearly evident themes running through the responses. A tally was taken, and 4 of the 24 respondents referred to the students with disabilities as 'normal'.

However, it was clear that, whether the mainstream pupils perceived the students with disabilities as 'different' or 'normal', they were very concerned with their own abilities to manage the situation. Many of the comments they made appeared to connect their perceptions of students with disabilities with their own feelings around a lack of preparation for the experience. Pupils spoke of their feelings of inadequacy regarding their own abilities, feelings of unfamiliarity both with the situation and with the students with intellectual disabilities and feelings of vulnerability:

- *I was frightened, and not sure what to do*

- *I was frightened because I didn't know how they would react*

- *I didn't know how to approach them – I was apprehensive – didn't know what to expect from them*

- *The first time I saw them, I was shocked. How are you meant to act around them? What are you meant to do? I was worried*

- *Not sure whether I could talk to them or whether they would attack me.*

From analysis of the data set, further categories were identified and coded. What appeared to emerge were mainstream pupils' perceptions of difference and normality, together with their own feelings of inadequacy (I), within a context that was unfamiliar (U), which left them unable to predict (P) the future with any sense of certainty. The ways in which theory emerged from this set of data could not have been predicted at the outset of the project. It had been anticipated that mainstream pupils would respond to this particular question by discussing how they perceived young people with disabilities. This was evidently explored by the pupils initially, with reference to perceptions of normality and difference, but they then moved on to discuss their own position in relation to that.

Through analysis of the remaining interview responses, it was possible to build up a picture which demonstrated a change in pupils' perceptions as a result of the project. This change was positive, but clearly dependent upon being able to integrate and work alongside students with disabilities, to gain practical skills and knowledge, and to feel supported by adults who knew the students with disabilities well and could demonstrate many of the skills the mainstream pupils required to interact with them.

Through utilising the grounded theory approach, it was possible to code and identify statements which gave rise to themes. These themes were then reduced to an overarching concept which addressed the original research question. It was possible to

Identify that, prior to working inclusively, mainstream pupils had held views about young people with intellectual disabilities and ASD which were based on poor factual knowledge and little experience. Mainstream pupils perceived themselves (not originally a question on the interview schedule!) as inadequately skilled. Through working on the project, they gained practical knowledge (as opposed to factual knowledge) which helped them to overcome those initial fears and to work effectively alongside students with disabilities. In addition to providing an answer to the original research question, this method enabled a concept to emerge regarding prerequisites which may enable mainstream pupils to change their perceptions and work inclusively.

*Dominant and emergent themes from Phase 1*

1. Dominant theme: limited factual knowledge

- *I didn't know whether they would have mild or severe dyslexia.*

- *My cousin had brain damage, so I had some explanation of autism.*

- *I knew because one of my family members had a brain tumour and was unable to do things.*

2. Dominant theme: mainstream pupils did not see young people with intellectual disabilities as people

- *I knew they existed.*

- *I'd seen a couple of them before, but not really worked with them.*

- *I'd seen people like that at [a local shopping centre].*

- *Sometimes I didn't see them as people.*

3. Dominant theme: perceptions of difference

- *I thought they were strange and different – they were strangers, and I wasn't used to them, but they were different to normal strangers.*

- *They are completely different to us.*

4. Dominant theme: lack of understanding

- *They weren't like us – I thought they would be more delicate.*

- *I thought they'd be walking around not knowing anything.*

- *I thought they were different, and I was scared to touch them… I thought I may get what they get if I touched them.*

5. Dominant theme: questioning their own abilities

- *I was frightened and not sure what to do… I didn't know how they would react.*

- *I didn't know how to approach them – I was apprehensive – didn't know what to expect from them.*

- *The first time I saw them, I was shocked.*

- *How are you meant to act around them? What are you meant to do? I was worried.*

- *Not sure whether I could talk to them or whether they would attack me.*

6. Emergent theme: practical vs factual

- *I think knowing more about them helps – like knowing what they can and can't do.*

■ *I know what they're like, so I can cope with it.*

■ *I don't know more about their condition, but more about the person.*

■ *I think they are normal people, and I treat them exactly the same.*

7. Emergent theme: shift in understanding

■ *They have problems, but they're all different. You have to know each one to know how to treat them and how to talk to them.*

■ *They're normal – you see past the disability, and don't just judge them by that.*

### Table 11.2. Summary of findings from Phase 1: mainstream pupils

> • Perceptions of young people with disabilities were more positive, but this was not related to increased knowledge of disabilities *per se*.
>
> • Practical skills acquired were more important than factual knowledge.
>
> • Pupils' own abilities to manage the situation were more important than their understanding of disability.
>
> • Feelings of their own lack of preparedness and the unfamiliarity of the situation did not enable them to predict the future context.

### Phase 2: What facilitated a change in perception and what do pupils think is important to facilitate inclusion?

Follow-up interviews with the mainstream pupils were conducted as group interviews, as opposed to individual interviews, as the pupils had formed strong alliances within the groups designated for 'The Monkey King' performance. It was felt that the strong group ties which had facilitated bonding between the young people through a shared experience would enable them to feel supported and confident to share understandings with the researchers. Findings from Phase 1 provided the framework for the interview schedule and findings were fed back to the pupils for validation. Phase 2 focused upon the mechanisms which had facilitated a change in perception, and factors which were important to the young people involved in the inclusion project.

### Table 11.3. Phase 2 interview questions: mainstream pupils

> • What helped you overcome your initial concerns?
>
> • What did you enjoy about working on the project?
>
> • What did you find difficult about working on the project?
>
> • Would you like to work with students with intellectual disabilities again?
>
> • What kind of things are helpful for pupils and teachers to know before embarking upon an inclusion project?

*How do perceptions change?*
It was clear from interviews in Phase 1 that mainstream pupils had been able to make the transition from a place where they felt awkward, unprepared, worried and vulnerable to a place where they could comfortably interact and work alongside students with disabilities. It was important to investigate what had helped them to make this journey – how had they been supported and what mechanisms had been important to facilitate this transition?

*Dominant themes from Phase 2:*
1. Dominant theme: role models
Pupils felt that the whole process of getting to know the young people from Sunfield, gradually over a long period and consistently, was important. Through working with the young people and watching staff who knew the children with disabilities well, they were able to copy the behaviour of staff, learn new communication strategies, and find out things they had in common. Mainstream pupils had been surprised at the level of autonomy demonstrated by the students with disabilities – that staff had encouraged the students to employ their own calming strategies, for example. Building upon this, the mainstream pupils recognised and felt empowered by the knowledge of staff working with the students at Sunfield:

■ *You got to know them more…it helped working with [M.]…if there were problems then you looked at staff for the way they worked with him*

■ *It was helpful with the Sunfield workers – the people with the children told you all about the children… We could watch the way they were, and how they spoke to them – we picked up on that*

■ *We saw how the Sunfield people worked with them, and put it together with how we would do things – it was like child-to-child bonding.*

2. Dominant theme: pupil 'mind set'
Pupils stated that the performance and the opportunity to work with students with intellectual disabilities were the things they had enjoyed most about the project. However, they commented that when they had first been told of the project by their school a lot of pupils volunteered who later withdrew after they had attended the first session:

■ *With the original group at the very beginning of the project lots of them left because they were frightened of the Sunfield kids – they just dropped out. When [other pupils from the local middle school] came to watch the performance, they were scared because they didn't understand.*

Importantly, this pupil goes on to say:

■ *When something is different people fear it.*

Clearly, the group of pupils who committed themselves to the project possessed certain attributes despite their feelings of inadequacy, unfamiliarity and lack of skills:

■ *Nothing was challenging – unless you have a challenging angle, it's not challenging. You've got to be willing to give it a go.*

<u>3. Dominant theme: teachers and pupils working together</u>
Sometimes pupils find it difficult to say what helped them work together in an inclusive way because questions are phrased subjectively – they are too close to the situation and may avoid answering objectively. To enable objective answers to be elicited, the groups were presented with a scenario whereby pupils were asked to give advice to a local school whose pupils were about to embark upon an inclusion project. Pupils divided their advice into that which related to pupils and that which related to teachers:

*Pupils*
Responses again related to practical skills/knowledge; being friendly, having patience and getting to know the students were all prioritised:

■ *Start off friendly – get to know them – don't ignore them because it will make it harder later*

■ *Don't expect too much from them, because they might not be able to do it*

■ *You must speak first – initiate the interaction*

■ *Talk to them as you would your friends.*

*Teachers*
Pupils felt it was very important that the teaching staff at the mainstream school were aware of the level of disability of the students, were prepared and able to adapt to the situation by using a different set of resources, and that the mainstream pupils could look to, and feel empowered by, their teaching staff:

■ *The teachers also need to know more – the teachers told [D.] off but children like [D.] are not the same as us so they shouldn't use the same technique – it's not helpful*

■ *We needed our teachers to guide and reassure us – we wanted them to give more practical help and more involvement in what we were doing.*

**Table 11.4. Summary of findings from Phase 2 – mainstream pupils**

| |
| --- |
| • Having role models, sustained contact and time to get to know individuals empowered pupils. |
| • Having the right attitude/mind set is important. |
| • Both teachers and pupils should be prepared to work inclusively. |

*Conclusion to Phases 1 and 2*
Clearly there is a need to prepare mainstream pupils well before embarking upon an inclusion project. However, this principle is not restricted solely to pupils, but must extend to a whole-school ethos approach, involving teachers as well as pupils. Inclusion must develop as a dynamic process in which teachers engage (Carpenter, 2001). Inclusion, as such, is therefore an evolutionary process: 'it is a pervasive approach intended to influence, develop and change not only schools but also Society itself (Carpenter and Shevlin, 2004). If we can empower young people with the skills and resources they need to be able to work alongside young people with disabilities and, in doing so, can help them to move away from perceptions of

difference based on uninformed judgments to perceptions of understanding gained from experience, we can help to create and support environments which are enabling.

The findings from Phases 1 and 2 facilitated development of a 'Process for positive social construction' (see Figure 11.1). The mainstream pupil is placed in the centre and is supported by *enabling environments* together with *tools and resources* which enable them to become *skilled individuals* developing *positive social constructions of disability.* The cyclical nature of the process ensures the evolving positive social constructions feedback into, and strengthen, the enabling environment to support future development.

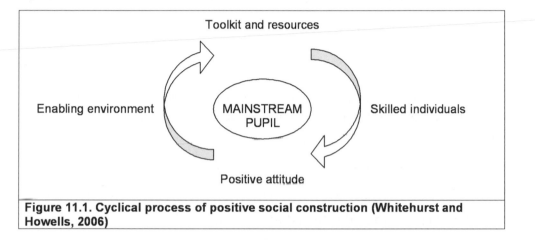

**Figure 11.1. Cyclical process of positive social construction (Whitehurst and Howells, 2006)**

Demystifying the inclusion experience for mainstream pupils begins to create a context which is much more familiar to them; one within which they can engage and develop adequate skills. A 'Model of support for inclusion' has been developed based on the mainstream pupils' feedback. By turning around their feelings of inadequacy, unfamiliarity and lack of predictability, we can create a basis of support for students, enabling them to benefit from and enjoy the inclusion experience.

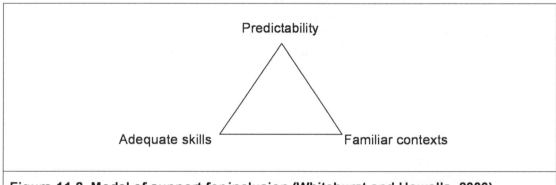

**Figure 11.2. Model of support for inclusion (Whitehurst and Howells, 2006)**

### Phase 3: What do students with intellectual disabilities feel is important to them about working on an inclusion project?

Ensuring that the students with disabilities who participated in the project were able to feedback on their experiences of inclusion was of paramount importance.

*Focus of the research interview*

Students were asked about their feelings in relation to what they had enjoyed or disliked about the project. They were given prompts to aid them such as talking about the music, the dancing and the theatre – all supported by photographs. In addition, it was important to explore the extent to which they felt comfortable working with young people they did not know and had been able to make new friends.

**Table 11.5. Special school interviews**

- What did you enjoy about 'The Monkey King'?

- Did you enjoy working with young people you didn't know?

- Did you make friends with the young people from [the mainstream school]?

- Was there anything you didn't like?

*Findings*

Five of the six students involved in the project gave a positive response to being involved in 'The Monkey King' project. Some students were able to elaborate on this stating:

- *I liked working with the girls*
- *The theatre was impressive*
- *I liked the children from [the mainstream school]*
- *I liked being video'd.*

One student was able to relate the experience to inner emotions, stating that he felt nervous about being at the theatre. He also recalled the pretence element involved, remembering how he had to 'pretend to be asleep' on the stage and the feelings of being hot when dancing. Similarly, most students indicated that they had enjoyed working with young people from another school, recalling names of particular pupils to demonstrate this. Although they gave examples of mainstream pupils they had worked with, the concept of 'making friends' was complex for them. They immediately pointed to photographs of students from Sunfield stating that they were friends but, when asked if they had made friends with the mainstream pupils, they were more hesitant. In response to this question, one student recollected:

- *The girls, I shake their hand.*

The student who had no verbal skills was observed to segregate all the photographs of people he knew from those he did not know. This topic was pursued by the speech and language therapist, who asked which group he liked to work with. He replied by indicating the more familiar group of people.

All but one of the students indicated that they had enjoyed working with new people, and one student in particular was sad that the project had finished.

The sensory aspects of the drama project made a distinct impression upon the students ,and give us clear evidence that we need to be aware of when embarking upon such a project. Students recalled:

- *I did not like the music...it was too loud... I did not like the sound of the piano*

- *I did not like the theatre...it was too crowded... People were banging doors.*

One student was very adamant in her dislike of the project. She had very limited verbal skills, and relied entirely on the Talking Mat to respond to the questions. In response to each aspect of the project, she selected the category of 'Dislike'.

To contextualise the information that students gave and to provide a more detailed picture of the impact of their involvement in terms of personal and social development, residential care and education staff were asked to reflect on the students' progress during the drama project. To highlight the way in which this information has been used to support individual student accounts, two case studies have been developed focusing on the student who did not enjoy the inclusion project and one who did.

### Case Study 1: Jenny

Jenny, a young lady with a diagnosis of profound ASD, had been observed by staff as becoming agitated and stressed during rehearsals. This was noted by overt behaviours such as frequently asking for the toilet, frequently needing to wash her hands, and using self-calming strategies such as playing with Blu-tack. Education staff noted that, when in class, Jenny preferred to be separated from timetabled social activities and to have structured time on her own in a different room. Residential care staff had raised concerns with staff involved in the project questioning what Jenny would gain from being included in the drama production. Consequently, they had arranged to observe rehearsals to ensure the student's well-being was maintained. Despite these challenges, Jenny remained in the project, and performed at the Birmingham theatre with very little difficulty. Interestingly, although she responded extremely negatively during the interview, residential care staff had commented that as her involvement in the project continued, she demonstrated new skills with regard to choice. Although Jenny has few verbal skills, as the inclusion project progressed she was able to demonstrate a greater level of assertiveness and enhanced abilities regarding choice.

### Case Study 2: Tony

Tony is a young man with a diagnosis of severe intellectual disability. He was thrilled with the opportunity to visit another school and to mix with new people, especially girls! He took great care with his appearance prior to rehearsals, gelling his hair and wearing his latest gear! He participated eagerly in group activities and made many friends. He has moderate verbal skills and was always chatty and pleasant. Residential care staff reported that Tony had matured and developed as the project progressed, and for his off-site college course had chosen to attend a drama programme at a mainstream college. A carer commented:

> *The final performance was so great – it was lovely to see Tony's sense of achievement. It brought tears to my eyes seeing him holding his arms up in the air and shouting, 'We did it!'*

*Conclusion to Phase 3*
Despite the difficulties inherent in eliciting the views of students with severe and complex intellectual disabilities, it is clear that the benefits outweigh the problems. While it arguably requires more meticulous planning and implementation, greater consideration of ethical issues and enormous care with interpretation of findings, these issues should constrain, but not deter the researcher from including students with such severe difficulties. If we continue to hear only the voices of others, we continue to do *unto* this population and ignore the messages they have for us. Traditional methods of triangulation, involving the views of others, are significant in allowing us to build up a picture of students in different contexts and to consider their development, but this picture is meaningless without the accounts of those at the centre of inclusion.

This study has demonstrated that young people with severe intellectual disabilities have the same range of preferences and fears as mainstream children. They, too, are hesitant about making new friends and prefer their more familiar peers, but are equally excited by new challenges and new horizons

**Final reflection**
Young people are young people first – it is *their* right and *our* obligation to ensure that when we talk about inclusion we take their views into account. Young people are young people first – we need their voices to inform our practice. Only then can we say we are truly working inclusively.

**References**

Beveridge, S. (1996) 'Experiences of an integration link scheme: the perspectives of pupils with severe learning difficulties and their mainstream peers', *British Journal of Learning Disabilities*, 24 (1), 9–19.

Cameron, L., Watson, J. and Murphy, J. (2004) 'Talking mats: a focus group tool for people with learning disability', *Communication Matters,* 18 (1), 33–35.

Carpenter, B. (2001) 'Inclusive societies: inclusive families'. Paper given to the National Institute for Learning Difficulties, Trinity College, Dublin (April).

Carpenter, B. and Shevlin, M. (2004) 'Creating an inclusive curriculum'. In: P. Noonan Walsh and H. Gash (eds) *Lives and Times: Practice, policy and people with disabilities.* Bray, Co. Wicklow: Rathdown Press.

Department for Education and Skills (2004) *Removing Barriers to Achievement: The Government's strategy for SEN.* Nottingham: DfES Publications.

Department of Education and Science (1978) *Special Educational Needs: Report of the Committee of Enquiry into the Education of Handicapped Children and Young People (The Warnock Report).* London: Her Majesty's Stationery Office.

Detheridge, T. (2000) 'Research involving children with severe learning difficulties'. In: A. Lewis and G. Lindsay (eds) *Researching Children's Perspectives.* Buckingham: Open University Press.

Fox, S., Farrell, P. and Davis, P. (2004) 'Factors associated with the effective inclusion of primary-aged pupils with Down's syndrome', *British Journal of Special Education,* 31 (4), 184–191.

Hastings, R.P. and Oakford, S. (2003) 'Student teachers' attitudes towards the inclusion of children with special needs', *Educational Psychology,* 23 (1), 88–94.

Kinder, K. and Harland, J. (2004) 'The arts and social inclusion: what's the evidence?', *British Journal of Learning Support*, 19 (2), 52–65.

Lewis, A. (2002) 'Accessing, through research interviews, the views of children with difficulties in learning', *Support for Learning*, 17 (3), 110–116.

Lewis, A. (2004) '"And when did you last see your father?": exploring the views of children with learning difficulties/disabilities', *British Journal of Special Education*, 31 (1), 3–9.

Lewis, A. and Porter, J. (2004) 'Interviewing children and young people with learning disabilities: guidelines for researchers and multi-professional practice', *British Journal of Learning Disabilities*, 32 (4), 191–198.

Martinsen, H. and von Tetzchner, S. (1996) 'Situating augmentative and alternative communication intervention'. In: S. von Tetzchner and M.H. Jensen (eds) *Augmentative and Alternative Communication: European perspectives*. London: Whurr/Wiley.

Murphy, J. (1997) *Talking Mats: A low-tech framework to help people with severe communication difficulties express their views*. Stirling: University of Stirling.

Porter, J. (2003) 'Interviewing children and young people with learning disabilities', *The SLD Experience*, 36, 14–17.

Robson, C. (2002) *Real World Research*. Oxford: Blackwell.

Shevlin, M. and O'Moore, A.M. (2000) 'Fostering positive attitudes: reactions of mainstream pupils to contact with their counterparts who have severe/profound intellectual disabilities', *European Journal of Special Needs Education*, 15 (2), 206–217.

Stalker, K. (1998) 'Some ethical and methodological issues in research with people with learning difficulties', *Disability and Society*, 13 (1), 5–19.

Whitehurst, T. and Howells, A. (2006) '"When something is different, people fear it": children's perceptions of an arts-based inclusion project', *Support for Learning*, 21 (1), 40–44.

Yazbeck, M., Mcvilly, K., and Parmenter, T.R. (2004) 'Attitudes toward people with intellectual disabilities', *Journal of Disability Policy Studies*, 15 (2), 97–111.

# PART 5
# The **SIECCA** Curriculum

# CHAPTER 12

# Implementing TEACCH in Support of a 24-Hour Curriculum

*Iain Chatwin and Val Harley*

## Introduction

In 1998, Sunfield introduced an autism-specific provision with a 24-hour curriculum approach. There was an increasing proportion of young people with a diagnosis of autistic spectrum disorder (ASD) being admitted to the school, and in response to national initiatives (see Chapter 1) the Sunfield Integrated Education and Care Curriculum Approach (SIECCA) (Carpenter, Chatwin and Egerton, 2001) set out to provide a holistic programme for the education of young people profoundly affected by an ASD. The decision to introduce this ASD-specific provision was based upon the need to develop a core skill base among staff and develop a model of practice that could be used to re-integrate young people who had been excluded from other educational settings. Inclusion in a dedicated provision would be the stepping stone to wider community inclusion once individually tailored support had been developed.

Eight years after the original concept for SIECCA was launched, its underlying principles, originally developed for two designated residential house–classroom pairings, now underpin practice throughout the school. The core tenets of SIECCA are the use of structured teaching, functional behaviour analysis, alternative and augmentative communication, and a transdisciplinary approach to delivering a consistent curriculum across all areas of provision, not exclusively within the classroom environment.

## The needs of young people with ASD

The starting point for developing the approach was the needs of young people with ASD, severe and complex learning needs, and challenging behaviours. The impact of the triad of impairments in ASD (Wing, 2002) for this group of young people means that they need an approach that supports complex communication needs, provides opportunities to engage in meaningful social interaction, including play (see Chapter 3), and enables them to generalise existing skills to novel situations. An awareness of inherent sensory and perceptual dysfunctions (Bogdashina, 2003) supports a range of environmental and therapeutic interventions that have a significant effect on behaviour and engagement. The SIECCA programme uses consistency of approach across all areas of intervention to reduce anxieties experienced by the students and enhance self-esteem and learning potential.

## Implementation of the SIECCA programme

Two residential groups of eight students each were established, and a specific classroom was allocated for each house so that student groupings in residential care and school remained constant. Each group was supported by a staff team working across residential care and education environments, jointly led by a senior teacher and residential care team leader. The staff team consisted of a teacher, a residential care team leader and deputy, learning support workers, night care support workers and a psychology assistant. In addition, an occupational therapist was employed to support the SIECCA provision.

With staff teams being constituted from diverse professional backgrounds, it was important to provide training across a wide area of knowledge and skills. The whole SIECCA staff team undertook a common training programme covering core practice areas such as 'Treatment and Education of Autistic and related Communication-handicapped Children' (TEACCH), child protection, behaviour management, and alternative and augmentative communication. A central policy is that all training is offered to all staff, allowing staff from different professional disciplines to work toward the same qualifications, including university-accredited courses. Refresher training and work-based advisory sessions have also been essential in supporting staff to implement new knowledge and counteract loss of treatment integrity (see Chapter 13).

## Description of the SIECCA programme
### *Structured teaching*
Structured teaching strategies were developed using the TEACCH model (Mesibov and Howley, 2003; Mesibov, Shea and Schopler, 2005; Schopler, Mesibov and Hearsey, 1995). Structured teaching provides the framework for a range of educational, leisure, self-help and daily living activities, through environmental adaptations and developing individual skills (Mesibov, Shea and Schopler, 2005). The TEACCH model of structured teaching recognises that the effects of ASD are unique to an individual person, and so takes a person-centred approach to assessment.

The content of a structured teaching programme is individually formulated and refined by on-going assessment to build upon the strengths, needs and interests of the individual, creating a framework within which an Individual Education and Care Plan (IECP) can be delivered. 'Structure' refers to timetabling (routines and schedules) and visual and physical structure (boundaries to tasks, time and environments), which address the anxieties that students with ASD have around predicting what will happen next, and the problems that they have with visual and conceptual discrimination, distractibility, excessive focus on detail and difficulties with organisation and sequencing (Aarons and Gittens, 1999). Supported by clear and meaningful visual information within an organised and structured environment in which distraction is minimised, the student with ASD is better able to understand their environment and its boundaries, and to learn more effectively. Structured teaching can have dramatic effects on reducing a student's frustration and anxiety, and consequently can reduce the challenging behaviours they present, thereby providing a support for behaviour management.

### *Physical structure*
In their classrooms, students may have individual, clearly identified work stations and dedicated one-to-one teaching areas. Most classes have one or more rest areas and a central table for group association including snack. Work stations may be screened off from the main room to minimise distraction and anxiety for students, and student-specific colour coding may be used to provide visual clarity. Work systems provide visual and structural clarity of the order for tasks to be worked on, and a specific area is identified for work finished.

In the residential accommodation, much of the physical structure is provided by the layout of the house – a dining room for eating, an activity room for structured leisure, etc. Although the house may have an activity station, similar to a work station, to enable students to take part in chosen activities without distraction, the physical structure relates to daily living skills; for example, a low screen may be provided to give privacy to a student who finds it difficult to eat when disturbed by others, or a taped square on the floor may indicate to a student where they should put their cushion to watch television without getting too close to the screen.

*The schedule*
The schedule provides a visual key to the sequence of activities that a person is involved in, and is devised for each individual using suitable prompts to represent activities or locations. The prompts on the schedule are at an appropriate conceptual level for each student to ensure they can understand what is being communicated, and may be objects of reference, photographs, symbols or written words; a combination of two may be combined to help a student develop from one mode to another.

Before being used on the schedule, the association between the prompt and the object that it stands for has to be taught. Initially students may be directed by staff handing them a visual prompt to signify that it is time to begin the next activity, but the aim is to enable all students eventually to use a schedule.

Schedules can be placed at a fixed location on a wall-mounted board, shelf or as boxes on a table; or they may be portable in the form of a clipboard, binder or book. Activities are typically sequenced either left to right or top to bottom depending on the natural preference of the individual. Dependent upon how much information a student is confident with, the schedule may describe anything between the current and next activities, up to a whole day of activities. Each student then follows their schedule, removing or checking-off prompts as activities are completed.

Transition between locations or activities can be a difficult and disturbing scenario for people with ASD due to their difficulties with selective processing of information (Aarons and Gittens, 1999). A student with ASD may become distracted on their way to a destination (e.g. by noises or light effects), become disorientated and then be unable to recall what they were doing or where they were going leading to a situation of stress and confusion. Whereas a verbal instruction is impermanent, a visual prompt acts as a concrete reminder of their original intention. Prompts on schedules, which may then be matched to duplicates in place at their destination indicating that the transition is at an end, can lessen anxiety and uncertainty. Environmental signposting or restructuring, and the routine of schedule checking, can make transitions easier to achieve.

Schedule sequences incorporate both essential activities and periods where the student can choose what they wish to do at the time. Choices are offered in the form of a board (to which prompts relating to available choices are attached), folder or book. This format provides the basis for developing expressive communication by the students, using prompts that can be extended to enable them to convey physical and emotional needs.

*Work systems*
Work systems, also referred to as activity systems, provide the framework by which educational or daily living tasks are structured temporally and visually according to

the skills and developmental level of the student. Work systems follow either a left-to-right or top-to-bottom progression and teach the student independent working and an understanding of when the activity is finished. An essential element of any work system is that it effectively communicates to the user:

- What work to do
- How much work to do
- A clearly defined end to the activity
- What to do next.

The sequence in which the tasks are to be completed is identified by matching cues (e.g. colour tokens, shapes, pictures, numbers, letters or words) arranged on the work system to duplicates on tasks, or by following written lists. The amount of work to be completed is related to the concentration span of the student, and is visually identified by the number of cues on the work/activity system. A 'finished box' is often used for completed work with students at earlier developmental stages, while more able individuals may be expected to return completed work to a variety of locations. If the next task or activity has strong appeal for the student, then motivation to complete work tasks will be greater. The student will be able to develop independent working through the use of their work system, and work or activity stations within the class, home, leisure or vocational setting may be designed to meet the support needs of the individual. Physically structured to support on-task habits and minimise distraction, work stations provide visually clear organisation, and support the progression of independent working on tasks previously taught in one-to-one teaching sessions.

*Tasks and activities*
Tasks are organised activities with a clear beginning and end that the student can complete without guidance from staff. They may involve operations such as measuring, matching, sorting, assembling, reading, maths, domestic chores, self-care, vocational or leisure activities. Visual structure is achieved through a variety of means including placing relevant materials in containers or limiting an area, sequencing components, colour coding, highlighting, labelling and using layout jigs. The end point of the task should be made clear to the student (e.g. by all the materials being used up or all questions answered). Making the task meaningful and interesting for the student will provide motivation for completion, although, for many students with ASD, the completion of a task is a reward in itself. Tasks may be developed over time by making changes to the instructions, increasing the complexity or duration, adding a checking element or a communicative component.

It is important to remember that the structured support provided for students is the key to their increased confidence and independence. In a familiar environment, a student's increasing independence in carrying out an activity may mean that physical and visual structure can be progressively reduced or modified to promote independence *within that environment* (e.g. screens may be lowered or removed, a student might progress from an object-based communication system to one that uses photographs, etc.). However, it should be recognised that if elements of the context change (e.g. due to the introduction of a new student, a change in classroom layout, illness or an upsetting incident), the structure may need to be increased again to compensate for the student's heightened levels of anxiety. If a student is asked to carry out a familiar task with slightly different components or in another setting, often their 'weak central coherence' (Frith, 2003) means that they may find it difficult to appreciate the similarity of the task and to transfer skills. Therefore, a certain level of structure may need to be reinstated to enable them to attain success. If the structure is not reinstated, the student's anxieties may result in the re-emergence of their previous difficulties.

### Functional behaviour analysis

Functional behaviour analysis underpins our approach to meeting students' behaviour support needs, and is described by Drudy (2001) as 'analysing the function or purpose of a behaviour in order to understand it'. Where a behaviour may be ineffectively meeting a student's needs, or is inappropriate to the current situation, an assessment is carried out. This assessment involves systematically recording observations of the behaviour exhibited, and the events and stimuli in the environment both before and after the behaviour occurs. This is recorded as antecedent (the stimulus or stimuli the student responds to), behaviour (the observed actions the student exhibits) and consequences (the stimulus or stimuli that the student receives, or is no longer exposed to, as a result of this behaviour) on an incident analysis form.

Incident analysis forms are analysed by the psychology team to investigate trends in the occurrence of stimuli that may be provoking, and needs that may be fulfilled by, the behaviour. A behaviour development plan (BDP) is then drawn up, in consultation with education and residential care staff, which focuses on altering the antecedents and consequences influencing the student's behaviour to minimise the forces driving it and help the student achieve a meaningful outcome through more appropriate means.

A range of strategies may be employed to help the student to cope with stimuli, including calming routines, picture stories (see Chapter 5) and calm books. Routines are taught when the student is calm and responsive, and reinforced positively so that they are not perceived as punishment. Picture stories can reinforce the link between action and effect, and present options to the student to help them to resolve situations positively. Scrap books with pictures or tangible items that relate to pleasurable experiences can help to calm individuals and reinforce positive interactions.

### Alternative and augmentative communication[1]

Effective communication is central to the TEACCH approach. Many young people with ASD are made anxious when they encounter uncertainty and cannot predict what is to happen next (Jackson, 2002). Students also need a way in which they can communicate their needs with those who care for them. If they do not have a means of communication, anxiety or frustration can lead to withdrawal or challenging behaviours.

Most people with ASD receive information more easily if it is presented visually (Dettmer, Simpson, Smith Myles and Ganz, 2000; Quill, 1997). An emphasis is therefore placed on providing visual information about what is happening now, how and when it will finish, and what will happen next. Where this is not appropriate for individuals, tactile or audible information may be used.

Most students with ASD at Sunfield are non-verbal and use visual modes of communication; others use electronic communicators (e.g. Vocaflex). Some of the students appear to have well-developed expressive verbal skills when conversing on their own terms, although due to echolalia, difficulties with word-finding and meaning, and a reduction of communicative ability under stress, they also may need to rely upon a visual system to communicate with another person effectively.

The role of effective communication in reducing anxiety and stress may be enhanced by introducing approaches such as the Picture Exchange Communication System (PECS; Bondy and Frost, 2002).

### The 24-hour curriculum and the transdisciplinary approach

Within the SIECCA provision, a transdisciplinary approach (Davies, 2007) has been established to provide a unified service focusing on the individual needs of each young person, in order to provide the most flexible and beneficial learning environment possible for them. Teaching, residential care, psychology and specialised therapy professionals work closely with the young people and their families. Each member of the transdisciplinary team brings their specific skills to work with the students, but they are also encouraged to transcend the boundaries traditionally created by single professional discipline approaches:

> ...in a transdisciplinary team the roles are not fixed. Decisions are made by professionals collaborating at a primary level (rather than at a secondary level as in a multi-disciplinary team). The boundaries between disciplines are deliberately blurred to employ a 'targeted eclectic flexibility'. (Pagliano, 1999)

Within the 24-hour curriculum, skills learnt piece-by-piece in the classroom can be extended and combined within the social setting. Underpinning the 24-hour curriculum is the central concept of 'consistency': consistency of individual interactions with students, consistency between team members in their approach and expectations, and consistency of provision. The school's Office for Standards in Education report (Ofsted, 2006) acknowledged that this was:

> ...a genuine 24-hour curriculum in which pupils flourish because it is meticulously planned and implemented by dedicated teams of staff.

Key factors in the approach are that all staff understand the 'culture' of autism (Mesibov, Shea and Schopler, 2005) and the principles on which SIECCA is based. Parental collaboration helps to develop a total support network for the student allowing them to use their skills not just within the structured environment of Sunfield, but also within the family home or in a holiday setting.

### Communication within the staff team

Effective communication between staff is important for ensuring consistency of approach, and providing a means by which staff can raise issues of concern. Regular staff meetings and individual supervision of staff by line managers in residential care, education and therapy settings allow issues relating to the support of the young people to be highlighted and may provide the basis for issues being taken to the full staff and transdisciplinary teams. In addition to student-focused teams, structured teaching representatives from across site also meet termly to ensure consistency of approach and provide an opportunity to share ideas.

### Collaborative working within the programme

During the first weeks of a student's placement at Sunfield, the key worker works closely with the teacher and psychology assistant to set up schedules and work systems. All intervention is based upon thorough assessment to ensure that support is appropriate to both the 'exceptional' needs related to ASD and the 'individual' needs of the student (Norwich, 1996), and aimed at maximising the student's independence.

An important part of the assessment process is the completion of the IECP. Planning of individual targets is a fundamental area of collaboration with families, though only one of the ways in which we endeavour to be partners with the families of our students. Working from the objectives identified in the student's Statement of Special Educational Needs (SSEN), five areas of skill development are identified to be worked upon as cross-site targets for the current term. Alongside education targets (e.g. for literacy, numeracy, etc.), these targets may relate to self-care, daily living and social presentation skills; family, identity and social relationships; being healthy; or emotions and behaviour.

The staff team is able to support the students in residential care and education environments, providing consistency of assessment and delivery of each IECP, following either the National or Further Education Curriculum. Teaching of daily living, social and leisure skills is undertaken in the most appropriate environment, encouraging the individual to mature and develop their capacity for interdependent and independent living as adults.

In order to provide consistency of presentation, skill-teaching programmes have a fixed structure and set order for completion of tasks. Attainment may be recorded on a chart for evaluation and future planning purposes, and backward chaining techniques (Arnold and Yeomans, 2005) are often used to ensure success. Though each student's programmes are co-ordinated by their key worker, the implementation is carried out by the whole team. Specific therapy programmes are devised by the appropriate professional, but are then delivered by any member of the staff team or family, following the programme design and structure on a transdisciplinary basis (Doyle, 1997). Individual adaptation of items of equipment and environmental adjustments (e.g. provision of screens) may be employed for some students to allow them to function more effectively within certain situations and gain confidence within group settings.

Staffing levels may vary over the duration of the day to reflect the demands made upon students, and the need to facilitate small group activities. During the night, there are always at least two staff awake, and it is essential that they are part of the overall team implementing a consistent approach. Schedules, work systems and calming strategies rely on consistent application, whenever they may be used during the 24-hour period.

*Collaboration with families*
The nature of residential provision places a particular emphasis on family contact, support and involvement. Effective collaboration requires dedicated services that are able to respond to a variety of individual needs and circumstances. We adopt the premise that families should be self-defining; it is up to the student and their family to identify who the significant people are in their home life (Carpenter, 2000). 'Family' does not have to be solely blood relatives. Often neighbours and friends have had a significant role in a student's life, and these contacts need to be recognised and maintained.

The teacher and key worker share responsibility for liaison with the student's family. This includes discussion of how structured teaching strategies similar to those used at Sunfield may support family outings or be used in the family home. The degree to which any of the components of structured teaching may be used in the home setting varies greatly, so our emphasis is on enabling whatever is appropriate for an individual family. Video tapes are frequently used as part of the education review process, and provide a further means for families to be informed about their son or daughter's life at school and to see how structured teaching is employed.

Places on training courses are made available to parents at reduced cost, and specific TEACCH workshops to support home implementation are also delivered at the school for families. Whenever a new student joins the school, parents have the opportunity to discuss the SIECCA approach, and an information booklet describing TEACCH and its implementation at Sunfield is available for families. TEACCH trainers, residential care and education staff advise and support families with home implementation, and can provide some resource material and possibly outreach visits to advise further on strategies for use in the home.

The Family Centre at Sunfield provides opportunities for families to stay on the school site without charge. Families can choose whether their son or daughter stays with them or returns to the residential house at night or for periods during the day. The centre also enables families to practice using systems in an environment where there are always staff on hand to support if needed. This has been of great benefit in supporting family visits and enabling family outings to run smoothly and pleasurably (Carpenter, Attfield and Logan, 2006).

## Facilities – on and off site

The structured teaching approach enables students to take part in a range of social and leisure activities, both on and off site. Opportunities for students to access community activities and facilities have been developed through individualised schedules. Appropriately individualised programmes support the needs of students across the whole day, enabling them to participate in group and individual activities. Structured walks and fitness trails provide a meaningful format for exercise, and team games are adapted to incorporate individual levels of participation. Effective management of group work presents particular challenges. 'Jigsawing' (Howley and Rose, 2003), a strategy in which each student is given their own task within a group which must be completed for the whole activity to succeed, is combined with structured teaching techniques within the classroom and leisure domains. Domestic group routines, such as mealtimes, incorporate individual work systems presented as most appropriate for the student. Periods when students listen to music as a group may be used to provide a clear transition period between activities such as morning domestic routine and going to class; or following snacks and evening hygiene before going to bed. The nature of routines varies with age group, and progress to support the changing needs of individual students.

## Conclusion

The aims of the SIECCA model of practice have been to provide appropriate residential educational services for young people profoundly affected by ASD. The inherent uniqueness of an individual student's experience means that they cannot be representative of all young people with ASD. But for those students for whom it has been most difficult to find appropriate services, a consistent, 24-hour, integrated curriculum using the SIECCA approach has been proven to enable individual achievements of a greater degree than ever before in these young people's lives.

An assessment-based, 24-hour intervention, with consistency of approach underpinned by transdisciplinary practice, has delivered successful outcomes for a group of young people who had previously been excluded from existing services. A key factor in this success has been the use of the TEACCH model of structured teaching (Mesibov, Shea and Schopler, 2005) within a coherent model of provision, with a clear emphasis on collaboration with parents and families (Carpenter, Chatwin and Egerton, 2001).

Surveys of parent views (see Chapter 10) have confirmed that the strengths of the SIECCA approach are recognised and valued by families. The most important factors in the service we provide as a residential school were identified by families as a high level of care that values the student, an understanding of the student's ASD, and good home–school communication (Carpenter, Conway and Woodgate, 2003). These correspond with the factors identified in a study of parents using a short-term residential service incorporating TEACCH (Preece, 2000), suggesting that they should constitute general aims for social provision for children and young people with ASD.

Further developments will include refinements of building design for both residential (Sunfield, 2006) and school environments, with a new school building project soon to commence. Structured support strategies will be further extended into larger community settings, enabling meaningful inclusion.

As understanding of ASD has continued to grow, and through attempting to view the world from the perspective of a person with ASD, strategies devised to meet their unique neurological needs have created visible changes in interaction, communication and independence. An environment that is based less on language and more on visual information does not have to inhibit social interaction and engagement. Indeed, for people with ASD, the reverse has been demonstrated.

Though the approach discussed here is implemented with a 6- to 19-year-old school population, our current understanding of the benefits of early intervention would suggest the need for developing and implementing integrated structured systems of support in early years services and home-based support. Equally, we are actively promoting the integration of structured teaching systems in adult services who will assume continuing responsibility for the young adults leaving us. It is never too soon or too late to make a difference.

## References

Aarons, M. and Gittens, T. (1999) *Handbook of Autism: A guide for professionals (2nd edn)*. London: Routledge.

Arnold, C. and Yeomans, J. (2005) *Psychology for Teaching Assistants*. Stoke-on-Trent: Trentham.

Bogdashina, O. (2003) *Sensory Perceptual Issues in Autism: Different sensory experiences – different perceptual worlds*. London: Jessica Kingsley.

Bondy, A. and Frost, L. (2002) *A Picture's Worth: PECS and other visual communication strategies in autism*. Bethesda, MD: Woodbine House.

Carpenter, C. (2000) 'Sustaining the family: meeting the needs of families of children with disabilities', *British Journal of Special Education*, 27 (3), 135–144.

Carpenter, B., Attfield, E. and Logan, N. (2006) 'Communicating with Families', *The SLD Experience*, 45, 21–25.

Carpenter, B., Chatwin, I. and Egerton, J. (2001) 'An evaluation of SIECCA: an intensive programme of education and care for students with profound autistic spectrum disorders', *Good Autism Practice*, 2 (1), 52–66.

Carpenter, B., Conway, S. and Woodgate, A. (2003) 'Happy families', *Special Children*, November/December, 34–37.

Davies, S. (2007) 'Why is transdisciplinary team practice the preferred model in early childhood intervention?'. In: Kurrajong Early Intervention Service (ed.) *'Team Around the Child': Working together in early childhood intervention*. Wagga Wagga, Australia: Kurrajong Early Intervention Service (KEIS).

Dettmer, S., Simpson, R., Smith Myles, B. and Ganz, J. (2000) 'The use of visual supports to facilitate transitions of students with autism', *Focus on Autism and Other Developmental Disabilities,* 15, 163–169.

Drudy, S. (2001) *Educational Provision and Support for Persons with Autistic Spectrum Disorder: The report of the Task Force in Autism.* [Online at: http://www.sess.ie]

Doyle, B. (1997) 'Transdisciplinary approaches to working with families'. In: B. Carpenter (ed.) *Families in Context: Emerging trends in family support and early intervention*. London: David Fulton.

Frith, U. (2003) *Autism: Explaining the enigma (2nd edn)*. Oxford: Blackwell.

Howley, M. and Rose, R. (2003) 'Facilitating group work for pupils with autistic spectrum disorders by combining jigsawing and structured teaching', *Good Autism Practice,* 4 (1), 20–25.

Jackson, L. (2002) *Freaks, Geeks and Asperger Syndrome: A user guide to adolescence*. London: Jessica Kingsley.

Mesibov, G. and Howley, M. (2003) *Accessing the Curriculum for Pupils with Autistic Spectrum Disorders*. London: David Fulton.

Mesibov, G., Shea, V. and Schopler, E. (2005) *The TEACCH Approach to Autism Spectrum Disorders.* New York: Kluwer Academic/Plenum.

Norwich, B. (1996) 'Special needs education for all: connective specialisation and ideological impurity', *British Journal of Special Education*, 23 (3), 100–103.

Office for Standards in Education (Ofsted) (2006) 'Inspection report: Sunfield School (2–5 October 2006)'. [Online at: www.ofsted.gov.uk]

Pagliano, P. (1999) 'Designing the multisensory environment', *PMLD–Link,* 12 (2), 2–6.

Preece, D. (2000) 'An investigation into parental satisfaction with a short-term care service for children with an autistic spectrum disorder', *Good Autism Practice*, 1 (2), 42–56.

Quill, K. (1997) 'Instructional considerations for young children with autism: the rationale for visually cued instruction', *Journal of Autism and Developmental Disorders*, 21, 697–714.

Schopler, E., Mesibov, G. and Hearsey, K. (1995) 'Structured teaching in the TEACCH system'. In: E. Schopler and G. Mesibov (eds) *Learning and Cognition in Autism*. New York: Plenum.

Sunfield (2006) *Designing Living and Learning Environments for Children with Autism*. Clent: Sunfield Publications.

Wing, L. (2002) *The Autistic Spectrum: A guide for parents and professionals (updated edn)*. London: Robinson.

**Endnote**

[1] Information can be found online at: http://www.inclusive.co.uk/infosite/aac.shtml

# CHAPTER 13

# Transfer of Training into Practice

## The TEACCH Training Programme at Sunfield

*Iain Chatwin and Deb Rattley*

## Introduction

Creating change in a classroom or residential care setting, and sustaining these new practices, is known to be challenging (Little and Houston, 2003). A number of variables will impact upon the transfer of training into practice, including individual trainee characteristics, such as motivation and ability to learn, and the correlation of training conditions to the practice setting.

Resources, including time, invested in ineffective training, or training unsuited to practice, are resources that could be directed to training in an alternative approach with greater potential for success; and therefore carry what economists term an 'opportunity cost'. Making the correct initial decision about training is therefore important. Once the decision is taken, ensuring effectiveness of the chosen action is crucial for successful outcomes. However, this is not always well addressed in practice. We know that success will be achieved not only through effective training programmes, but also through the implementation of learning support thereafter. One of the key questions for trainers remains whether the knowledge and skills gained from training translate into improvements in practice (McKenzie et al., 2000), and research suggests that this has been infrequently achieved (Showers, 1990).

This chapter explores how a model for evaluating the impact of training on practice was developed, and how this evaluation shaped trainer involvement in post-lecture room learning. This example focuses on a training programme for education and residential care staff working with children and young people with autistic spectrum disorders (ASD). The specific training considered here is the Treatment and Education of Autistic and Related Communication-handicapped Children (TEACCH) approach (Mesibov, Shea and Schopler, 2005). However, this model will generalise to many intervention training programmes.

The school provision for students with ASD has been developed around key tenets, including the TEACCH model of structured support for living and learning, within a 24-hour curriculum (Carpenter, Chatwin and Egerton, 2001). Sunfield's commitment to training and the quality of training provided have been recognised through our selection as a recipient of a National Training Award. The level of training attended is dependent upon the role of the staff member, but there is an emphasis on staff from all departments having a common foundation.

The desired outcome of training is the implementation of new knowledge and skills in practice, ultimately to stimulate a quality-of-life benefit for the young people we work with. However, the evaluation of training is not a straight forward process. A number of questions arise regarding what to evaluate, when to evaluate it, how to evaluate it, and what to do with the evaluation results. Further questions of importance are: 'How have staff used what they have learnt?', 'How has this benefited our pupils?' and 'What is the trainee supposed to be able to do as a result of the training?'

An additional consideration is who should carry out these evaluations. During the training event, this is typically the trainers; but, when considering effectiveness in practice, evaluations are often carried out by someone removed from the training delivery process. There is clearly a responsibility for managers, through regular supervision and appraisal, to consider training impact and build on reflective practice. However, there are limitations to self-evaluation, and evaluation by managers outside the training role.

Firstly, how will this evaluation be fed back to the training providers? For training delivered in-house, this may be addressed through including, within staff appraisals, an opportunity for feedback about training which can later be anonymised and relayed to professional development co-ordinators. A second limitation is that this process may not reveal discrepancies between practice and the training model. Clearly, the effectiveness of the TEACCH approach will be affected by how accurately it is interpreted. This phenomenon of variation in 'treatment integrity' or 'therapist drift' (Jordan and Powell, 1996) has implications for the effectiveness of practice, and is also a critical element for investigation in the evaluation of training.

In this respect, observational assessment by trainers has clear benefits. Observation by a TEACCH trainer, alongside consultation and discussion, can provide a valuable control over accurate implementation. These considerations mean that evaluation of training must not only be end-user focused, but also employ multiple levels to support continuous improvement of practice and training.

### Developing a model for evaluating training

In seeking to conceptualise a model for evaluating in-house training, it is worth exploring some existing concepts and models of evaluation.

Donald Kirkpatrick (1994; Nickols, 2003) provides a model that, while originally developed over 40 years ago, maintains credibility and regular application to today's training arena. Kirkpatrick identifies four stages of evaluation:

Stage 1    *Reactions:* the training event and immediate delegate responses to its effectiveness; were needs met, and how do trainees plan to use what they have learned?

Stage 2    *Learning:* that has taken place in terms of measurable new knowledge, skills, etc.; have attitudes changed, and by how much?

Stage 3    *Behaviour:* observable improvements in workplace performance, behaviour and techniques that reflect what was learned during the training.

Stage 4    *Results:* improvements in organisational impact.

A criticism of the Kirkpatrick model may be that it does not provide a diagnostic element to support analysis when the training does not produce the desired result(s), or to identify if the same result could be achieved in less time or for less cost. Phillips (1994) promotes evaluation beyond Stage 4 with a focus on measuring 'return on investment', to determine whether or not the training was appropriate and is achieving its objectives.

Gaines-Robinson and Robinson (1995) promote the notion of trainers as 'performance consultants', a model which places emphasis away from the training event itself and seeks evaluation of the implementation of interventions resulting from this process.

Based upon these considerations and Kirkpatrick's original four stages, a model for in-house organisational training evaluation was developed around six potential stages of evaluation (Figure 13.1).

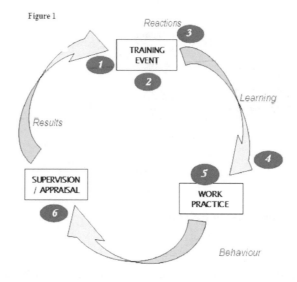

**Figure 13.1. Six stages of evaluation**

Stage 1   *Point of entry*: formal or informal measures of existing knowledge may be obtained; can inform content and delivery style of training event

Stage 2   *During training event*: formal or informal measures of acquisition of knowledge and skills, and effectiveness of training methods; gives feedback to allow modification of content and delivery style of training process if required

Stage 3   *End of event*: formal or informal measures of the value of training to trainees indicating gains in knowledge or skills; gives feedback to allow modification of content and delivery style for future training events, and inform practice support needs

Stage 4   *Return to practice*: formal or informal measures of relevance/transferability of knowledge and skills to practice

Stage 5   *Continuing practice*: formal or informal measures of individual and collaborative implementation of knowledge and skills to practice; end-user benefits identified

Stage 6   *Supervision and appraisal*: formal review of training effectiveness and application of knowledge and skills to practice; identification of benefits for organisation.

It is at Evaluation Stages 5 and 6 where we are most likely to become aware of any short-comings of the training programme in terms of preparation for practice.

While represented above as a cycle, the professional development process is normally typified by new experiences building on previous knowledge and skills, and so could more accurately be represented as a helix of training events, work practice and reflection (see Figure 13.2).

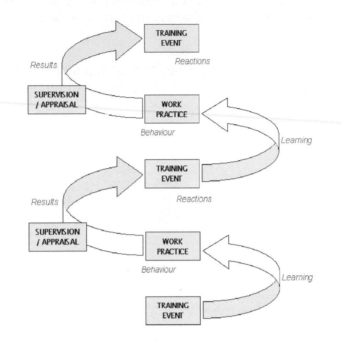

**Figure 13.2. Helix of professional development**

## Applying the model to practice

With regard to the TEACCH training considered here, this helix evolves from an Induction Day briefing, through a two-day TEACCH course for all practitioners, to a five-day TEACCH course for senior practitioners. Within this process, complementary training courses such as 'Behaviour management', 'Autism awareness' and 'Communication' will all have an influence on increasing skill levels. Beyond the five-day course, there is potential for more individual progression, through working toward trainer status or as an underpinning knowledge for higher education qualifications.

The overall effectiveness of a five-day TEACCH course, and subsequent benefits in practice, will therefore have some relationship to previous training and experience of participants, as well as in turn supporting subsequent training. The development of knowledge through induction and foundation courses (including two-day TEACCH training) would support the argument that five-day courses should be for experienced senior practitioners. However, there then needs to be an effective cascade of knowledge to colleagues from this level in the organisation. Part of this evaluation process, therefore, asks course participants how dissemination has been achieved.

In the education department, there is a staff team of approximately 80, who work with over 200 residential care staff, plus therapists and psychologists, to provide support for a 24-hour curriculum. All teachers and senior teaching assistants attend the five-day course, as do the team leaders and deputy team leaders from the residential care department. Teaching assistants and residential care support workers attend the two-day course. There is, therefore, an emphasis on cascading knowledge within classroom and residential care teams. Experience has shown that trying to cascade learning through a limited number of trained staff has the potential to lead to misinterpretation and rigidity of application, instead of the flexibility that the TEACCH approach offers.

Application of the above evaluation model to the TEACCH five-day training programme is achieved through:

Stage 1    Applicants providing information on professional background and qualifications, which is reviewed by training team to inform trainee group composition

Stage 2    Small group discussion between trainees and trainer; observation of trainee performance by training team; evaluation of completed training tasks

Stage 3    A formal evaluation questionnaire completed by trainees; training team meeting

Stage 4    Completion of an in-service training evaluation, which includes asking the trainee to look at how they will use the training in the future; meetings with TEACCH trainers; dissemination to colleagues

Stage 5    TEACCH trainers visit residential settings/classrooms for observation of individuals and teams; consultancy and small group meetings with trainees

Stage 6    Formal supervision and annual appraisal meetings between trainee and line manager with feedback to professional development co-ordinators/TEACCH trainers. All staff at Sunfield are encouraged to be reflective practitioners, and this process should involve a critical analysis of the impact of training on practice.

The first three stages of this process are reported through evaluation of questionnaires, and have consistently shown a high level of satisfaction with course delivery and pertinence to practice. Alterations to the training programme have been informed through this process over several years, and the training event ranks very highly: 90% of course evaluation forms filled in by participants designate it 'very good'.

Stage 4 has been achieved through trainees reviewing the event with their line manager, with dissemination being achieved through team meetings and workplace demonstration. A fundamental element in maximising the benefits of TEACCH training is transferring the learning into the students' various life settings. Research into the transference of skills from the training room to practice settings highlights the difficulties that can occur during the process and consequently reduce the effectiveness of the training (Smidt, Balandin, Reed and Sigafoos, 2002).

The development of support for the effective transfer of skills into practice, and strategies for sustaining this, led to a focus on the previously unexplored area of evaluation at Stage 5.

Evaluation was conducted through a range of observational, interview and question-naire methods. Observations were conducted semi-formally in residential settings, partly using a formative assessment checklist based upon the tri-level assessment (Wall, 2001) used by Division TEACCH. These were later compared to observations made in classrooms using a similar checklist devised for classroom use.

A 25% sample of staff who had attended the five-day course and who were still work-ing at the school were sent questionnaires for self-completion, and two staff each from the residential care and education departments were interviewed to provide fur-ther qualitative responses to inform the questionnaire data.

Interviews and questionnaire responses provided the following reflection on the strengths of the training course for practice:

- Provided positive skills for applying principles to practice

- Awareness of pre-existing corruption of TEACCH model

- New appreciation of student needs

- More confident in talking to parents and professional visitors.

Issues that had arisen when applying knowledge and skills within the work setting included:

- Uncertainty in applying assessment formats from the course

- Difficulty in transferring own learning to junior staff

- Five-day course very intensive – needed more time to think through implementa-tion in own setting

- Things forgotten over time, and need for refresher sessions.

Additional requests included:

- *In situ* support with setting up new systems

- An 'ideas' resource for tasks

- Trainer-led group discussions.

These findings have informed the pattern of support provided to staff across depart-ments. Residential accommodation-based sessions were conducted, and follow-up meetings for newly trained staff were established, alongside a photographic resource of task ideas on the internal computer network.

Residential setting-based sessions were carried out both in response to requests from residential care staff and to trainer selection. Observations were supported by written feedback and consultation advice sessions. In one residential setting, this led to two additional sessions being delivered to support new staff awaiting attendance on a two-day training course, and to provide a discussion forum for the staff team.

Follow-up meetings were arranged approximately six weeks after completion of the training course to review how participants had applied their learning, and to ascertain the nature of on-going support that they felt would best meet their needs. Responses indicated that having TEACCH trainers on-site and available for informal consultancy was invaluable. The follow-up meeting itself provided a template for meetings with trainers and other course participants to provide a useful discussion forum around individual issues.

The emphasis for follow-up meetings was on newly trained staff, but it was suggested that some form of refresher training should be available for all staff. It was felt that the meetings were worthy of trainer time investment as a method of following up and maximising the benefits of training, and ensuring that all staff develop their understanding of the issues for their colleagues in other parts of the organisation. Follow-up interviews with participants on more recent courses has identified that access to support from trainers is highly valued.

**Consultancy advice for practice**

Supporting training into practice has been based on a consultancy advice model to enable us to assist the transference of skills from TEACCH training more creatively. The TEACCH approach employs a range of strategies to support students in a breadth of academic and vocational activities (see Chapter 12). Consultation approaches help productive application of skills and, by focusing on trouble-shooting and reinforcement of training topics, minimise the potential discomfort for practitioners of being evaluated on their practice (Mesibov, Shea and Schopler, 2005).

This training can improve the quality of teaching and learning, and it has provided a creative approach to assessment and on-going teaching diversity. Sunfield's aim is to support Wall's (2001) proposition that:

> *A TEACCH affiliated classroom…is a changing, dynamic entity because children served are unique, changing people who are hopefully moving constantly towards realization of their full potential.*

To deliver this requires us constantly to review the physical structure, type of instruction and the tasks that are set for our students, together with a commitment to develop their independence within school and, indeed, their life.

However, we also know that this is not an easily achieved goal and that commitment to the process must be on-going. It can be achieved only if staff understand the TEACCH approach, and have on-going advisory support available as they endeavour to bring good practice into their work setting. As Baker (1998) highlights, it is not typical for orthodox training sessions alone to effect change in staff performance to a level that benefits their clients.

It appears clear that a consultancy advice model can provide a framework for the development of successful TEACCH systems because:

■ TEACCH practice is now embedded in all our processes across the 24-hour curriculum of both education and residential care departments

■ The TEACCH philosophy and practice has been promoted among all our staff

■ All key staff have been TEACCH trained

■ There is a core team of three independent trainers whose expertise can be made available to staff (with two other staff in training as trainers).

The philosophy is that whatever the level of the TEACCH training undertaken by a staff member, TEACCH trainers become their consultant support with a commitment to supporting the individual as they develop their practice following the completion of their training course.

The following case study illustrates how the model works in practice. The example is based in a classroom setting, but could equally be applied elsewhere.

**Case study: Colin[1]**

Colin is 14 years old and a day student at the school. Colin moved from a highly structured TEACCH class in Key Stage 3 (11–14 years) to a Key Stage 4 (14–16 years) class. With the onset of adolescence, a change in his medication, the complexities of his autism, and slightly reduced physical and visual structure in his new class, Colin was beginning to exhibit more challenging behaviour; and the frequency and severity of these behaviours was rapidly increasing. As a result, Colin was threatening to staff, easily distracted and completing very little work. His educational progress was severely impaired. Colin also found it difficult to transition around the classroom and spent long periods of time in the bathroom.

The staffing in the class at this time consisted of a newly qualified class teacher awaiting TEACCH training, a senior teaching assistant who, although recently trained on the five-day course, did not feel confident to promote and deliver the TEACCH approach, and two teaching assistants who had attended the two-day training.

The TEACCH approach acknowledges that people with an ASD are most often visual learners; this is reflected in the use of symbols,[2] objects, pictures and photographs to support communication. These strategies were evident in the classroom, and the TEACCH trainer was asked to provide support as a consultant to advise on setting up the broad structure required to meet Colin's needs.

In the first instance, this involved speaking to the previous class teacher to ascertain the level of structure Colin had previously relied on. As the current class teacher was new to the school, a meeting was established, involving a TEACCH trainer and Colin's previous class teacher. This approach – informally utilising the strengths of all staff – identified areas of development that were responsive to Colin's needs. This is an important issue to address, as there is a need to instil a supportive culture where staff can openly and easily identify their own strengths and areas for development, so that appropriate training and mentoring can be more easily put in place.

The meeting was very successful. It included a discussion of Colin's needs and setting up the classroom, while ensuring minimal disruption to other students in the class.

The process involved:[3]

- Putting physical structure in place with 'independent work', 'one-to-one teaching', and 'choice' areas

- Setting up a work system (number-matching (two tasks), finished box)

- Setting up a schedule (symbol cards to match to areas of the room, e.g. snack table, group table, etc.)

- Re-arranging the room to suit Colin's requirements and the needs of the other students

- Suggesting that an experienced TEACCH practitioner (senior teaching assistant), who had taught Colin before, support the class team and Colin on a temporary basis, thus fostering good practice and building the confidence of the newly trained senior in the class.

The follow-up to this involved both class teachers and the trainer informally supporting the class team during the first week, and arranging to meet with them at the end of this period. Further meetings were planned to take place over the subsequent months.

The outcomes were that:

- Colin now completes up to five tasks in his work station at any given time

- He is settled and relaxed within the classroom environment

- Fewer incidents of challenging behaviour occur

- He transitions around the classroom with very few difficulties

- There is a significant reduction in time spent in the bathroom during the school day

- He will sit appropriately at the group table for snack and group activities.

Staff recognised that Colin's surroundings now made sense to him and that, as a result, he understood where he had to go and what he had to do throughout the day. He has continued to work well within class, and staff are now asking questions about how they can implement a similar programme for other students in the group.

This model of support, although effective and successful, was not without remaining issues which needed to be addressed, including:

- Some staff members lacking confidence and feeling an inability to express this

- More experienced TEACCH-trained staff needing to learn to work in new ways, sharing their expertise with colleagues beyond their own classroom

- Demands on trainer/consultant time could be excessive

- The need for continual investment in TEACCH training for all staff.

In response to these issues, the trainer/consultants have implemented a refresher course, established TEACCH representatives from residential and educational settings, and devised a recording form.

Refresher training attended by staff who have attended the two-day course was devised by the TEACCH training team. Attendance has been by open application; however, the rolling programme will be monitored to ensure that all staff attend and maintain up-to-date knowledge and skills.

A refresher course for five-day TEACCH-trained staff is conducted in collaboration with Division TEACCH on a biennial basis. Managers identify staff to attend based on individual and organisational priorities. The course focus is on further developing individual skills by reviewing the concepts and components of the structured teaching model, and using discussion and activities to identify progressive support strategies. This has added a further element to the professional development helix, extending reflective practice opportunities.

A forum has been established, consisting of the TEACCH trainers and staff representing each residential and educational setting. The TEACCH representative role includes acting as the identified point of contact and collaboration between residential care, school, families and TEACCH trainers. Meetings are held termly, and provide an opportunity for staff to pool ideas and discuss potential solutions to problems encountered in practice. This has been of benefit in identifying and sharing good practice, and building confidence in using and developing structured teaching approaches.

The representative ensures that for each student an assessment is carried out and a summary form completed and distributed. School staff teams complete TEACCH set-up forms for their students. The set-up form contains information regarding physical structure, schedule, work system, visual structure, communication system and additional information. As students move through school, the information is updated and shared with new staff, and these forms have facilitated a smoother transition for students from class to class.

The forms are working documents which are amended regularly, and team collaboration in compiling the forms has led to a greater understanding of students' individual support needs and awareness of their long-term targets. Regular TEACCH trainer visits are used to review the TEACCH set-up with staff and discuss current issues. Staff confidence has improved as a result. The form provides a tool for both trainer and staff to reflect critically on the individual set-up and helps to ensure that all student needs are addressed.

## Conclusion
Benefits for trainers of working to a consultancy advice model have been:

- Clearer understanding of implementation levels across site
- Ability to provide individualised and targeted response to practice issues
- Feedback for training day content and delivery style
- Opportunity to articulate guiding principles
- Improved cross-site development and transdisciplinary implementation.

There may be considerable time constraints on trainer availability, and monitoring may need to take place as a component of other tasks. However, mentoring of practice has helped to maintain integrity of implementation, and to ensure that the focus of TEACCH implementation is maintaining the benefits for Sunfield's students. Five-day TEACCH-trained staff now work together more closely with all staff to prepare for new students or to support existing students, and this collaboration has been of benefit to all: promoting positive relationships, widening the skill base and relieving time pressures on trainers.

A number of research studies have identified that 'work environment factors' may significantly impede the application of training in human services (Clarke, 2002). In other words, there needs to be a supportive culture in place (Smidt, Balandin, Reed and Sigafoos, 2002). The role of the training team, both inside and outside the training room, needs to include the fostering of a culture that enables sustained development of TEACCH practices. Any ASD will present differently depending on the individual. It is therefore unlikely that one singular intervention will be successful for all individuals with ASD (Jordan, Jones and Murray, 1998), and it is important that staff are enabled to assess and individualise student support.

Though the end-of-course evaluations confirm the effectiveness of the five-day training, it is only with continuing consultancy, advice and further training that staff will move forward in their practice interventions, and that the key principles will become embedded. Opportunities for practising skills learnt in the training room must be actively linked to working practices and maintained.

This chapter has sought to identify the key issues affecting sustainability of the training experience in practice. The results of this process have been used to improve internal training programmes, develop appropriate resources, inform the role of trainers as consultants, and develop support roles within teams.

## References

Baker, D. (1998) 'Effects of video-based staff training with manager-led exercises in residential support', *Mental Retardation*, 36 (3), 198–204.

Carpenter, B., Chatwin, I. and Egerton, J. (2001) 'An evaluation of SIECCA: an intensive programme of education and care for students with profound autistic spectrum disorders', *Good Autism Practice*, 2 (1), 52–66.

Clarke, N. (2002) 'Job/work environment factors influencing training transfer within a human service agency: some indicative support for Baldwin and Ford's transfer climate construct', *International Journal of Training and Development*, 6 (3), 146–162.

Gaines Robinson, D. and Robinson, J. (1995) *Performance Consulting: Moving beyond training.* San Francisco, CA: Berrett-Kohler.

Jordan, R. and Powell, S. (1996) 'Therapist drift: identifying a new phenomenon in evaluating therapeutic approaches'. In: G. Linfoot and P. Shattock (eds) *Therapeutic Intervention in Autism.* Sunderland: University of Sunderland Autism Research Unit.

Jordan, R., Jones, G. and Murray, D. (1998) *Educational Interventions for Children with Autism: A literature review of recent and current research.* Sudbury: Department for Education and Employment.

Kirkpatrick, D. (1994) *Evaluating Training Programs: the four levels.* San Francisco, CA: Berrett-Koehler.

Little, M. and Houston, D. (2003) 'Research into practice through professional development', *Remedial and Special Education*, 24 (2), 75–87.

McKenzie, K., Paxton, D., Patrick, S., Matheson, E. and Murray, G. (2000) 'An evaluation of the impact of a one-day challenging behaviour course on the knowledge of health and social care staff working in learning disability services', *Journal of Learning Disabilities*, 4 (2), 153–165.

Mesibov, G., Shea, V. and Schopler, E. (2005) *The TEACCH Approach to Autism Spectrum Disorders.* New York: Plenum.

Nickols, F. (2003) 'Evaluating training: there is no cookbook approach'. [Online at: http://home.att.net/~OPSINC/evaluating_training.pdf]

Phillips, J. (1994) *Handbook of Training Evaluation and Measurement Methods (2nd edn).* Houston, TX: Gulf.

Showers, B. (1990) 'Aiming for superior classroom instruction for all children: a comprehensive staff development model', *Remedial and Special Education*, 11, 35–39.

Smidt, A., Balandin, S., Reed, V. and Sigafoos, J. (2002) *Staff Training: An overview of recent research on residential care staff supporting people with intellectual disabilities with communication difficulties and challenging behaviour.* Conference papers from 'Disability and diversity: successful living', Westmead, Sydney, Australia (March).

Wall A.J. (2001) *TEACCH Structured Teaching Approach Checklist: Tri-level consultation goals.* Charlotte, NC: Division TEACCH.

**Endnotes**

[1] Names have been changed to protect identity.

[2] Symbols are generated using the 'Writing with Symbols' software package, available from Widgit Software (http://www.widgit.com/products/wws2000/index.htm).

[3] Refer to Chapter 12 for a more detailed explanation of specialist terms and rationale.

# PART 6

# Preparing for the Future

# CHAPTER 14

# Preparation for Adulthood

## Pathways in Recognised Attainment

*Maureen Porter*

## Introduction

In the last century, education in UK schools for young people between the ages of 14 and 19 years has been described as a 'one-size-fits-all' approach (Morris, 2002) in which curriculum delivery took little account of the individual learner; if the student could not learn within the education system, then it was their problem. However, with an increasing number of students becoming alienated from the learning system, the Tomlinson report (1996), the first national inquiry in England into further education provision for students with disabilities and/or learning difficulties, laid the responsibility for student engagement at the feet of those delivering the curriculum.

Recognition of the importance of providing young people with intellectual disabilities with access to continuing education and training opportunity came with the Warnock report (1978), while the Further and Higher Education Act (1992) placed a duty upon the Further Education Funding Council to take their requirements into account. However, almost 20 years on from the Warnock report, Tomlinson found that the overall quality of learning for students with disabilities was poorer than for other students, and many disabled people were not receiving any further education[1] at all. He identified the need for a more inclusive further education sector (Dunn, 2003), proposing that provision and support should match the needs of individual learners:

> *The aim is not for students to simply take part in further education but to be actively included and fully engaged in their learning. At the heart of our thinking lies the idea of match or fit between how the learner learns best, what they need and want to learn and what is required from the FE sector, the college and teachers for successful learning to take place.*

Tomlinson's report marked the beginning of an on-going, focused commitment by the UK government to reform further education (Dearing ,1997; Kennedy, 1998; Department for Education and Employment (DfEE), 1999, 2000; Department for Education and Skills (DfES), 2002a,b, 2003a, 2005, 2006; Learning and Skills Council, 2005).

As a preliminary development, the government reconfigured the curriculum to meet their concerns about the low numbers of students in the UK who continued in school beyond the age of compulsory schooling (16 years), which was among the lowest in the developed world (DfES, 2006). Prior to this, there had been discontinuity between the Key Stage 4 curriculum (i.e. for students between the ages of 14 and 16 years) and the further education curriculum (for students age 16–19 years), with courses being discrete within each curriculum. New '14–19' curricular planning encouraged courses with learning progressions which spanned Key Stage 4 and the further education. This meant that students intending to complete the course of learning would automatically aim to stay at school beyond the age of 16 years. More recent government objectives also aim to create increased continuity between Key Stage 3 (i.e. for students between the ages of 11 and 14 years) and Key Stage 4 curricula (DfES, 2005) and between school and college courses.

On 21 January 2003, the Government published its vision for transforming the way the education system caters for young people in *14–19: Opportunity and excellence.* It set out a staged process of reforms, designed to offer a more personalised learning route for all students so that they would develop increased skills for life, work and further learning, and could fulfil their potential. The report recognised the educational phase between 14 and 19 years as critical for young people, being a time when earlier learning was consolidated and used to prepare for adult life and employment. It called for greater choice and quality:

> *...excellent provision that responds to [students'] needs, enables them to progress in their learning and prepares them for the modern workplace;*

and identified the current 14–19 curriculum as needing:

- Greater coherence and continuity between earlier learning and skills for adulthood to allow smooth transition between these life stages

- Greater subject breadth, with vocational subjects being valued equally with academic subjects

- Tailored learning to meet the individual needs and aptitudes of students.

It stated that expectations of student capability and achievement should be high, and that schools should:

> *...ensure that all young people have an experience of learning which stimulates, motivates and stretches them so they achieve their full potential.*

While core rafts of subjects were required for Key Stage 4 and further education students, there was to be a greater emphasis on work-related and enterprise learning and 'experience beyond the curriculum...which can enrich learning whilst developing and expressing creative and practical skills and interests'.

School links with further education colleges, the community and the world of work were encouraged, together with more out-of-classroom learning. There was also greater emphasis on effective assessment, monitoring and accreditation which would take account of different learning and teaching styles and ensure on-going curriculum relevance for individual students.

This person-centred approach within further education was further underpinned by wider government policy. Both *Improving the Life Chances of Disabled People* (Prime Minister's Strategy Unit, 2005) and *Removing Barriers to Achievement* (DfES, 2004a) articulated a commitment to inclusion of young people with disabilities in further education. *Every Child Matters* (2003b, 2004b) stated the need for services to maximise opportunities and minimise risks for all children and young people, and focus more effectively on the family. *Valuing People* (Department of Health, 2001) emphasised the importance of rights, independence, choice and inclusion for people with disabilities, and the Special Educational Needs and Disability Act (2001; now 'Part 4' of the Disability Discrimination Act 2005) introduced new rights for learners with disabilities and responsibilities for education providers.

Alongside young people's rights to an individually planned, appropriate curriculum, these documents emphasised the need for staff training to support the delivery of such a curriculum (Tomlinson, 1996).

### Sunfield's 14–19 curriculum

Sunfield provides education for students between 6 and19 years with severe and complex learning needs, and it aims to offer all its students a broad, balanced, relevant and coherent curriculum. How this is interpreted for students across the school differs according to their age. In the lower school (ages 6–13 years), schemes of work are derived from the UK National Curriculum programmes of study. These provide continuity, progression and appropriate learning contexts for students. The upper school caters for students between the ages of 14 and 19 years, through the Key Stage 4 and the further education curricula (the '14–19 curriculum'). The upper school gives students access to opportunities for learning, while aiming to confer adult dignity through greater access to relationships, choice, autonomy and self-advocacy.

Sunfield began to reform its approach to further education[2] from 1997 onwards. Previously, the emphasis had been on a student-centred, therapeutic curriculum, which prepared students for adulthood by equipping them with creative skills (e.g. crafts) which would have occupied them in the old-style residential homes for adults with intellectual disabilities. There had been no links with further education colleges or work placements, no system of accreditation, and the curriculum had lacked the breadth, balance and continuity now in place.

After being promoted to head of 14–19 education in 2001, the writer realised that although substantial improvements had been made, the Sunfield further education curriculum was a document much in need of revision. It had become very subject-led, rather than student-centred, with the National Curriculum subject focus in the lower school continuing into further education. Additional extra-curricular activities (e.g. external sports activities) had been randomly linked at various times. Some students had opportunities to study modules at college, and others were involved in on-site work placements; various accreditation schemes had been adopted by different classes. However, student opportunity and implementation of accreditation schemes were inconsistent, and there was little coherence. In some classes, each student would be using a different accreditation scheme, which was unworkable for the teaching staff. The curriculum lacked framework, purpose and consistency, and did not adequately prepare students for the opportunities, responsibilities and experiences of adult life.

The formulation of the new further education curriculum became a focus of research. The aim of the study was to review arrangements in the light of the current policy context, and investigate potential developments in respect of the 14–19 curriculum for students. While the policy perspective provided the driving force for the reform of

Sunfield's 14–19 curriculum, there was scope for individualisation to meet the needs of our students with severe and complex learning needs.

As a residential school, Sunfield had a variety of settings in which students had the potential to learn – in the classroom, in the residential care houses, in the extensive grounds, in the community. It was therefore decided that a 24-hour curriculum would be implemented. Supported learning across the range of contexts, delivered by residential care, education, psychology and therapies staff, ensured that students' learning experiences were not fractured, but were consolidated within 'real life' situations.

## Methodology

An evaluative survey was carried out (Robson, 2002) to obtain the opinions of the Sunfield teachers and residential care leaders who were responsible for the learning of students between the ages of 14 and 19 years. They were asked about the 14–19 curriculum as it was at that time, and for their ideas about what a reformed 14–19 curriculum might and might not include. A project diary was also kept.

## Participants

Differentiated questionnaires were sent out to nine school teachers and six residential care team leaders who had varied responsibility for students' education between the ages of 14 and 19 years at Sunfield. Among the eighteen students in the further education department, eight students had an understanding of the purpose of the investigation. All eight were invited to take part in a supported survey and communicate their curriculum likes and dislikes, either through speech or rebus symbols. The needs of the remaining students, as perceived by staff, were articulated through staff questionnaires.

## Data collection

Data was gathered over a three-month period using questionnaires, and interviews and participant/non-participant observations which were recorded in a project diary.

*Questionnaires*

Three questionnaires were designed. They used a combined approach, of both open and closed questions, to allow the respondents to express a broad range of ideas about the current further education curriculum and how this curriculum might be improved in the future.

■ The questionnaires were designed for teachers in two different departments – those with classes of age range 14–19 years and those with a 16–19-year age range, with the first ten questions being common to the two departments; the remaining questions were specific to the age range taught.

■ The second questionnaire was sent to the staff working in the students' residential care.

■ The final questionnaire was designed to be completed by the participating students with support from staff.

Before being sent out to staff, the questionnaires were trialled with a small group of teachers not concerned with the actual research, and this led to some amendments being made.

*Project diary*

The project diary was used to note comparisons between the whole department curriculum delivery and a class-based model. Observations (participant and non-participant), key points of informal conversations and discussions, and any curriculum changes made with reasons and their outcomes, etc. were also recorded. The outcomes of informal interviews with residential care staff were noted in the diary.

Following data collection using these methods, a focused discussion was held with the head of education during which a long-term plan for 14–19 curriculum reform at Sunfield was developed, future delivery was addressed, and the potential for incorporating an external accreditation programme within the curriculum was discussed.

## Ethical considerations

Ethics are a central principle of research practice, and it is important that the researcher is absolutely clear about the nature of their agreement with the research participants in terms of research focus, consent, privacy, confidentiality, participant rights and the benefits, practical application and dissemination of the research (Opie, 2004; Robson, 2002; Wellington, 2000). In this research project, fully informed permission was obtained at organisational level as well as from all persons individually involved – staff, parents for the students, and the students themselves as far as they were able. The promise of confidentiality and a statement of the right of participants to withdraw from the research at any time were placed on all questionnaires, and no names or identifying details were required. The focused discussion with the head of education was audiotaped and transcribed, and she was aware of her right to check and approve the resulting transcript.

## Analysis of results

*Questionnaires*

Of the nine questionnaires sent out to teachers, seven were returned; of the six sent out to team leaders, five were returned; and all eight students agreed to take part and completed their questionnaires.

### *The education perspective*

The questionnaires circulated to teachers comprised questions concerning classroom management (five questions), policy/guidance awareness (one question) and teaching and learning (eleven questions). In this chapter, the results and discussion have been based upon the questions related to 'Teaching and learning', which have been categorised according to the key features derived from the literature survey.

*Student needs*

Teachers were asked to identify priority learning needs for each of the students in their class, giving a total of 76 responses. In summary, these were:

- Communication/listening skills (34 responses) + (2* responses)

- Independence skills (17 responses) + (2* responses)

- Co-operation skills (13 responses)

- Behaviour development strategies (9 responses)

- Range of experiences (2* responses)

Two teachers (*) listed needs for their class as a whole rather than for individual students.

*Curriculum relevance*

Teachers articulated their sense of responsibility for making the curriculum relevant for their students, stating that they wanted to make the curriculum meaningful to individual students (four statements; n=18), and that they expected students to achieve and progress (five statements). However, they were concerned about the relevance of the curriculum subjects to their students (three statements) and, in particular, the approach to the teaching of literacy and numeracy (six statements). All four further education department teachers stated that they delivered literacy and numeracy in appropriate contexts rather than in timetabled sessions.

Teachers of 16–19-year-old students were asked to indicate which of a range of subjects they considered should be included in their curriculum. The results are shown in Table 14.1 below.

**Table 14.1. Subjects which teachers considered appropriate within a curriculum for students aged 16–19 years**

| Number of teachers indicating appropriateness of subject | | | | |
|---|---|---|---|---|
| **4** | **3** | **2** | **1** | **0** |
| Application of number, Communication, Creative arts, Current affairs (relating to immediate environs), Home management, Improving own learning, Information technology, Leisure/recreation, Personal, Social and Health Education, Problem-solving, Relating to others | Citizenship, World of work | Literacy, Numeracy, Technology | Careers | History, Modern foreign languages, Science |

Alongside Home Management, already listed in Table 14.1, teachers found the following areas of the existing curriculum to be particularly useful:

■ Community access outings

■ College placements

■ Work experience.

However, they found that some sensory-based learning options were not useful (e.g. the soft play area (three statements; n=17), sensory suite (four statements)), and some out-of-classroom areas were also deemed not useful (e.g. farm classroom (six statements), games room (two statements), food technology room (two statements)).

When asked for suggestions for additional curriculum activities, two teachers asked for specific exercise programmes modelled on gym/fitness suite activities, and two teachers suggested that the food technology room should be improved so that practical life skills could be more realistic.

*Curriculum continuity*

Teachers of Key Stage 4 students were asked about priority skills which would aid the transition of their students to the further education curriculum. In response (n=8 responses), teachers thought that communication (three responses), broadening of experience (three responses) and behaviour development strategies (three responses) were the most important areas.

*Teaching approaches*

Teachers employed a number of approaches to increase learning opportunities for the students in their classroom, including structured teaching (TEACCH model), small group teaching and sensory approaches.

When asked which aspects of the curriculum they found most successful for their students, they identified aspects which came within the vocational, daily life skills, social and leisure areas:

- College placements/work experience (eleven responses; n=27)
- Cross-curriculum extension through off-site visits (seven responses)
- Home management (five responses)
- Sensory curriculum (three responses)
- Circle time (one response).

*Assessment and accreditation*

Student assessment

The questionnaire revealed that there were a number of different assessment/evaluation methods used by teachers educating the 14–19 year age group: three teachers used 'P' levels;[3] four used subject levels; and seven used Integrated Curriculum targets (n=14).

Accreditation

There were also a number of accreditation schemes being used across the 14–19 department, including the Award Scheme Development and Accreditation Network's (ASDAN) 'Towards Independence' (two teachers; n=7), 'Transition Challenge' (one teacher) and 'Further Education Level Up Awards' (one teacher), while two teachers used the 'Accreditation for Life and Living' (ALL) scheme from Oxford, Cambridge and Royal Society of Arts (OCR).

All teachers valued accreditation schemes, and articulated a variety of reasons for this. There were thirteen responses focusing on the schemes' benefits to the students – that it gave the students a sense of achievement/purpose (seven responses; n=16), allowed students to achieve at their own level (three responses) and celebrate small steps towards larger achievements (three responses). All seven teachers said that students and their parents enjoyed the recognition they received on Prize-giving Open Day, some adding that the certificates gave the students a concrete indication of achievement (three comments).

Two responses identified the curricular benefits, saying that it gave extra breadth to the curriculum.

Teachers also commented (n=10 comments) on the organisational benefits of using the schemes in terms of long- and medium-term planning (seven comments), and on the benefits of differentiated levels within the schemes (three comments). Key Stage 4 teachers appreciated the ideas given within the schemes for cross-curricular teaching.

When asked about disadvantages associated with external accreditation schemes, teachers articulated (n=14 comments): problems with gauging the correct levels of evidence (two comments); gathering/organising evidence (five comments); and meeting the moderation deadlines (five comments). Two Key Stage 4 teachers commented on the difficulty of running the dual system of National Curriculum alongside accreditation.

*Further comments concerning the 14–19 curriculum*
Teachers made a number of suggestions (three comments; n=6) directly relating to improving the 14–19 curriculum. These included:

- The creation of opportunities for skills specialists to support different curriculum areas more intensively

- The provision of more information about age-appropriate resources

- The development of opportunities for students to focus on skills which were relevant to their transition to adult life.

### The residential care perspective
The questionnaires circulated to residential care leaders comprised 10 questions, all relating to teaching and learning within the residential care environment.

All leaders (five) said that it was their responsibility to provide a good, caring and enjoyable experience for the young people in their care. In addition, comments were made (n=11) about the need to provide a link between students' family homes and residential care environments (four comments), to provide role models for daily living (three comments), to prepare young people for adulthood (three comments) and to encourage independence (one comment).

They identified each young person's specific needs (n=124 comments) within the residential care environment, which were categorised as follows:

- Self-help and independence skills (30 comments)

- Communication skills (29 comments)

- Awareness of danger (22 comments)

- Behaviour development strategies (17 comments)

- Community skills (16 comments)

- To learn tolerance of others (10 comments).

Leaders' responses to the question about encouraging student self-advocacy related to the students' ability to communicate their opinions – one leader pointed out the difficulties of making sure the students who were less assertive were also listened to.

*Activities*
Students had access to a wide variety of activities, although there were limitations related to level of staff support needed by students in the community. The focus of teaching/learning in the residential care houses (n=5) related to personal and group leisure activities (e.g. computer games, bike-riding, etc.), both on- and off-site, and to specific targets for the Integrated Curriculum (four responses), external accreditation (one response) and Personal Social and Health Education (one response).

*Accreditation*
Of the five residential care houses, one house used an external accreditation scheme, and found the continuity provided for students' learning between the education and residential care environments useful; four had specific times set for students to work on ACCESS targets. One house used out-of-school activities to enhance Personal Social and Health Education. One house stated that it was difficult to allocate responsibility for different targets between education and school, and to provide acceptable evidence.

*The 24-hour curriculum*
While all leaders agreed that the young people needed to learn to generalise skills across a variety of settings, involving different people, places and equipment, and felt that cross-setting targets were a good idea, their additional comments (n=11) suggested that the strategies currently in place to support this were not adequate. Some indicated that the Integrated Curriculum targets were not totally appropriate, and that target-setting was confusing (four comments); others expressed difficulties in liaising with education staff (two comments).

*Further comments relating to a 14–19, 24-hour curriculum*
Two comments were made – one suggesting that school staff might make occasional visits to the residential care houses during out-of-school hours, and the other reflecting positively upon an improved relationship with school staff after implementing shared learning targets for students: 'We feel more as if we're working as a team now.'

### The student perspective
The questionnaire given to students gave them the chance for self-advocacy, for as Clare (1990) states, the core components of self-advocacy are:

- Being able to express thoughts and feelings

- Being able to make choices

- Being able to make changes.

It is important that students learn that they have choices and there is the possibility of choice. This is where this questionnaire had its starting point.

The students were introduced to the questionnaire in a group lesson. They discussed each question, one by one, and after each discussion they were asked to fill in the answers. Teaching staff were on hand to give assistance with the questions about lessons 'liked best' and lessons 'not liked', and with writing. Of the twelve students involved, eight were able to answer the questions reliably.

Of the eight students, five were currently taking part in work experience, and three had done so in a previous term. Four students went to college.

They were asked questions about what they did and did not like about the curriculum, and their answers are tabulated below (see Table 14.2).

**Table 14.2. Students' (n=8) curriculum likes and dislikes**

| Subject / Opinion | Environment | Cooking (Cookery Room) | Computers (Computer Room) | Art /painting | Making things | Minibus outings | Writing | 'Doing work' | Sitting down (for a long time) | College | Visiting the farm | Games room | Working on targets |
|---|---|---|---|---|---|---|---|---|---|---|---|---|---|
| Like | 7 | 6 (4) | 7 (4) | 7 | 7 | 8 | 4 | – | – | – | – | 5 | 4 |
| Don't like | 1 | – | – | – | – | – | 4 | 7 | 4 | 1 | 3 | – | – |

When asked for their opinions on what they would like to do in school, the students offered three suggestions:

- *Play my CDs*
- *Watch TV*
- *Play my games on the computer*!

## Analysis and discussion
### Responsibilities of staff towards students
Both teachers and team leaders identified responsibilities towards students appropriate to their setting, with team leaders predominantly expressing their role in terms of supporting contact with families, providing role models in the residential environment and preparing the young people for adulthood. Teachers saw their responsibilities as curriculum focused – making sure the curriculum was relevant and accessible to their students and that they could progress. While residential staff saw their contribution in terms of providing continuity for students, both in terms of maintaining family links and teaching life skills in preparation for adulthood, teachers were concerned with providing access to learning and development. In terms of the governments' recommendations for further education, the two perspectives needed to be brought together to bring about meaningful progression and learning within the context of preparation for adulthood.

### Student priority learning needs
Teachers and team leaders identified similar priority learning needs for their students, with the two categories of highest importance – 'Communication/Listening skills' and 'Independence skills' – differing only in the order in which they were placed by the two groups. Behaviour development strategies also featured in both lists. In the context of a shared curriculum, this suggests that common targets could easily be implemented across both settings.

Shared targets were already in place between some houses and classes. Where this was happening effectively, the team leader felt that it had created a better working relationship between the two staff groups; however, two team leaders said that students' key workers had experienced difficulties in liaising with teachers about targets, and some found the Integrated Curriculum confusing, and questioned its relevance.

This suggested that while there was potential for teaching responsibilities to be shared between the classrooms and houses, the targets and system needed to be reviewed.

### Teaching approaches

Differentiated teaching approaches were being used widely across site (e.g. structured teaching (TEACCH model; see Chapters 12 and 13), split groups), and it would be necessary to recognise these in planning the curriculum.

### Curriculum content

The subjects prioritised by teachers for inclusion in any future 14–19 curriculum corresponded with recommendations in the policy literature (DfES, 2005), being strongly vocational and related to daily life. While 'Literacy' and 'Numeracy' as subjects were considered important by only two teachers each, their practical application was considered important by the majority of teachers via 'Application of number' and 'Communication'. This concern for relevance is reflected in the literature (DfES, 2005) where teachers using the 14–19 curriculum are recommended to introduce core subjects in meaningful, 'real life' contexts. However, informal notes from the project diary suggested that many teachers found delivery in context difficult to confirm, and there was a lack of evidence of assessment of progress. This would need to be addressed within the revised curriculum, and training delivered if necessary.

The documents relating to curriculum reform stress the duty of schools and other service providers to provide focused training for staff, stating that they cannot be expected to deliver an appropriate curriculum without training (Tomlinson, 1996). It would be important to explore areas of the curriculum in which further training could be offered to staff. The project diary records the suggestion of some teachers that staff with particular skills could share them with other classes.

The subjects within the existing curriculum which the teachers listed as most valuable for students (see above) were practical and non-classroom based. This was also a feature recognised in the literature (DfES, 2003a) as desirable within the 14–19 curriculum. Half the students responding to the questionnaire also said that they did not like 'sitting down' (for a long time). This being the case, it was surprising that some teachers found that non-classroom based areas (e.g. the soft play room, the sensory suite, the farm, the food technology room) were not useful. It was important to include these areas within a broadly based, balanced and relevant curriculum, but also to investigate the reasons for these areas being under-used, and to arrange for training if appropriate.

The more academic subjects of 'Science', 'Modern foreign languages', and 'History' were considered important by none of the teachers responding to the questionnaire. However, science remained a requirement of the core curriculum in both Key Stage 4 and further education. In addition to indicating a lack of belief in its relevance, teachers' opinions might also reflect a lack of confidence in delivery and in making it accessible to students.

### Resources

In addition to under-utilisation of some across-site resources, the project diary notes indicated that there had been a number of instances where resources were being used which were not appropriate to the students' ages, which would need to be addressed.

### *Assessment*

In the focused interview with the head of education, it was requested that the area of within-class, student assessment should be addressed to ensure it was fit for purpose and built into curriculum expectations.

### *Accreditation*

Teachers' and team leaders' felt that externally moderated accreditation schemes were very beneficial for both students and staff for a wide variety of reasons. However, responses to questions about accreditation revealed the variety of different schemes which were used within the school and within the same classroom. This could impose an almost unworkable burden on teaching staff, a fact noted by one Key Stage 4 teacher trying to fulfil the demands of multiple accreditation schemes and the National Curriculum. This therefore indicated that the implementation of accreditation schemes needed to be reviewed; with so many parallel schemes in operation there was a danger that continuity of learning for students would be lost due to teacher overload.

Accreditation schemes needed to be made relevant and accessible across the range of students' abilities. The head of education also asked for the planning of accreditation to be introduced formally into the curriculum and across the department to avoid repetition or duplication of modules by either classes or houses. The implementation would also include the keeping of records showing planning, progress and attainment. The accreditation schemes adopted would be extended into the residential care setting and the Key Stage 4 curriculum to provide continuity of attainment for students.

### *College/work placements*

Teachers stated that college and work placements were valuable for students; however, informal discussions recorded in the project diary revealed that the more able students appeared to have better opportunities for college placements, and students at a lower developmental stage appeared not to have equal opportunity to access all the types of work experience on offer. Team leaders also articulated difficulty with engaging students at a lower developmental level in terms of role modelling. The differentiated inclusion of these young people was something that needed to be addressed when planning the 14–19 curriculum.

### Outcomes

The information gathered from the questionnaires and project diaries, and the focused discussion with the head of education, resulted in the following recommendations being made regarding the 14–19 curriculum, which were specifically relevant to the further education curriculum, but also had implications for the Key Stage 4 curriculum:

1. **The construction of a three-year further education curriculum** which:

    a. Meets the needs of all students

    b. Optimises the use of resources

    c. Is delivered in an appropriate learning environment

    d. Achieves good accreditation results

e.   Is of the highest quality

f.   Secures continuity of education for students between ages 14 and 19 years.

This was achieved by:

- Comparing three existing schemes (Byers and Rose, 1996; Dorchester Curriculum Group, 2002; Equals, 1999; Further Education Unit/Mencap, 1995) and taking elements from each to create a curriculum for students that would 'prepare them to live as able and informed citizens' (Dearing, 1997)

- Using the staff suggestions from the further education questionnaire to include the following subjects:

  - □ 'Environment', 'Creative development' and 'Current affairs', which were grouped as 'Knowledge and understanding of the world'.

  - □ 'Personal, social and health education (PSHE)', 'Community' and 'Home management', which were grouped under 'Life skills'

  - □ 'World of work' and 'Careers education', which were grouped under 'Vocational studies'

  - □ 'Key skills' replaced 'Literacy' and 'Numeracy' and included the following elements: 'Communication', 'Application of number', 'Information Technology', 'Relating to others', 'Improving one's own learning and performance' and 'Problem-solving'. These were be taught in relevant contexts.

The curriculum was designed to be a three-year, rolling curriculum, covering the same curriculum areas and subjects each year, but with a different and specific emphasis in each term and year. Table 14.3 shows an example of a Year 3 curriculum area within 'Life skills'

- Assessment was addressed by producing nine level descriptors for each subject within a study area. These were used in conjunction with record sheets for each level, thereby producing a record of progress within a subject for the three years a student would be in the further education department.

2.   **To introduce external accreditation pathways** to

a.   All classrooms and residential care houses for students in the age range 14–19 years.

- Accreditation was associated with the subject and topics for each year. It had built-in differentiation, offering different accreditation pathways for all levels. These were categorised under 'core', 'support' and 'extension'

- The accreditation schemes selected were:

  - □ *For the 'core' students*: 'Towards Independence' from ASDAN[4]

  - □ *For the 'extension' students*: 'Level Up Award' from ASDAN, which offers progression to Further Education Level 1 and Key Skills at 'Entry Level'[5].

  - □ *For the 'support' students and Key Stage 4*: The 'Accreditation for Life and Living (ALL)' programme from Oxford, Cambridge and Royal Society

**Table 14.3. Example of a differentiated Sunfield further education curriculum area ('Community') for 'Year 3' of 'Life Skills', and the associated level descriptors**

| LIFE SKILLS | Autumn | Spring | Summer |
|---|---|---|---|
| COMMUNITY | *Areas for activity* | *Religions* | *International environment issues* |
| CORE (all students) | ← TI The world around us → | | |
| SUPPORT (some) | **Transition Challenge** Independent living 9 Positive self-image 9 Personal development 9 **ALL** Community: Introductory module (½) First module (½) | **Transition Challenge** All modules: Activity 7 | **Transition Challenge** Positive self-image 9 |
| EXTENSION (a few) | FEAS level 1/level 2 FEAS bronze award | | |

| LEVEL DESCRIPTORS |
|---|

**Community**

At each level, the student will:

**Level 1**
- Experience a range of local services pertinent to their own needs
- Accept the presence of another person

**Level 2**
- Demonstrate an awareness of changes in their own environment
- Acknowledge the presence of other people

**Level 3**
- Recognise a range of services within the school
- Express likes/dislikes within an immediate environment
- Initiate an interaction with another person

**Level 4**
- Request a service to meet a need within the home or school situation
- Contribute to an environmental/community project alongside others

**Level 5**
- Identify a local environment/community problem and suggest solutions
- Comment positively and negatively on services they receive

**Level 6**
- Recognise a range of features which identify an environment
- Show an understanding that the environment can be changed for better or worse through the actions of other people
- Identify a range of roles which people can take in a community

**Level 7**
- Know the existence of and how to contact local services such as Citizens Advice Bureau, departments for issuing bus passes, etc.
- Contribute to and participate in an event or enterprise that helps other people

**Level 8**
- Recognise environmental issues which occur at national and international levels
- Recognise the purpose and consequences of rules and regulations in society

**Level 9**
- Recognise the main features of an area and explain how they contribute to its function
- Recognise how they and the community interact and how it can influence their life and that of others.

of Arts (OCR).[6]

As suggested through the questionnaire responses, the core accreditation scheme offers formal recognition for small steps in achievement towards a larger goal. It presents a framework of activities through which personal, social and independence skills can be developed. Some accreditation models were spread over a term, some two terms, and some covered the academic year. Therefore every student had access to accreditation at levels commensurate with their ability.

3.   **To integrate the post-16 curriculum with Key Stage 4**

- ■   Transition Challenge was also introduced within the Key Stage 4 curriculum at age 14 years. It can be undertaken with as much support as necessary, thus encouraging progression as students become more independent through their learning. This supported the aim of smooth transition between Key Stage 4 and the further education department. This also ensured that achievement was recorded across the range of statutory programmes of study, contributing to the 'Skills of adult living' recommended by the Dearing Review (1997) in relation to provision for students aged 14–19 years.

- ■   The head of care, care managers and staff in residential care houses were approached about sharing the responsibility for collecting evidence for accreditation and working towards specific targets to achieve this for individual students.

**Conclusion**

This research has had a beneficial impact on students' learning at Sunfield. Outcomes from the research have informed aspects of the Key Stage 4 curriculum, and the revised further education curriculum is now being used across the further education department on a three-year rolling plan. Within both these curricula, there are expectations that students will achieve externally moderated awards.

Since this review of Sunfield's 14–19 curriculum was carried out, the government has published further influential documents aimed at 14–19 reform, and these continue to reflect the concerns raised, and encourage the reforms set out, in *14–19: Extending opportunities, raising standards* (DfES, 2002b) and *14–19: Opportunity and Excellence* (DfES, 2003a).

Sunfield's main and further education curricula were assessed in 2006 by the UK Office for Standards in Education[7], and we are proud of the accolade we received:

> *The curriculum is outstanding. It is broad in range, but specifically targeted at the individual needs of each pupil... The curriculum for older pupils is enhanced through links with local colleges. Pupils are supported in these placements and the impact of their social development is significant. The greatest strength of the curriculum is that its provision and planning are totally enmeshed. All elements are mutually supportive of each other and the impact of these is rigorously monitored.*

However, management of the Key Stage 4 and further education curricula is an ongoing challenge. An effective curriculum is one which is permanently under review, and continually modified to meet the changing nature and demands of the students to whom it is delivered. For this reason, no curriculum will ever be conclusive, but will rather reflect the policy situation at a particular time and the changing needs of our changing student population. At Sunfield, teaching, training and learning is at the heart of what we do, and we believe that it is the right of every learner to receive excellent teaching and training (DfES, 2002a) which will allow them to look forward to a life which has 'prospects, dignity and a sense of control' (Prime Minister's Strategy Unit, 2005).

## References

Byers, R. and Rose, R. (1996) *Planning the Curriculum for Pupils with Special Educational Needs.* London: David Fulton.

Clare, M. (1990) *Developing Self-Advocacy Skills with People with Disabilities and Learning Difficulties.* London: Further Education Unit.

Dearing, R. (1997) *Higher Education in the Learning Society: Report of the National Committee of Inquiry into Higher Education.* London: DfES. [Online at http://www.leeds.ac.uk/educol/ncihe/]

Department for Education and Employment (1999) *Learning to Succeed: A new framework for post-16 learning.* Norwich: The Stationery Office. [Online at: http://www.skills.org.uk/lts-wp.pdf]

Department for Education and Employment (2000) *Freedom to Learn: Basic skills for learners with learning difficulties and/or disabilities.* London: DfEE. [Online at: http://www.lifelonglearning.co.uk/freedomtolearn/report.pdf]

Department for Education and Skills (2002a) *Success for All – Reforming Further Education and Training: Our vision for the future.* [Online at: http://www.success-forall.gov.uk/downloads/ourvisionforthefuture-76-109.pdf]

Department for Education and Skills (2002b) *14–19: Extending opportunities, raising standards.* Norwich: Her Majesty's Stationery Office. [Online at: http://readingroom.lsc.gov.uk/pre2005/research/responses/14-19-extending-opportunities-raising-standards.pdf]

Department for Education and Skills (2003a) *14–19: Opportunity and excellence.* Annesley: DfES Publications. [Online at: http://www.qca.org.uk/downloads/14-19oppex.pdf]

Department for Education and Skills (2003b) *Every Child Matters.* Annesley: DfES Publications. [Online at: http://www.everychildmatters.gov.uk/_files/EBE7EEAC90382663E0D5BBF24C99A7AC.pdf]

Department for Education and Skills (2004a) *Removing Barriers to Achievement: The government's strategy for SEN.* Annesley: DfES Publications [Online at: http://www.teachernet.gov.uk/_doc/5970/removing%20barriers.pdf].

Department for Education and Skills (2004b) *Every Child Matters: Change for children.* Annesley: DfES Publications. [Online at: http://www.everychildmatters.gov.uk/_files/F9E3F941DC8D4580539EE4C743E9371D.pdf]

Department for Education and Skills (2005) *14-19 Education and Skills.* Norwich: Her Majesty's Stationery Office. [Online at: http://www.dfes.gov.uk/publications/14-19educationandskills/pdfs/14-19WhitePaper.pdf]

Department for Education and Skills (2006) *Further Education: Raising skills, improving life chances.* Norwich: The Stationery Office. [Online at: http://www.dfes.gov.uk/publications/furthereducation/docs/6514-FE%20White%20Paper.pdf].

Department of Education and Science (1978) *Special Educational Needs (The Warnock Report).* Norwich: HMSO.

Department of Health (2001) *Valuing People: A new strategy for learning disability for the 21st century.* London: DH. [Online at: http://www.archive.official-documents.co.uk/document/cm50/5086/5086.pdf]

Dorchester Curriculum Group (2002) *Towards a Curriculum for All.* London: Fulton.

Dunn, S. (2003) *Return to SENDA?: Implementing accessibility for disabled students in virtual learning environments in UK further and higher education.* London: City University. [Online at: http://www.saradunn.net/VLEreport/index.html]

Equals (1999) *Moving On.* North Shields: Equals.

Further Education Unit/Mencap (1995) *Learning for Life.* London: FEU.

Kennedy, H. (1998) *Learning Works: Report of the Further Education Funding Council Widening Participation Committee* Coventry, FEFC

Learning and Skills Council (2005) *Through Inclusion to Excellence.* Coventry: Learning and Skills Council. [Online at: http://readingroom.lsc.gov.uk/lsc/2005/research/commissioned/through-inclusion-to-excellence.pdf]

Morris, E. (2002) 'Foreword'. In: Department for Education and Skills (2002a) *14–19: Extending opportunities, raising standards.* Norwich: Her Majesty's Stationery Office. [Online at: http://readingroom.lsc.gov.uk/pre2005/research/re-sponses/14-19-extending-opportunities-raising-standards.pdf]

Opie, C. (ed.) (2004) *Doing Educational Research.* London. Sage.

Prime Minister's Strategy Unit (2005) *Improving the Life Chances of Disabled People.* London: PMSU. [Online at: http://www.strategy.gov.uk/downloads/work_areas/disability/disability_report/pdf/disability.pdf]

Robson, C. (2002) *Real World Research: A resource for social scientists and practi-tioner researchers (2nd edn).* Oxford: Blackwell Publishers.

Tomlinson, J. (1996) *Report of the Further Education Funding Council Learning Diffi-culties and/or Disabilities Committee.* Coventry: FEFC [Summary online at: http://inclusion.uwe.ac.uk/csie/tmlnsn.htm].

Wellington, J. (2000) *Educational Research.* London: Continuum Books.

## Endnotes

[1] 'Further education' is education beyond the age of 16 years. This is not to be confused with 'higher ed-ucation', which is education towards qualifications above 'Advanced' ('A') level.

[2] The further education department at Sunfield includes students aged between 16 and 19 years.

[3] Information available online at: http://www.qca.org.uk/8798.html

[4] Online at: www.asdan.co.uk and www.asdan.co.nz

[5] 'Entry Level' means that the syllabus is approved by government Ministers as meeting the criteria for a 'National Entry Level Award'. The award is designed for candidates at age 16 and above who are work-ing at typical 8-year-old level and below in the National Curriculum. The award is intended to encourage progression to higher level qualifications with national recognition.

[6] Online at: http://www.ocr.org.uk

[7] Online at: http://www.ofsted.gov.uk/reports/117/117033.pdf

# CHAPTER 15

# Transition Solutions

## Looking to the Future

*Jo Egerton*

## Introduction

It is recognised that young people with severe intellectual disability have more stressful experiences than other young people with disabilities during their move from school to an adult provision (Cope, 2003; Department for Education and Skills (DfES), 2004). This is both in terms of the barriers encountered during the transition planning process and in terms of young people's experience of the physical process (Kim and Turnbull, 2004). As a residential school for young people with severe and complex intellectual disabilities (aged 6 to 19 years), Sunfield is concerned with facilitating a smooth and seamless transition to adult services for its school-leavers, and regularly reviews its transition procedures.

Sunfield is also concerned to support parents, who have the primary responsibility for identifying a provision which may become their son or daughter's home for the whole of their adult life. Many parents are naturally apprehensive about both the actual move and understanding the complex processes involved (Carpenter, 1997). In order to find out how the school might better support parents over this period, Sunfield has carried out three investigations: the first, a survey of parents of Sunfield alumni – the 'Alumni Project' (Smart, 2004); the second, comprising in-depth follow-up interviews with some of the same group of parents – 'From the Far Side' (Egerton, 2005); and the third, current, exploratory study – the 'Transition Solutions Project' (Millward, 2006).

The three projects demonstrate a progression in Sunfield's support for parents: an evaluation of the situation experienced by parents whose sons and daughters left Sunfield between 1998 and 2001, and how they felt this could be improved; Sunfield's stepped implementation of transition support strategies as a result of parent feedback; and, finally, proactive planning for innovative future developments in transition support for students and families.

## The Alumni Project (Smart, 2004)

In 2001, Melanie Smart, then researcher at Sunfield, carried out a survey of parents of Sunfield students who had left Sunfield between 1998 and 2001 (Smart, 2004). The survey asked about their experience of transition planning, their own involvement and whether the adult provision had met the needs of their son or daughter, including possible reasons for placement breakdown where relevant. It aimed to capture parent perceptions of their son or daughter's transition, from the beginning of the planning process (age 14 years) through to their current situation in an adult provision.

The questionnaire was sent out to 47 parents, of whom 17 agreed to take part in the survey. The four sections of the questionnaire asked about: details of the young people's diagnoses and needs; information about their current provision, transition experiences and aspects of the adult provision; about long-term transition planning; and about placement breakdown (if applicable). All of the 17 young people who were the focus of the questionnaires had a diagnosis of severe learning disabilities usually alongside other conditions, the most prevalent of which was autism (8).[1]

The survey found that 14 parents believed their son/daughter to be happy in their adult placement. For parents, the most important characteristics of the adult service included 'atmosphere and environment', 'level of independence/support', 'proximity to parental home' and 'social/leisure opportunities'. This was corroborated by both positive and negative comments, which also referred to the skill and motivation of staff and communication of the service with parents. This corresponded with Heslop, Mallet, Simons and Ward's (2002) finding that 'social and leisure opportunities' was one of four key areas about which parents in their study had requested information.

When asked about their sense of preparation for their son/daughter's transition, ten parents said they had felt prepared and five had felt unprepared. Parents suggested that they had needed more information about transition earlier on in the process, and advice about '*what* [the child] should have, *who* should be providing it and *when* it should happen'.

Commenting on transition planning from age 14 years (DfEE, 1994; DfES, 2001) and pre-transition preparation, thirteen parents described themselves as being 'very much involved' in the planning process, although only one parent said the same of their son/daughter. However, many parents described their experiences of transition in terms of worry, stress and 'fighting' – for funding, placement confirmation, information and responses from outside agencies. While eleven parents felt they were 'very supported or supported' by Sunfield, four felt 'unsupported' and one felt 'very unsupported'.

Parents of the four young people who experienced placement breakdown were asked about their son/daughter's experience. All cited the level of challenge the young person's behaviour posed to the service (and vice versa) as the trigger for exclusion from the service or removal by parents. However, parents variously identified the causes for the young person's behaviour as: inappropriateness of placement, arising needs (e.g. illness, mental health needs) or poor or unprepared staffing.

Following discussion of the findings and their implications, the report concluded:

> *Even when the placement is appropriate for the young person and their needs are being met, the period of transition is still disruptive and confusing for young people with severe learning disabilities in long-term care.*

## From the Far Side (Egerton, 2005)

In the course of the 2001 survey, Smart had asked parents if they would be willing to take part in follow-up interviews, but left Sunfield before she was able to carry them out. Therefore, the follow-up project was carried out by the present writer. Fifteen parents had indicated that they would be prepared to take part in an in-depth interview about their experiences of their son/daughter's transition, and 12 were able to take part in interviews carried out during 2005. This report summarises the findings from semi-structured interviews.

Smart's (2004) research indicated that one element which parents considered may be critical in young people's ability to settle in adult provisions was consistency of approach. Therefore, it was decided that the follow-up research should focus upon the way information was shared between Sunfield and the young person's adult provision to promote that consistency. The aims of the research were to find out whether, in parents' opinions, there were any improvements that Sunfield could make to the information-sharing process to increase the ease with which young people settled in their adult provision, and to share with parents of forthcoming school leavers the perspectives of parents who had been through the process of transition.

## The questionnaire

The interview questionnaire was designed to lead parents and the interviewer into a focused discussion on information-sharing, and to give parents opportunities to raise issues about other areas of transition important to them.

The first part of the questionnaire asked for factual information. Part 2 asked parents to think about what had been important for their son/daughter in helping them to settle and whether any particular aspect was more important in information-sharing than others. Part 3 asked parents their opinions of the information-sharing that had taken place between Sunfield and adult provision staff and for any suggestions for the future. Part 4 asked for comments on any additional concerns around transition and asked if they had any advice for future families going through transition.

## Analysis of data

The semi-structured interview transcripts were analysed using categorical qualitative content analysis (Gillham, 2005) and, in the analysis, the researcher focused upon 'distinct and potentially generalisable features of the data' (Gillham, 2005). Most of the themes identified by the researcher had an association with specific chronological stages of transition:

- Parents' search for and identification of an adult provision for their son/daughter

- Preparation for the young person's transition to the adult provision

- The transition itself, and the young person's settling-in and/or pre-exclusion period.

However, a number of themes were evident in more than one stage.

## Findings related to information-sharing

Sunfield has a variety of ways of sharing information with adult provisions – in permanent form (e.g. documented records, including personal history files, minutes of review meetings and supplementary written information, photos, etc.), and in verbal form (e.g. telephone calls, informal meetings, exchange visits by both staff groups to each other's provision, informal training sessions). All parents recalled one or more different ways of sharing information as helpful to their son/daughter in settling.

### Was the Information-sharing satisfactory?

Eight of the ten parents whose son/daughter had transitioned directly from Sunfield to the adult provision were satisfied with the information-sharing about their son/daughter between Sunfield and the adult provision. Of these, four parents were very positive, describing the transitions as 'brilliant' (2)[2] 'hugely supportive' (1) and 'very good' (1), and four other parents stated that Sunfield could not have done more, although they suggested improvements when asked.

Three parents thought that Sunfield could have communicated more accurately with the adult provision and parents about their son/daughter's abilities or likely levels of challenge to services. They felt that an overemphasis on positive achievement had led to a misplacement of the young person.

Two suggested that parents should be given detailed information about young people's challenging behaviours in advance of their search for an adult provision so they could make a suitable choice of future placement. One of these parents explained:

> You don't want to be giving negative vibes to parents the whole time, and, let's face it, that's not what you want to hear as a parent. But I think sometimes we don't quite understand on a day-to-day basis how the behaviour is manifesting itself, and what's behind it.[…] It might have helped possibly with the choice of where [my son] went […]. (Parent 3)

One parent also suggested that Sunfield should have an expectation that young people's behaviour would regress due to the stress of transition and advised that the adult provision be made aware of their son/daughter's history of challenging behaviours and the strategies which had been successful in addressing it.

> Skills learnt at [Sunfield] doesn't come after a day. It comes after lots of work with the child, and when they move to another place which is going to be very different, and all that structure disappears, they are bound to return to whatever behaviour they had before. Probably made worse with age as well. (Parent 8)

Commenting on the adult provisions' assimilation and utilisation of information, two parents said that they did not think that the adult provision could have done more, although four thought that they could have done.

Two parents suggested that the parents' role in information-sharing should be formalised:

> […] then at least that gives the parent the feeling that he can actually do something about it. Rather than being seen as interference with internal business or whatever. So if the parents get an official role, then at least that can't be swept under the carpet, as it were. (Parent 1)

However, two others felt that Sunfield and adult provision staff would be able to talk more freely and give fuller information about the young person without parents present.

### Personal history files

Personal history files contained, in the words of one parent, *'the history of all [my son's] life at Sunfield and more besides'* (Parent 2). Three parents remarked that the file had been important for their son/daughter's period of settling because it had helped adult provision staff to maintain consistency for the young person. However, only one parent, who had been given her son's Personal History File to pass on to the adult provision, said she was aware of the detail of the information shared between Sunfield and the adult provision within the file.

### Person portraits

Four parents suggested that A4 summary sheets prefacing the files were or would have been useful in addition to the files which were described by one parent as useful but *'enormous'*. These A4 sheets would provide adult provision staff with immediate access to crucial information which some adult provisions had overlooked, e.g. medical needs, successful strategies for working with and encouraging the young person, and descriptions of typical days and achievements. Two parents had provided these summary sheets themselves. One parent observed that adult provision staff had failed to pick up key points about his daughter's care from her personal history file, and had felt that a prefacing A4 summary sheet would have prevented this occurring.

### Verbal sharing of information

Nine of the 12 parents mentioned at least one form of verbal sharing of information between staff from Sunfield and the adult provision as being particularly important for their son/daughter in settling within the adult provision. Opportunities for sharing information verbally had included telephone conversations and reciprocal visits – with and without the young person – before, during and after transition. In some cases, Sunfield staff had offered hands-on training for adult provision staff to promote consistency of approach for the young person.

### Refinement of transition support – parent suggestions and current developments

Most parents expressed satisfaction with the way in which Sunfield shared information with their son/daughter's adult provision. Suggestions for improvements included development of specific expectations around the form, content and timing of information-sharing; formal involvement of parents in three-way information-sharing with Sunfield and the adult provision in recognition that parents are the enduring custodians of information about their son/daughter (this would also set the precedent for continuing parent–adult provision communication); documentation of information shared between Sunfield and the adult provision; offering parents an in-depth briefing about their son/daughter's needs and challenging behaviours prior to their search for a suitable adult provision; and extending the range of background information presented to parents prior to their search for a suitable adult provision.

In 2005, Sunfield appointed a Transition Solutions Adviser as part of the Transition Solutions research project (see below). Part of her remit is offering guidance and support to Sunfield care workers in sharing information about the young people effectively. The following suggestions for improvement are dovetailed with information about current practice promoted by the Adviser.

### Guidance on the different ways of sharing information

Interviews with the 1998–2001 parent group suggest that their experience was that sharing information with adult provisions about young people was individually driven by staff, and that there was no organisational procedure at that time which covered this. However, discussions have taken place in Sunfield's periodical Transition Review meetings about standardising the different opportunities for sharing information. Carers could be made aware of all the different ways they might share information about the young person with the adult provider, and parents could be told of the different ways in which information had been shared with the adult provider about their son/daughter.

Parents mentioned pen portraits and A4 summary sheets as particularly useful in affording adult provision staff immediate access to essential information about their son/daughter. Sunfield's Transition Solutions Adviser is currently trialling symbolled[3] information sheets which will give adult provision staff immediate access to information about the young person's medical and social needs, likes and dislikes, and how staff can manage their anxiety.

### Inclusion of parents in information-sharing

This would increase families' awareness about the information which was being shared between Sunfield and the adult provision. Ways in which this could be done may be to send parents copies of written information shared with the adult provision sent to parents, and offer families the opportunity to take part in informal verbal information-sharing alongside Sunfield staff (e.g. families could be invited to Sunfield when adult provision staff were visiting).

Since her appointment, the Transition Solutions Adviser, who supports school leavers and their families during transition, acts as a point of communication for parents, Sunfield care workers, adult provision staff and Social Services, and keeps everyone included in and informed of developments. She has suggested that she could routinely involve parents with pre-transition visits to the adult provision and send out summary paperwork to parents.

### Detailed, realistic and historical information about young people's challenging behaviour

Prior to parents beginning to search for an adult provision for their son/daughter (i.e. at age 17 or before), they could be given in-depth information about their son/daughter's likely challenge to services to enable them to identify an appropriate provision. Once the young person's adult provision had been identified, the provision staff could be given a historical summary of behaviour management and development from the time of the young person's arrival at Sunfield onwards and details of successful strategies used. This would give the new provision an indication of behaviours the young person might display due to anxiety in an unfamiliar environment, and give them strategies which have been effective in supporting the young person in the past.

It is now Sunfield protocol that there should be regular, objective behaviour management updates presented at Annual Reviews, and that the adult provision should be provided with a summary of the young person's behaviour development over their time at Sunfield and details of successful strategies used.

### *Parents could be routinely advised what to expect from young people after transition*

The parents in the 'From the Far Side' study had not been aware of how their son/daughter would react to a new residential environment after, in some cases, many years at Sunfield. Information that parents gave at interview suggests that school leavers may experience:

- A short honeymoon period (one to three weeks), followed by an average of nine months to settle, although periods of up to eighteen months were described.

- The possibility of a recurrence of challenging behaviours previously resolved

- The possibility of a temporary regression in level of skills.

Since 2003, Sunfield has offered information days for parents whose son/daughter is approaching transition presented by an autism consultant who is also an ex-Sunfield parent. These information days focus particularly on legislation and community care assessments. The Transition Solutions Adviser suggested that other information needed by parents around their expectations of adult services could be run in an additional workshop.

### Further findings

Heslop, Mallet, Simons and Ward (2002) assert that:

> Young people's experiences of the transition to adulthood are helped (or hindered) by factors that are more connected to the environment and context in which transition occurs, than on the actual transition process itself.

Despite the original, narrower, focus of this research on information-sharing between Sunfield and the adult provision, their statement appears to be supported by the focus of concern of this parent participant group – both in terms information which would have helped them identify a suitable placement and their focus upon adult provision characteristics which supported or compromised their son/daughter's ability to settle.

Most parents identified the need that they had felt for more comprehensive information around the time they were beginning to search for a suitable adult provision for their son/daughter. They had felt unprepared for the search in terms of information about the process, having realistic expectations of adult services and specifically about potential adult provisions.

> I felt that I was the one who was having to ask questions, to find out what was going to happen, what I could do to help, taking names, taking contact details and following up. I don't think that parents should have to go through that. They should have a responsible person who does that for them. Now whether that is Social Services, whether that is Sunfield, whether that's a mixture of the two… (Parent 9)

Some parents also said that it would have been useful to talk to parents with experience of transition. All parents offered advice for parents of forthcoming school-leavers – variously about: who to talk to; what to be prepared for; characteristics of adult provisions to look out for; and the need to challenge unfavourable decisions by agencies.

> *You've got to be clear in your own mind, as much as you can be, about the sort of place that you think would be suitable for your son or daughter, because what Social Services come up with may not be what you had in mind. I know you're always limited by what's out there, but as myself and my husband have demonstrated, if you fight enough, as long as you get the funding, you can get somewhere for your child that you're happy with.* (Parent 9)

Some parents' perceptions that, in order to manage their son/daughter's severe and complex needs (e.g. in terms of specific communication systems and styles, behaviour support, individualisation of support and community/activity access) adult provision staff needed to be well-trained, supported by a well-organised management, and highly motivated is borne out by the literature (Felce, 1999; Maudslay, 2002; Simpson 2000; Whittaker and McIntosh, 2000). Mansell (2000) describes such staff as being able to offer 'active support' – a more organised and structured approach particularly suited to young people with ASD and developmental disabilities.

Parents also expressed opinions, borne of their experiences, about the characteristics of adult provisions which they felt had been important factors in their son/daughter's ability or inability to settle. These included the approach the adult provision had taken to level of choice, setting of parameters, level of independence, continuity of approach between and within provisions, individualisation, activities, staffing characteristics and environment. Key to parent satisfaction and opinion of the adult provision's effectiveness of approach to their son/daughter was the extent to which that adult provision individualised approaches and their recognition of the parent voice as important. Parents who were not valued by adult provisions were concerned by their inability to make changes for the better in their son/daughter's lives. For those who were valued by adult provision staff, the months of struggle to find the right place for their son/daughter were made worthwhile. This parent, whose son was excluded from his first adult provision, subsequently found one which met his needs:

> *[Adult provision staff] would gather the problematic areas, if you like, at one of our meetings, and then we would discuss it together, and they would ask me, 'What do you do in this case?' and 'This is what we would do. Do you think this would work or not?' So really it's a discussion all the time. [...They say] 'You know him better than we do, therefore you tell us.' [...] And it works [both ways] [...] If we've got problems, there is always somebody at the end of the [telephone] line when he's at home. It's the nearest thing to perfection that I have seen it, really, this place.* (Parent 8)

## Conclusion

When parents described a successful placement for their son/daughter, they invariably mentioned that the adult provision assimilated and utilised information provided by Sunfield and the parents. All parents felt that information shared between Sunfield and the adult provision about their son/daughter was valuable, and over half of the group made suggestions for improvement of the information-sharing process. However, the weight of parent evidence seems to suggest that unless the adult provision has a prevailing ethos which recognises the importance of continuity of support for young people over and beyond the transition period, information shared is likely to be discarded.

This research has provided a vehicle for examination of a wider, intricate and reciprocal information-sharing network operating around transition, and of the issues which were of particular importance for these parents. Interviewing parents on the 'far side' of transition allowed the researcher, and other parents, entré to their specific concerns for their individual son/daughter in unique situations. While it is not possible to generalise the experiences of such a small parent group to the wider population of parents of young people with severe and complex intellectual disabilities, these parents have described a spectrum of situations and responses which Sunfield and parents of young people going through the transition process can consider in the context of their own particular journey.

**Looking to the future – the Transition Solutions Project (Millward, 2006)**
Transition Solutions is a three-year research project, funded by West Midlands Regional Partnership and the Home Farm Trust. Within an action research design, its aim is to address issues raised by Sunfield's previous transition research (Egerton, 2005; Smart, 2004) and to explore with parents, staff and young people at Sunfield innovative ways of supporting transition to improve the experiences of young people and their families. In 2005, a transition solutions advisor was appointed to head up the project.

The Transition Solutions project is developing strategies to promote awareness and expectations of transition among Sunfield's population of young people with severe and complex learning disabilities in ways suited to their cognition, style of learning and needs. It has adopted a 'reach back/reach out' approach which supports continuity and consistency of approach between services, maintains links between past and present students, and monitors students beyond Sunfield by maintaining contact with adult services and offering support where necessary. The aim of the project is to develop guidelines for families, to support staff and refine practice to prepare students better, to enable Sunfield to be proactive in supporting students and families, to develop a directory of adult provisions and to establish links with adult providers who are able to meet the complex needs of young people at Sunfield.

To date there have been interesting and exciting outcomes which will have considerable impact on the transition experience of young people and their families in the future. The project will report in 2008, and the results will be disseminated from Sunfield.

To date, much of the emphasis on transition from children's to adult services for young people with learning disabilities has been on planning that transition. However, as Wood and Trickey (1996) comment, the tendency for procedures to dominate processes is a common one with parallels in a number of everyday events (e.g. marriage, retirement) where people 'plan carefully for [the event]…but often not for the period of adjustment which follows'. This is the concern underlying the present research at Sunfield. Through the Transition Solutions project, Sunfield aims to be able to bridge the gulf which can develop for young people between their adult and child provisions to provide the seamless service which our children need.

**References**
Carpenter, B. (1997) *Families in Context: Emerging trends in family support and early intervention.* London: David Fulton.

Cope, C. (2003) *Fulfilling Lives: Inspection of social care services for people with learning disabilities.* London: Department of Health.

Department for Education and Employment (1994) *Code of Practice on Identification and Assessment of Special Educational Needs.* London: Her Majesty's Stationery Office.

Department for Education and Skills (2001) *Special Educational Needs Code of Practice.* London: DfES.

Department for Education and Skills (2004) *Removing Barriers to Achievement: The special educational needs strategy.* Annesley: DfES Publications.

Egerton, J. (2005) *From the Far Side: Parents' perceptions of information-sharing to support transition for young people with severe and complex learning disabilities (Unpublished M.Sc. dissertation).* Birmingham: University of Birmingham.

Felce, D. (1999) 'Enhancing quality of life for people receiving residential support', *British Journal of Learning Disabilities, 27,* 4–9.

Gillham, B. (2005) *Research Interviewing: The range of techniques.* Milton Keynes: Open University Press.

Heslop, P., Mallett, R., Simons, K. and Ward, L. (2002) *Bridging the Divide at Transition: What happens for young people with learning difficulties and their families.* Kidderminster: BILD.

Kim, K.H. and Turnbull, A. (2004) 'Transition to adulthood for students with severe intellectual disabilities: shifting towards person–family interdependent planning', *Research and Practice for Persons with Severe Disabilities, 29* (1), 53–57.

Mansell, J. (2000) 'Time to raise standards', *Community Care* (10 August).

Maudslay, L. (2002) 'Research into practice', *Community Care,* (9 August).

Millward, J. (2006) 'Transition solutions: a three year project focusing on supporting families of young people with complex learning needs moving from a residential school to adult services' (Explanatory leaflet). Clent: Sunfield.

Simpson, M.K. (2000) 'Programming adulthood: intellectual disability and adult services'. In: D. May (ed.) *Transition and Change in the Lives of People with Intellectual Disabilities.* London: Jessica Kingsley.

Smart, M. (2004) 'Transition planning and the needs of young people and their carers: the Alumni Project', *British Journal of Special Education, 31* (3), 128–137.

Whittaker, A. and McIntosh, B. (2000) 'Changing days', *British Journal of Learning Disabilities, 28* (1), 3–8.

Wood, D. and Trickey, S. (1996) 'Transition planning: process or procedure?', *British Journal of Special Education, 23* (3), 120–125.

## Endnotes

[1] Numbers in brackets represent the number of young people to whom the previous statement applies.

[2] Numbers in brackets represent the count frequency of parents making statements which could be categorised by this statement type.

[3] Sunfield uses a computer program to generate line drawings with associated words. The program, 'Writing with Symbols', can be purchased from Widgit Software (http://www.widgit.com).

# CHAPTER 16

# Research Tools for Evidence-Based Practice

*Teresa Whitehurst*

## Introduction

Research has many faces; it can mean many things to many people. Above all research is the search for answers. Scientific research continues to make daily progress in unravelling the complexities and causes of disability. This gives practitioners a more stable basis upon which they can build interventions and develop new pedagogies. Academic research articulates theories to explain the complexities that emerge from these scientific discoveries. Nevertheless, for practitioners, such scientific and academic foundations, however solid, do not always readily translate into their everyday working practices. For practitioners, the value of research lies in its ability to equip them with a toolkit of resources which are responsive to the ever changing needs of children with whom they work under the conditions imposed by their environment.

The concept of research emerging from the grass roots, being defined and driven by practitioners, is not new. However, the concept of research emerging from a special school, driven by the population *within*, rather than being prescribed, guided and undertaken by *others* is relatively rare. The model developed at Sunfield School embraces a unique situation where the components of research come together to create a dynamic force which is greater than the sum of its parts. Creating an evidence base through research leads to professionally informed practice, providing resources and guidelines for real and specific issues faced by today's practitioners.

## What is special about research in intellectual disabilities?

Traditionally, researchers have belonged to the world of science and academia, whose results may be accessed by practitioners. Supporting practitioners to become researchers involves more than just giving them to tools to carry out research. Sunfield School has set about creating a culture where research is valued, supported, relevant, accessible, applicable and, above all, do-able.

## Structures supporting research

Central to an understanding of how research can be conducted within special schools is an appreciation of the foundations upon which such a culture is built and how that culture is nurtured and supported. Research can only flourish when those working within an organisation have an appreciation of its value and where a common dialogue has been established.

The launch of the Sunfield Research Institute in January 2005 was the culmination of a long-term commitment (from 1998) by Sunfield to encouraging practitioner research. This process began gently in the early stages, encouraging a few interested practitioners. The post of 'research and development officer' was created, identifying a dedicated member of staff responsible for conducting project work. A core knowledge base began to build among staff through Sunfield's Professional Development Centre. In 2003, the decision was taken to create the post of 'research officer', to harness and guide the enthusiasm of staff at Sunfield and to give direction to the research process. In addition to supporting staff undertaking individual projects, many practitioners explored research as part of their courses and professional development. In-house dissemination and external research publication enabled messages to be shared with wider audiences. An internal research framework developed, reflecting the needs of Sunfield's practitioners and supporting their research pathways. Expansion of the evolving research culture, and recognition of this by Sunfield's trustees, culminated in the launch of the Research Institute and the associated International Advisory Board.

At grass roots level, making research accessible to practitioners necessitates the creation of a common language where research can be discussed in terms of its value to their practice and to the children and families with whom they work. Sunfield's research officer works to ensure that these dialogues take place in a way which is meaningful to a diverse range of staff.

This process is supported by a regular Innovations Forum where the whole organisation is invited to listen to new ideas, new ways of working or share findings from research undertaken by colleagues. These presentations are conducted by a wide variety of staff including speech and language therapists, outreach workers, psychologists and psychology assistants, teachers, teaching assistants and Sunfield's counsellor. This ensures current knowledge and research are shared, valued and eventually embedded within practice.

### Ethical considerations

The issues of consent, confidentiality and anonymity are paramount in all aspects of research. Protection of the most vulnerable populations, such as children with intellectual disabilities and those in residential settings, requires even greater consideration. No child, whatever their abilities, can give fully informed consent to taking part in research as they cannot be aware of the wider implications or consequences of agreeing to participate. Therefore the consent of parents/guardians is needed, and it is the responsibility of the researcher to give parents/guardians and children full information about the project in a form they can understand and make them aware of their rights. In the same way that a researcher would give a typically developing child the choice of whether or not to take part in research, it is important that children with intellectual disabilities also are given this choice at a developmental level appropriate to them. Although many children with intellectual disabilities have communication impairments, even those who are most severely affected can usually indicate choice at some level if only by their reaction to a situation. Where children are living away from home, often approval from a social worker may also be necessary.

Sunfield has taken special consideration of these factors in developing its own Code of Ethical Conduct. This document is given to all members of staff prior to commencing a research project to give them guidance. It not only ensures research is conducted to a high standard of rigour, but that the children and families it seeks to help are protected at every stage of the research process.

## Research scholarships

With the support of funding through Sunfield's trustees, research scholarships are available to *any* member of staff wishing to explore an area of their practice. Research scholarships are currently being undertaken by music therapists exploring the use of 'body percussion' techniques to enhance the proprioceptive experiences of children with autistic spectrum disorders (ASD); by the heads of the Education and Care Departments considering a new 24-hour, cross-site curriculum within the framework of *Every Child Matters* (Department for Education and Skills (DfES), 2003, 2004); by a psychology assistant exploring the experiences of siblings of children with disabilities; by an assistant head teacher and the IT training officer developing a new resource to address the emotional needs and strengthen the mental well-being of children with severe and complex needs (see Chapter 8). Research scholarships provide a small amount of financial support to help staff to develop and implement their ideas. It enables cover to be provided for their role and the expenses of the project to be met. Finance for larger projects is sought through external funding from charitable trusts.

All projects need to be scrutinised by an informed professional panel to consider their merit, validity, rigour and ethics. The Research and Ethics Committee provide the forum for this discussion and meet termly to consider the progress of existing projects and take decisions on the inception of new projects. These proceedings operate with reference to Sunfield's Research Policy and Code of Ethical Conduct. All projects are then closely monitored and supported by the research officer.

In addition, the Research Institute has the support of a number of 'research associates' and the benefit of a 'virtual' International Advisory Board. Research associates are external colleagues who contribute to Sunfield's research process by working alongside the organisation in a research capacity. The Institute currently has four such associates: one supporting a project to consider the pedagogy around delivery of Sherborne Developmental Movement Programme to children with ASD (see Chapter 4); one conducting research around thinking, feeling and will in children with ASD (see Chapter 9); one delivering mental health training to front line staff working with children with severe and complex needs (see Chapter 6); and one who previously conducted 'the Alumni Project' around the experiences of families and students during transition (see Chapter 15). Meanwhile, the unique creation of a 'virtual' International Advisory Board affords the opportunity for all research to be scrutinised by experts from around the world. The willingness of no less than 30 such experts lends incredible strength to the research process.

## Methodologies

Before commencing any research project, staff are encouraged to think carefully about what they seek to find out. What aspect of their work do they wish to investigate? Do they think something can be measured or do they want to find out about someone's experiences? Researchers select their approach from a range of methodologies, each one appropriate to different situations and associated with a specific collection of tools and strategies. The methodology they choose gives them the framework and scope to search for the knowledge they seek. Key to this process is a thorough literature search around their chosen area. This systematic procedure ensures they are aware of other research which may have been conducted by other practitioners looking at the same or similar area, population or issue.

A good literature search will provide a practitioner embarking upon a piece of research with studies which are similar to theirs (thus enabling them to consider advantageous features of someone else's work) and studies which are different (enabling them to consider how they would like to change or adapt studies to suit different needs). This level of critical thinking around the chosen research area prepares the practitioner researcher by sensitising them to current debates and grounding their work with relevance to the body of knowledge which already exists.

Certain populations within society, usually the most vulnerable, have often been marginalised not only by the way society views their situation, but also by the approach of those who conduct research. These populations have typically involved the elderly, ethnic minorities, families and people with disabilities. Researchers from outside the research population and their environment rarely understand the culture or constraints operating on them. When research populations are incomplete or are not consulted throughout the research process, there is a danger that important issues will be ignored, irrelevant questions asked, relevant questions omitted and invalid interpretations of data made. Historically, this is one of the reasons much academic research aimed at changing practice has remained on the library shelves rather than being assimilated within practice. Although arguably more open to bias, practitioner research is valuable because practitioners have a deeper understanding of their research environment. Practitioner researchers can not only explore effective means of mediating academic research recommendations, but can also explore research questions whose significance to the research population has been overlooked by the academic community.

Sunfield promotes a participatory/emancipatory stance to research. A participatory approach encourages and facilitates people who are part of the research population to work *alongside* researchers. From this perspective, a partnership is formed which is empowering and emancipatory; it values the contribution of each individual as an equal partner in the process, and in so doing enables the voices of those traditionally silenced to be liberated.

## Qualitative or quantitative?
Methodologies based upon these principles are primarily qualitative and focus on the multiple realities shaped by social, political, cultural, economic, ethnic, gender and disability values. They differ from the scientific positivist paradigm which prefers a quantitative, 'objective', reductionist approach, placed within the realms of experimental design, and instead offers a research approach which explores feelings and behaviours through value-bound methods generating data which is rich, deep and valid. Often thought of as the 'soft' option, qualitative research has its own rigour and validity and has been more recently referred to as a 'flexible' design (Robson, 2002).

Reliability and validity within qualitative research are often thought to be compromised by the nature of its subjective and value-bound approach. However, these issues can be counteracted by researcher reflexivity and incorporation of triangulation into the research design. The degree of objectivity found in quantitative research itself is also debatable. Researcher reflexivity acknowledges the potential influence of the researcher on the focus of the study, taking account of issues such as their own gender, ethnic background, values and preconceptions. It is incumbent upon the researcher to acknowledge this potential bias, be aware of its influence and, where possible, take steps to reduce its impact upon the study.

Triangulation is a method used by researchers to check and establish validity in their studies. There are different types of triangulation. Validity is established when corroborative results are obtained from different data sources or through different methods of data collection. For example, interviews may be conducted with a range of stakeholders. This data could be triangulated by looking for outcomes which are agreed upon by all stakeholder groups. This strengthens reliability by providing different view points on the same issue.

Much of the research conducted at Sunfield aims to consider the experiences of its children, their families and the professionals involved in their care and education. However, this is not to the exclusion of quantitative methods. The design of each research project is meticulously considered and dependent upon the aim of the individual research question. The approach recognises the value of the data continually collected within the organisation from care, education and psychology, and utilising this data within the context of research. The use of small scale research is prohibitory only in terms of its generalisability to wider populations. Results from any such small scale studies may only relate to the population involved, but this should not deter organisations who may wish to share both process and outcome with wider audiences, thus informing the debate and ensuring practitioners learn from each other.

## A transdisciplinary approach

Sunfield's transdisciplinary approach to the care and education of its children is reflected in its research. The transdisciplinary approach differs from a multidisciplinary approach in which professionals of different disciplines are brought together for a common purpose, but maintain their separate roles. In contrast, the transdisciplinary approach allows each professional to transcend their traditional role and, with supervision and guidance from the discipline specialists in the team, embrace elements of other roles. This approach extends the resources available to the team (e.g. time, personnel), and reduces the level of intrusion into the lives of the research participants. It acknowledges the strengths and expertise of the professional specialist, but goes further to recognise, or encourage the development of, skills beyond their conventional, and often stereotypical, role. For example, under the tutelage of a psychologist, night care staff can implement programmes and carry out observations which are the traditional preserve of the psychology department.

## Models and methods

The research question adopted by the researcher influences the design of the research – e.g. an action research or exploratory study – and the methods or means used to collect information for analysis – e.g. tests, surveys, observation. It is important for researchers to be aware of the model being used and of selecting the appropriate methodology. Recognised research models and methodologies have been developed over many years, during which many early difficulties will have been eliminated. If an individual researcher generates their own, there is a danger that the resulting data may be compromised or invalid. Researchers also need to find out how other people have carried out any similar studies. If a similar methodology to that of an earlier study can be adopted, it may enable a comparison between the results of the two studies and may contribute to the validity of the conclusions.

There are many excellent text books giving clear and concise descriptions of models and methods (e.g. Cohen, Manion and Morrison, 2000; Robson, 2002; Denscombe,

2002). The following examples illustrate the ways in which a variety of approaches have been utilised at Sunfield.

### Collaborative exploratory single subject case study using mixed methods: Sunfield Nutrition Project

An exploratory study is used to investigate something about which little is known or to develop new ideas about a certain issue or topic. A case study focuses on an issue concerning an individual or group in a particular situation, and a range of information relevant to this issue is collected using different strategies. A mixed method has the advantage of generating both quantitative and qualitative data. For example, the researcher may use scores from a series of tests, together with data from semi-structured interviews with the participants.

Research suggests that gluten and casein have a toxicological effect in children with ASD who are not capable of correctly breaking down these products in their digestive systems. Sunfield wanted to explore the advantages of an adapted nutritional approach for its own student population, and to find out how this affected the young people's physical well-being, their psychological functioning, their capacity to learn, their levels of interaction and their social and verbal skills. A nutrition programme was constructed with the assistance of the Institute for Optimum Nutrition in London. It consisted of an individually tailored regime of supplements, together with a gradual reduction in the student's consumption of gluten, casein, sugar, soya and yeast.

This research was designed as an exploratory study involving a small group of 12 students living within the school's residential setting. (This was not an experimental design so no control group was established.). A single subject case study method was adopted, reflecting each student's unique and individual profile. This allowed the research to explore the effects of an adapted nutritional approach for each particular student over an eight-month period. Although direct comparisons could not be drawn between students due to their differing nutritional profiles, the within-student changes, evidenced through test scores and observations, could be recorded over time.

A mixed method approach to data collection was adopted. Baseline and post-intervention quantitative data were collected by both the nutritionists and the psychology team. In the case of the nutritionists, this was gathered by means of blood, urine and hair samples. The psychology team conducted tests on a range of each student's skills and functions. Monthly monitoring generated a statistical profile of each student's progression and compliance to the nutritional approach. At the conclusion of the intervention period, the nutritionists were able to compare their baseline data to the post-intervention data, enabling them to comment on changes in each student's nutritional status. Similarly, through comparison of test scores pre- and post-intervention, changes in each student's level of functioning could be ascertained. In addition to this quantitative data, interviews were conducted with all staff who had been involved in the project – including those from education, care, psychology and catering. This type of research enabled the experiences of those working on the project to be captured.

This mixed method approach was beneficial in that it allowed the researchers not only to see the outcomes for the student, but also to gain insight into how practitioners implementing the adapted nutritional programme had coped with changes and challenges. This is important information in terms of the continuing logistics and feasibility of such a venture long-term.

Importantly, this project was guided by a Nutrition Project Management Group which was attended by team leaders from the students' houses, teachers from the students' classes, the catering manager preparing the food and the psychologists conducting the monitoring. These members of staff were research partners working alongside the research team, learning together. They had the opportunity to be part of the process and feedback regularly about the changes they were seeing in the students and the difference that these changes were making, not only to the students' lives but to the practitioners' everyday working lives.

### Evaluation using focus groups, interviews and photography: Creating an ASD-Specific Living Environment

An evaluation is not a method, but a study of what has worked in a given situation using selected designs and methods within a systematic approach. It is important in terms of accountability for and assessing the value of any past or proposed changes.

In April 2004, eight boys and two groups of care staff moved into two adjoining houses designed specifically for young people with ASD. These buildings had taken 18 months and £1,000,000 to design and construct. It was important for the organisation to know how the modifications made to the design of the houses had changed the lives of the students and staff living there.

The research project was designed as an evaluation which focused on the lives and experiences of the people living in the houses on a daily basis. Semi- structured interviews with team leaders were conducted three months prior to the move, a month after the move and again after six months. This enabled them to consider their expectations, their concerns and their hopes for the students and for themselves. These ideas were then tracked over time to see how they had developed. In order to capture the experiences of other care workers in the new accommodation, a focus group was established which was held on a monthly basis for a period of three months.

The interviews and focus group generated very rich and detailed data from which themes emerged. These themes provided evidence of consistent experiences for a range of staff, reflecting how they felt the move had been beneficial to the students and the impact this was having upon their working practice (Whitehurst, 2006).

Obtaining the views of students with severe and complex learning needs is inherently complex, but vital to ensuring *all* the key stakeholders in the process were consulted. The Mosaic Approach (Clark and Moss, 2001) was used. This considers alternative ways of listening to students' 'voices' – in this case, through the use of photography. The more able students living in the new house were given a digital camera to take photographs of the things they liked about their new home. Adopting the Mosaic Approach enabled the data generated by the students' photographs to be set within the context of other data in much the same way as the triangulation method. Consequently, the research identified that the themes generated through analysis of the interviews and focus groups was supported through the photographs taken by the children (Whitehurst, 2007, in press).

## Survey using questionnaires: investigating the impact of TEACCH training

A survey is an excellent way of gathering data from a large number of people about one specific topic. Although this method generally makes use of a quantitative questionnaire with a variety of tick boxes, it can be extended to incorporate some short sentence qualitative feedback.

The head of teaching assistants at Sunfield wanted to investigate the impact of practice of the TEACCH (Treatment and Education of Autistic and related Communication Handicapped Children) training for her staff. She distributed a qualitative questionnaire to all teaching assistants who had received the training, asking them to comment on their perceptions of TEACCH prior to the training, what they thought they had gained during the training, and how they would put this knowledge into practice.

Data generated from this survey suggested the training had been an extremely positive experience, enabling staff to have a greater appreciation of the systems operating within the classroom and giving them confidence to engage in a common dialogue with teaching staff (Maiden, 2007, in preparation). This data will support the department in planning for future training.

## Action research

Action research is conducted by practitioners in their own setting. As Cohen, Manion and Morrison (2000) state, 'Action research is a powerful tool for change and empowerment at a local level.'

Through structured self-reflection professionals can investigate aspects of their own practice as they engage in that practice. This is usually depicted as a cyclical process – or, alternatively, a spiral process (Roberts-Holmes, 2005) – beginning with an idea which is trialled, monitored, evaluated and refined. This process then recommences any number of times until the initial thought, idea, or practice is re-defined or re-negotiated to the satisfaction of the researcher. Essentially action research is practical, cyclical and problem-solving in nature.

Music therapists at Sunfield are currently using action research to explore the use of a new technique with students with severe and complex learning needs. 'Body percussion' is a technique used with young people in Finland where rhythmic patterns are 'played' by using parts of the body as percussion. In this physical activity, the rhythms can then be sequenced and extended, involving attention, memory and coordination. Knowing that young people with intellectual disabilities often have proprioceptive and spatial problems, this technique is currently being trialled and adapted by the music therapists to address these problems.

## Conclusion

The way we explore the world around us is set within the context of what we already know. True research helps liberate our minds to explore new concepts, new ideas and new ways of working. In order to operate as responsible and responsive practitioners, we must continually seek to modify the way we work in relation to the needs of future generations. The fabric of any organisation has many diverse patterns, many textures and many uses, but common to all is the quality of the thread which runs through that fabric. When research becomes the thread within an organisation it weaves a strong fabric; a fabric which is flexible and adaptive; a fabric which practitioners from all disciplines may draw upon to provide them with the resources for their own practice. Ultimately, it is the strength and quality of the thread which will ensure the fabric we weave supports the lives and futures of our students, families and practitioners.

## References

Clark, A. and Moss, P. (2001) *Listening to Young Children: The Mosaic Approach.* London: National Children's Bureau.

Cohen, L., Manion, L. and Morrison, K. (2000) *Research Methods in Education (5th edn).* London: Falmer.

Denscombe. M. (2002) *Ground Rules for Good Research.* Maidenhead: Open University Press.

Department for Education and Skills (DfES) (2003) *Every Child Matters.* Nottingham: DfES Publications.

Department for Education and Skills (DfES) (2004) *Every Child Matters: Change for children..* Nottingham: DfES Publications.

Maiden, M. (2007, in preparation) 'Teaching assistant perceptions of the impact of TEACCH training upon their classroom practice' (working title).

Roberts-Holmes, G. (2005) Doing your Early Years Research Project. London: Paul Chapman.

Robson, C. (2002) *Real World Research.* London: Blackwell.

Whitehurst, T. (2006) 'The impact of building design on children with autistic spectrum disorders', *Good Autism Practice*, 7 (1), 31–38.

Whitehurst, T. (2007, in press) 'We're moving house', *Special Children.*